THE RE

Former Editors
Clifford Leech 1958–71
F. David Hoeniger 1970–1985

General Editors
E. A. J. Honigmann, J. R. Mulryne, D. Bevington
and E. M. Waith

THE LADY OF PLEASURE

THE REVELS PLAYS

ANON. *Arden of Faversham The Second Maiden's Tragedy*
Two Tudor Interludes: *Youth* and *Hick Scorner*
A Yorkshire Tragedy

BEAUMONT *The Knight of the Burning Pestle*
BEAUMONT AND FLETCHER *Philaster*★

CHAPMAN *Bussy d' Ambois*★ *The Widow's Tears*
CHAPMAN JOHNSON AND MARSTON *Eastward Ho*

DEKKER *The Shoemaker's Holiday*

FARQUHAR *The Recruiting Officer*

FORD *The Broken Heart 'Tis Pity she's a Whore*
The Lover's Melancholy

GREENE *James the Fourth*★

JONSON *The Alchemist*★ *Bartholomew Fair*★
Volpone The New Inn

KYD *The Spanish Tragedy*

MARLOWE *Doctor Faustus*★ *The Jew of Malta*★
The Poems Tamburlaine I and II

MARSTON *Antonio's Revenge The Fawn The Malcontent*
MARSTON AND OTHERS *The Insatiate Countess*

MIDDLETON *Women Beware Women*★
MIDDLETON AND DEKKER *The Roaring Girl*
MIDDLETON AND ROWLEY *The Changeling*★

PEELE *The Old Wives Tale*

SHIRLEY *The Cardinal* *The Lady of Pleasure*

SKELTON *Magnificence*

TOURNEUR *The Revenger's Tragedy*★

VANBRUGH *The Provoked Wife*

WEBSTER *The Duchess of Malfi*★ *The White Devil*★

WYCHERLEY *The Country Wife*

★ available in paperback

Richard Perkins, leading actor for Queen Henrietta Maria's men;
portrait by an unknown hand in the Dulwich College Picture Gallery.

THE REVELS PLAYS

THE LADY
OF PLEASURE

JAMES SHIRLEY

Edited by
Ronald Huebert

MANCHESTER
UNIVERSITY PRESS

Published by
Manchester University Press
Oxford Road, Manchester M13 9PL
and 27 South Main Street, Wolfeboro,
New Hampshire 03894–2069, USA

ISBN 0 7190 1539 1 *cased*

British Library cataloguing in publication data
Shirley, James
   The lady of pleasure.—(The Revels plays)
   I. Title   II. Huebert, Ronald
   III. Series
   822′.4   PR3144.L3

Library of Congress cataloging in publication data
Shirley, James, 1596–1666.
   The lady of pleasure.
   (The Revels plays)
   Bibliography: p.x
   Includes index.
   1. Huebert, Ronald. II. Title. III. Series.
PR3144.L3 1986   822′.4   86–2833

Typeset by August Filmsetting, Haydock, St Helens

Printed in Great Britain by Bell and Bain Ltd., Glasgow

Contents

LIST OF ILLUSTRATIONS   vi

GENERAL EDITORS' PREFACE   vii

PREFACE   ix

ABBREVIATIONS   x

INTRODUCTION

   1. The playwright   1
   2. The play   5
   3. The play in performance   23
   4. The text   35
      Notes   44

The Lady of Pleasure   51

APPENDICES

   A. The Cockpit in Drury Lane   189
   B. Press variants   198

GLOSSARIAL INDEX TO THE COMMENTARY   201

Illustrations

Frontispiece: Richard Perkins, leading actor for Queen Henrietta Maria's men; portrait by an unknown hand in the Dulwich College Picture Gallery. By permission of the Governors of Dulwich Picture Gallery.

Page 192: Architectural plan for the interior of a Jacobean or Caroline indoor playhouse; from a series of drawings by Inigo Jones and John Webb in the Library of Worcester College, Oxford. By permission of the Provost and Fellows of Worcester College, Oxford.

General Editors' Preface

The series known as the Revels Plays was conceived by Clifford Leech. The idea for the series emerged in his mind, as he explained in his preface to the first of the Revels Plays in 1958, from the success of the New Arden Shakespeare. The aim of the new group of texts was 'to apply to Shakespeare's predecessors, contemporaries and successors the methods that are now used in Shakespeare editing'. The plays chosen were to include well known works from the early Tudor period to about 1700, as well as others less familiar but of literary and theatrical merit: 'the plays included,' Leech wrote, 'should be such as to deserve and indeed demand performance.' We owe it to Clifford Leech that the idea became reality. He set the high standards of the series, ensuring that editors of individual volumes produced work of lasting merit, equally useful for teachers and students, theatre directors and actors. Clifford Leech remained General Editor until 1971, and was succeeded by F. David Hoeniger, who retired in 1985.

The Revels Plays are now under the direction of four General Editors, E. A. J. Honigmann, J. R. Mulryne, David Bevington and E. M. Waith. The publishers, originally Methuen, are now Manchester University Press. Despite these changes, the format and essential character of the series will continue, and it is hoped that its editorial standards will be maintained. Except for some work in progress, the General Editors intend, in expanding the series, to concentrate for the immediate future on plays from the period 1558–1642, and may include a small number of non-dramatic works of interest to students of drama. Some slight changes have been forced by considerations of cost. For example, in editions from 1978, notes to the introduction are placed together at the end, not at the foot of the page. Collation and commentary notes will continue, however, to appear on the relevant pages.

The text of each Revels play, in accordance with established practice in the series, is edited afresh from the original text of best authority (in a few instances, texts), but spelling and punctuation are modernised and speech headings are silently made consistent. Elisions in the original are also silently regularised, except where metre would be affected by the change; since 1968 the '-ed' form is used for non-syllabic terminations in past tenses and past participles ('-'d' earlier), and '-èd' for syllabic ('-ed' earlier). The editor emends,

as distinct from modernises, his original only in instances where
error is patent, or at least very probable, and correction persuasive.
Act divisions are given only if they appear in the original or if the
structure of the play clearly points to them. Those act and scene
divisions not found in the original are provided unobtrusively in
small type and in square brackets. Square brackets are also used for
any other additions to or changes in the stage directions of the
original.

Revels Plays do not provide a variorum collation, but only those
variants which require the critical attention of serious textual
students. All departures of substance from 'copy-text' are listed,
including any relineation and those changes in punctuation which
involve to any degree a decision between alternative interpretations;
but not such accidentals as turned letters, nor necessarily additions to
stage directions whose editorial nature is already made clear by the
use of brackets. Press corrections in the 'copy-text' are likewise
included. Of later emendations of the text, only those are given which
as alternative readings still deserve attention.

One of the hallmarks of the Revels Plays is the thoroughness of
their annotations. Besides explaining the meaning of difficult words
and passages, the editor provides comments on customs or usage,
text or stage-business—indeed, on anything he judges pertinent and
helpful. Each volume contains a Glossarial Index to the Commentary, in which particular attention is drawn to meanings for words not
listed in *O.E.D.*

The Introduction to a Revels play assesses the authority of the
'copy-text' on which it is based, and discusses the editorial methods
employed in dealing with it; the editor also considers his play's date
and (where relevant) sources, together with its place in the work of
the author and in the theatre of its time. Stage history is offered, and
in the case of a play by an author not previously represented in the
series a brief biography is given.

It is our hope that plays edited in this fashion will promote further
scholarly and theatrical investigation of one of the richest periods in
theatrical history.

E. A. J. HONIGMANN

J. R. MULRYNE

DAVID BEVINGTON

E. M. WAITH

Preface

Editors are made, not born. In my case, Dalhousie University has contributed in many ways, including the expenditure of money from the Research Development Fund; the Social Sciences and Humanities Research Council of Canada has been a benevolent patron; and the Huntington Library has assisted by awarding me a short-term fellowship. I am grateful to all, and to the libraries listed in Appendix B, for allowing me to consult, collate and explore.

Peter Davison first introduced me to the study of early printed texts, and without his teaching I could not have set up for an editor. F. David Hoeniger has read everything in these pages with the practised eye of a general editor, and his comments have pointed the way to many improvements; I have occasionally (though not adequately) recorded the generosity of his scholarship in the notes. Jonas Barish, Rick Bowers, D. F. Rowan and Rowland Smith have read portions of my typescript and have responded (variously) with much that I value: criticism, encouragement, advice. Peter Blayney, Judith Kennedy, T. J. King, Margaret Mikesell, M. G. Parks and S. E. Sprott have given patient and subtle answers to questions that baffled me. The late Elizabeth M. Yearling, while she was preparing her edition of *The Cardinal* for this series, allowed me to profit from her knowledge of Shirley through a helpful exchange of letters. G. R. Hibbard, who offered me the benefits and convivialities of being a speaker at the 1981 conference on Elizabethan Theatre at the University of Waterloo, has also given permission to include here some of the material appearing (as 'The Staging of Shirley's *The Lady of Pleasure*') in *The Elizabethan Theatre*, IX. And Tina Jones has produced a typescript, as if by magic, from assorted layers of raw material.

For collaborating in the study of Jacobean and Caroline drama, for inviting me to speak informally about editing to the Friday-at-four colloquium and for making it all seem worthwhile, I am grateful to the graduate students in English at Dalhousie, especially to those who have been members of English 545 (The Drama from Marlowe to Ford). For tolerating my obsession with *The Lady of Pleasure*, for teaching me to see beyond it, for sharing the love and the laughter of learning, I want to thank Elizabeth Edwards, my wife.

R.H.

Dalhousie University, 1984

Abbreviations

EDITIONS COLLATED

Q
: James Shirley, *The Lady of Pleasure: A Comedy* (London, 1637). For copies of Q collated, see Appendix B, p. 198. Qa indicates an uncorrected state of Q (prior to stop-press corrections); Qb indicates a corrected state.

Con. MS
: Manuscript annotations in the Library of Congress copy of Q.

Gifford
: *The Dramatic Works and Poems of James Shirley*, ed. William Gifford and Alexander Dyce, vol. IV (London, 1833).

Gosse
: *The Best Plays of the Old Dramatists: James Shirley*, ed. Edmund Gosse, Mermaid Series (London, 1888).

Neilson
: *The Chief Elizabethan Dramatists excluding Shakespeare*, ed. William Allan Neilson (Boston, 1911).

Schelling
: *Typical Elizabethan Plays*, ed. Felix E. Schelling (New York, 1926).

Spencer
: *Elizabethan Plays*, ed. Hazelton Spencer (Boston, 1933).

Baskervill
: *Elizabethan and Stuart Plays*, ed. Charles Read Baskervill, Virgil B. Heltzel, and Arthur H. Nethercot (New York, 1934).

Knowland
: *Six Caroline Plays*, ed. A. S. Knowland (London, 1962).

Harrier
: *An Anthology of Jacobean Drama*, ed. Richard C. Harrier, vol. II (New York, 1963).

Papousek
: Marilyn D. Papousek, 'A Critical Edition of James Shirley's *The Lady of Pleasure*' (Ph.D. thesis, University of Iowa, 1971).

WORKS OF REFERENCE, ETC.

Abbott
: E. A. Abbott, *A Shakespearian Grammar*, 2nd ed. (London, 1870).

Arber
: Edward Arber, *A Transcript of the Registers of the Company of Stationers of London, 1554–1640*, 5 vols. (London, 1875–94).

Bentley
: Gerald Eades Bentley, *The Jacobean and Caroline Stage*, 7 vols. (Oxford, 1941–68).

Burton, *Anatomy*
: Robert Burton, *The Anatomy of Melancholy*, ed. Floyd Dell and Paul Jordan-Smith (New York, 1927).

Cotgrave
: Randle Cotgrave, *A Dictionarie of the French and English Tongues* (London, 1611).

Cotton
: Charles Cotton, *The Compleat Gamester* (London, 1674).

Dolmetsch	Mabel Dolmetsch, *Dances of England and France from 1450 to 1600* (London, 1949).
Forsythe	Robert Stanley Forsythe, *The Relations of Shirley's Plays to the Elizabethan Drama* (New York, 1914).
Herbert	*The Dramatic Records of Sir Henry Herbert, Master of the Revels, 1623–1673*, ed. Joseph Quincy Adams (New Haven, 1917).
Jonson, *Wks*	*Ben Jonson*, ed. C. H. Herford and Percy and Evelyn Simpson, 11 vols. (Oxford, 1925–52).
King	T. J. King, 'Staging of Plays at the Phoenix in Drury Lane, 1617–42', *Theatre Notebook*, XIX (1964–5), 146–66.
Linthicum	M. Channing Linthicum, *Costume in the Drama of Shakespeare and his Contemporaries* (Oxford, 1936).
Markward	William B. Markward, 'A Study of the Phoenix Theatre in Drury Lane, 1617–1638' (Ph.D. thesis, University of Birmingham, 1953).
Marlowe, *Plays*	*The Complete Plays of Christopher Marlowe*, ed. Irving Ribner (New York, 1963).
Massinger, *Plays*	*The Plays and Poems of Philip Massinger*, ed. Philip Edwards and Colin Gibson, 5 vols. (Oxford, 1976).
Moryson	Fynes Moryson, *An Itinerary Containing his Ten Yeeres Travell*, 4 vols. (Glasgow, 1907–8).
M.S.R.	Malone Society Reprints.
Nason	Arthur Huntington Nason, *James Shirley, Dramatist: A Biographical and Critical Study* (New York, 1915).
O.E.D.	*The Oxford English Dictionary.*
Onions	C. T. Onions, *A Shakespeare Glossary*, 2nd ed. (Oxford, 1919).
Partridge	Eric Partridge, *Shakespeare's Bawdy*, 2nd ed. (London, 1955).
R.E.S.	*Review of English Studies.*
Revels History	*The Revels History of Drama in English*, ed. Clifford Leech and T. W. Craik, 8 vols. (London, 1975–83).
Robbins	Rossell Hope Robbins, *The Encyclopedia of Witchcraft and Demonology* (New York, 1959).
S.B.	*Studies in Bibliography.*
Shakespeare's England	Sir Sidney Lee *et al.*, *Shakespeare's England: An Account of the Life and Manners of his Age*, 2 vols. (Oxford, 1916).
Shirley, *Wks*	*The Dramatic Works and Poems of James Shirley*, ed. William Gifford and Alexander Dyce, 6 vols. (London, 1833).
Stone	Lawrence Stone, *The Family, Sex and Marriage in England, 1500–1800* (New York, 1977).
Strutt	Joseph Strutt, *Sports and Pastimes of the People of England*, 2nd ed. (London, 1810).
Sugden	Edward H. Sugden, *A Topographical Dictionary to the Works of Shakespeare and his Fellow Dramatists* (Manchester, 1925).

Tilley   Morris Palmer Tilley, *A Dictionary of the Proverbs in*
                                England in the Sixteenth and Seventeenth Centuries
                                (Ann Arbor, 1950).

My reference text for quotations from Shirley's plays and poems is the collected edition by Gifford and Dyce (Shirley, *Wks*). Shakespeare citations, unless
otherwise specified, refer to the revised Pelican text, *William Shakespeare:*
The Complete Works, ed. Alfred Harbage *et al.* (Baltimore, 1969). Titles of
Shakespeare's plays are abbreviated as in Onions, p. x. I have silently adopted
roman type for a few extended quotations from passages printed entirely in
italic (such as songs). And in quotations from old-spelling texts I have silently
modernised usage of *i/j*, *u/v* and long *s*.

Introduction

James Shirley's long life (1596–1666) bridges a drastic series of disruptions in the political, social, cultural and theatrical history of England. In the year of his birth, the Swan theatre was the newest showcase of stagecraft in Elizabethan London; by the year of his death, Nell Gwyn had already earned a place in the king's bed and in the hearts of Restoration playgoers. In terms of literary history, Shirley began his life as a contemporary of Spenser's, ended it as a contemporary of Defoe's. Through all of the radical changes, Shirley managed to survive: not always gracefully, but adequately and, to adopt a standard revered by the playwright himself, honourably.

The public record of Shirley's life is remarkably rich, partly because of the eloquent witness of his first biographer, Anthony à Wood,[1] and partly because of discoveries by modern scholars.[2] A middle-class Londoner by birth, Shirley was baptised at St Mary Woolchurch on 7 September 1596.[3] He attended the Merchant Taylors' School in London (1608–12), and may have proceeded briefly thereafter to St John's College, Oxford. Wood claims that he did so, and in one of the most tantalising anecdotes about the playwright, he reports that William Laud, then 'presiding' at St John's,

> had a very great affection for him, especially for the pregnant parts that were visible in him, but then having a broad or large mole upon his left cheek, which some esteemed a deformity, that worthy doctor would often tell him that he was an unfit person to take the sacred function upon him, and should never have his consent so to do.

The only fragment of this assertion that can be corroborated is the mole on Shirley's left cheek, which is discernible, though not prominent, in the two engraved portraits of the author.[4] If Shirley was ever an Oxonian, his presence has curiously disappeared from the records.

What does survive in official documents for the period after Shirley left grammar school is his own sworn testimony that for 'about two yeares or neere thereabouts' (1612/13–1614/15) he was employed as 'servant' to Thomas Frith, a London scrivener, who engaged in dubious moneylending schemes which ruined him in 1614.[5] Shirley's testimony is required because of the legal enquiries which Frith's shady dealings have precipitated, and in making his depo-

sition Shirley, perhaps prudently, shows remarkably little knowledge of Frith's financial affairs. Whatever the precise nature of
Shirley's service, it doubtless came to an end not long after Frith was
imprisoned in the autumn of 1614.

In the Easter term, 1615, Shirley matriculated at Catherine Hall,
Cambridge, where he earned his B.A. in 1617.[6] The yearning to be a
writer flourished during Shirley's Cambridge days, for by January
1617/18 he had prepared for publication his first literary work, *Echo
and Narcissus*,[7] no copies of which have survived, but which may well
be an early version of the long Ovidian narrative printed as *Narcissus,
or the Self-Lover* in Shirley's *Poems* (1646).

Even before he had access to a good fortune, Shirley was in want of
a wife. On 1 June 1618 at the age of twenty-two he married Elizabeth
Gilmet, the young daughter of a prominent St Albans family, whose
father and uncle took turns at being elected mayor of the town.[8] This
was a fortunate marriage in that it led indirectly to a comfortable
position as master of the grammar school in St Albans, and directly to
a family of several children: Mary (born in 1619), a second daughter
(who died in infancy), Mathias (born in 1624/5), Christopher, James
and Lawrinda. When and how this marriage came to an end is not
known, but Shirley was certainly married twice, to judge by the
bequests to 'my loveing wife, Frances' in his will.[9]

Shortly after his marriage to Elizabeth Gilmet, Shirley took steps
to ensure his financial solvency. On 2 November 1618 he secured a
written guarantee from the mayor and burgesses of St Albans that the
post of schoolmaster would be his on the death or retirement of the
incumbent, Thomas Gibson.[10] During the waiting period (on 19
September 1619) he took holy orders and was 'instituted to the
Curacy at Wheathampstead' in Hertfordshire, some five miles from
St Albans.[11] In January 1620/1 he took up his duties as master of the
grammar school, a position he held for the next four years.

Upon finding the 'employment' of teaching 'uneasy to him', in the
words of Wood's account, Shirley 'retired to the metropolis, lived in
Greys-inn, and set up for a play-maker, and gained not only a considerable livelyhood, but also very great respect and encouragement
from persons of quality, especially from Henrietta Maria the queen
consort, who made him her servant'. This radical transition began
when Shirley was twenty-eight, for by February 1624/5 his first play
had been licensed for performance and Shirley had moved, with his
family, to the parish of St Giles Cripplegate.

The School of Compliment, performed by the Lady Elizabeth's men at the Cockpit in Drury Lane, introduced the new playwright to his London public and began an association with Christopher Beeston, the theatrical manager, which lasted from 1624/5 until 1636. Near the beginning of this eleven-year span Beeston reorganised his company under the name of Queen Henrietta Maria's men, and it was to them that Shirley offered a long series of his best plays (normally two a year), including *The Wedding* (c. 1626), *The Witty Fair One* (1628), *The Traitor* (1631), *Love's Cruelty* (1631), *Hyde Park* (1632), *The Gamester* (1633), *The Example* (1634), *The Lady of Pleasure* (1635), and *The Duke's Mistress* (1635/6). Shirley's rising professional stature in these years may be measured in part by noticing Sir Henry Herbert's remarks, as Master of the Revels, on the occasion of a court performance (6 February 1633/4) of *The Gamester*; this play, says Herbert, was 'made by Sherley, out of a plot of the king's, given him by mee; and well likte. The king sayd it was the best play he had seen for seven years.'[12]

After the theatres were closed on account of the plague (12 May 1636), Shirley left London for Ireland, where he spent four years (1636–40) helping to establish the Werburgh Street theatre in Dublin.[13] For this troupe he wrote *The Royal Master* (1637), *St Patrick for Ireland* (c. 1639), and probably several other plays.

On his return to London in 1640, Shirley succeeded Massinger (who had recently died) as principal playwright for the King's men at Blackfriars. His sequence of plays for this company includes *The Cardinal* (1641) and *The Court Secret*, the last of which was not performed because of the closing of the theatres by parliament in 1642.

The years of Cromwell's hegemony were full of trouble for a playwright who had ostentatiously declared himself a royalist. After William Prynne's ill-advised if inadvertent attack on Henrietta Maria in *Histriomastix* (1633),[14] Shirley became an outspoken partisan of the queen's: he published an ill-tempered rebuke of Prynne as a dedicatory poem to Ford's *Love's Sacrifice* (1633), with heavy-handed irony he dedicated his own play, *The Bird in a Cage* (1633), to Prynne, and in collaboration with Inigo Jones and William Lawes he contrived the overstated splendour of a masque, *The Triumph of Peace* (1633/4), sponsored by the Inns of Court as a costly affirmation of loyalty to the crown.[15] Shirley's contribution to this last enterprise may be the reason for his being identified as 'one of the Valets of the Chamber of Queen Henrietta Maria' upon being admitted as an honorary member to Gray's Inn.[16]

'When the rebellion broke out', says Wood, 'he was invited by his

most noble patron William earl (afterwards marquess and duke) of
Newcastle to take his fortune with him in the wars, for that count had
engaged him so much by his generous liberality towards him, that he
thought he could not do a worthier act, than to serve him, and so
consequently his prince. After the king's cause declined, he retired
obscurely to London.' For his part in the wars, Shirley was inves-
tigated by the Committee for Compounding with Delinquents (in
January and February 1650/1) to whom he admitted his actions, declared his estate to be valued at £6, and sued for clemency. His plea
was granted in the form of a fine of £1 and the delivery of his goods
and person from the official threat implied in the term
'sequestration'.[17]

I have made no mention thus far of the most controversial statement in Wood's account, namely that Shirley 'changed his religion
for that of Rome'. Wood supposes such a conversion to have moti-
vated Shirley's renunciation of a career in the church in favour of the
schoolmaster's occupation. This question has occasioned a great deal
of research, from which no documentary proof in either direction has
emerged, and considerable debate the results of which remain incon-
clusive. While it can be stated with certainty that Shirley was a de-
voted and public royalist, if he was also a Catholic he kept his faith to
himself.

During the interregnum, according to Wood, Shirley returned to
'his old trade of teaching school, which was mostly in the White-
friers'. His publications during these years include a textbook and a
grammar designed for students of Latin, a collected edition of his
Poems, and various masques which may have been written for presentation by his schoolboys at Whitefriars.[18] One of these masques,
The Contention of Ajax and Ulysses for the Armour of Achilles, contains the most enduring lines which Shirley was ever to write:

> The glories of our blood and state
>   Are shadows, not substantial things;
>   There is no armour against fate;
>   Death lays his icy hand on kings:
>   Sceptre and crown
>   Must tumble down,
>   And in the dust be equal made
>   With the poor crooked scythe and spade.[19]

To the apparent public sentiment expressed in this dirge may be
added the personal feeling of a man who has faced hardship in the
service of his king.

By the time he made his will in July of 1666, Shirley was prosperous enough to bequeath £200 to each of his two surviving daughters and to his eldest son, sums of £100 and £150 to his other two sons, plus numerous token amounts to friends and acquaintances. The 'Remainder' of a presumably large estate, including 'plate, moneys, Jewells, Linnen, Woollen Bedding, brass, Pewter, or goods of any Kind whatsoever' were intended for the comfort of his widow.[20] This last bequest of Shirley's was never fulfilled, for, as Wood reports:

> he with his second wife Frances were driven by the dismal conflagration that happened in London an. 1666, from their habitation near to Fleet-street, into the parish of S. Giles's in the Fields in Middlesex, where being in a manner overcome with affrightments, disconsolations, and other miseries occasion'd by that fire and their losses, they both died within the compass of a natural day: whereupon their bodies were buried in one grave in the yard belonging to the said church of S. Giles's on the 29th of Octob. in sixteen hundred sixty and six.

For a playwright with a special gift for scenes of domestic pathos, and for a man who had lived his life at the mercy of the city of London, it was a fitting end.

2. THE PLAY

The first reader of *The Lady of Pleasure* to have recorded a critical response to the play is Abraham Wright, who at some time near the middle of the seventeenth century made the following notation in his commonplace book:

> Y[e] best play of Shirleys for y[e] lines, but y[e] plot is as much as none. y[e] latter end of y[e] 4th act y[e] scene twixt Celestine and y[e] lord is good for y[e] humour of neete complement. Aretina, who is y[e] lady of pleasure a good part for y[e] . . . expressing y[e] many waies of pleasure and expences. Celestine for y[e] same: both shewing y[e] pride and excesse in every thing of y[e] court ladies.[21]

Wright gives unusual prominence to Shirley, to judge by the space he allots in his commonplace book to quotations from and comments on eleven of Shirley's plays. By contrast, Beaumont and Fletcher are represented by six titles, Jonson and Shakespeare by two apiece. Thus Shirley's first literary critic is a sympathetic reader, and one whose standards of judgement are those common in his day rather than ours. *The Maid's Tragedy* is for Wright 'a very good play', better even than *A King and No King*, itself 'a good play . . . especially for y[e]

plot wch is extraordinary'. *The White Devil* is 'but an indifferent play
to reade, but for ye presentments I beeleeve good'; *A New Way to Pay
Old Debts* is 'a silly play'; and *Hamlet* 'but an indifferent play, ye lines
but meane'. However whimsical these judgements may seem today,
they are based on typical Caroline attitudes: a preference for tragi-
comedy over other dramatic forms, and a belief in the radical importance of plot.

Structure

Wright's claim that the plot of *The Lady of Pleasure* 'is as much as
none' ranks as his most interesting observation about the play.
What he means, no doubt, is that the play lacks a complicated in-
trigue, for this is what he praises in plays whose plots he admires.
The plot of *Hyde Park* is, according to Wright, 'best at ye last act',
and *The Duchess of Malfi* is to be commended 'especially for ye plot at
ye latter end'. Wright clearly has a taste for the bizarre coincidences,
reversals and contrivances which have disturbed many modern
readers of these plays, and he misses these artificial devices in *The
Lady of Pleasure*.

More importantly, he overlooks by the narrowest of margins the
structural axis which becomes apparent when the play is considered
not merely as a series of narrative events but as a social artefact.[22] In
drawing attention to Aretina's 'expences' and in commenting on 'y^e
pride and excesse in every thing of ye court ladies', Wright seems to
be reaching towards a concept such as conspicuous consumption or,
to use the language of the play itself, 'prodigality'. This impulse
governs the social behaviour of the characters in the play with such
alarming tyranny as to suggest that Shirley is observing and commenting on a pattern of life in the London society he intimately
knew.

The signs of prodigality in *The Lady of Pleasure* have almost nothing to do with the mere satisfaction of primary human appetites.
There is plenty of food in the world of the play, most of it made
available in the offstage banquets, taverns and ordinaries which
occupy a central place in the social lives of the gentry; but feasting in
this play is an acquired art in which competitive social nuances have
replaced gastronomical rumblings. When Alexander Kickshaw anticipates a tavern meal, he has in mind 'a dozen partridge in a dish'
along with pheasants, quails and sturgeon (IV.ii.148–51). When he
flatters himself with the prospect of dining at court, his desire is
explicitly 'not for the table' (V.ii.104) but for the pleasure of making a

favourable impression. The drinks which accompany such self-conscious meals may be sack or Rhenish or 'what strange wine else' (V.i.75), but never ale or beer. This is a world of sophisticated palates where Falstaff's traditional menus would be more likely to provoke derision than hunger.

The smells and savours associated with food in *The Lady of Pleasure* owe more to artifice than to nature. The appropriate symbol of refinement which alters and disguises natural food is the box of sugar-plums that Littleworth never tires of offering to the ladies. Equally telling is Kickshaw's resolution, on having discovered a lavish source of income, to 'forget there is a butcher' and rely instead on the advice of 'a witty epicure' in planning his meals (V.ii.105–7). Although food and talk about food are constantly crossing these characters' lips, there is nothing of the aromatic succulence which draws everyone in the direction of Ursula's passionately roasting pigs in *Bartholomew Fair*. Instead of simply appealing to the senses, food in *The Lady of Pleasure* is refined by art until it rivals the dreams of Sir Epicure Mammon.[23]

What is true about food holds even more conspicuously in the case of clothing. Here the extreme instance is that of Master Frederick, who arrives from the university in respectable academic dress only to discover that his aunt's fashionable pretensions have been mortified. Promptly consigned to the tutelage of Kickshaw and Littleworth, Master Frederick is transformed with great effort into a caricature of the over-dressed gallant. In a scene that amounts to a seventeenth-century fashion show (IV.ii), albeit one with a clumsy male model, Littleworth coaches Frederick in the conspicuous art of wearing his new clothes. The mundane considerations of comfort, cleanliness and utility are petulantly brushed aside in Littleworth's pursuit of pure ostentation. The wearer of truly fashionable clothing will find even his body altered, Littleworth claims: 'it is not / The cut of your apparel makes a gallant, / But the geometrical wearing of your clothes' (IV.ii.9–11). Good taste is hardly the point, and restraint is out of the question; the object of Littleworth's code of dress is flamboyance at any price.

The dressing of Master Frederick is only a slight exaggeration of what passes for normal elsewhere in the play. Lord Unready, whose name I have pilfered from Shirley's inadvertently appropriate stage direction,[24] makes his first two appearances while suffering the attentions of Master Haircut to such details of public life as his periwig. And Celestina, both wealth and youth on her side by virtue of being a

8 INTRODUCTION

widow at fifteen, broadens the principle of decorative ostentation to include her coach and sedan-chair. With an ingenuous honesty appropriate to her youth, Celestina admits that the purpose of lavish consumption is to be splendidly conspicuous: 'my balcony / Shall be the courtier's idol, and more gazed at / Than all the pageantry at Temple Bar' (I.ii.93–5). Celestina's desire to live in a world of 'silk and silver' (I.ii.21) may be shocking to her Steward, but it is simply the adolescent fantasy which corresponds to the values of her society at large.

Shirley's awareness of prodigality as more than an accident that happens to the rich – as a principle of human behaviour, in fact – can be deduced from his metaphorical application of the idea to the sexual experience of his characters. Kickshaw would like to be thought of as a sexual gourmet: hence, in alluding euphemistically to his female quarry, he prefers the term 'pheasant' (III.i. 140) to such traditional alternatives as 'mutton'. The note of bravado in Kickshaw's attitude towards women is a false one in the sense that it has nothing to do with sheer appetite or high spirits; his idiom belongs not to the locker-room but to the wine-tasting salon. The morning after his first meeting with Celestina finds Kickshaw enumerating her qualities with something of the collector's emphasis on status and scarcity: 'Such a widow is not common', he concludes, 'And now she shines more fresh and tempting / Than any natural virgin' (I.i.264–6).

But Kickshaw must not bear exclusive blame for an artificial and ornamental tone which is characteristic of sexual encounters and attitudes in the play as a whole. Madam Decoy is the broker in charge of conspicuous sexual consumption, and she has taken the trouble to provide her house with 'artful chambers, / And pretty pictures to provoke the fancy' (III.ii.20 1). Littleworth subscribes to an elaborately hierarchical theory of pimping (IV.ii.75–82), a view which lends credence to the rumour that some of the gallants 'are often my lord's tasters' (II.ii.92). Celestina, however skilful she may be in preserving her honour, is perfectly aware of the terms which society will place on her slightest gesture of sexual approval or discouragement:

> Some ladies are so expensive in their graces
> To those that honour 'em, and so prodigal,
> That in a little time they have nothing but
> The naked sin left to reward their servants;
> Whereas a thrift in our rewards will keep

> Men long in their devotion, and preserve
> Our selves in stock, to encourage those that honour us. (II.ii.66–72)

This is the language of an accomplished flirt. Celestina gains a reputation for chastity precisely because she knows how to manipulate her
suitors in order to provoke the maximum amount and the right kind
of conspicuous sexual adulation.

That Shirley himself wishes the notion of prodigality to be invoked
as a standard by which to judge the behaviour of his characters can be
inferred from the opening scene, in which Bornwell rebukes his wife
Aretina for taking up the fashionable patterns of town life with ex-
cessive and foolish enthusiasm. Bornwell is neither prudish nor avaricious; his case against the town rests partly on his instinctive preference for the life of a country squire, but it cannot be dismissed as
mere special pleading. He opposes Aretina's adopted way of life
because it is expensive, but this is only the surface of an argument
which cuts deeper. Prodigality is also artificial, competitive and tyrannical. It is artificial in the sense that even the rich materials of
Aretina's wardrobe 'dare / Not show their own complexions'
(I.i.91–2) but are covered in layers of ornament. It is competitive in
the sense that other fashionable women arouse in Aretina the fear of
being 'eclipsed' (I.i.279). And it is tyrannical in the sense that
Aretina does not have enough experience of high living to carry it off
casually:

> You make play
> Not a pastime but a tyranny, and vex
> Yourself and my estate by't. (I.i.109–11)

Thus, Bornwell's metaphors of prodigality as a form of suffocation –
an experience which can 'stifle' or which threatens 'choking' (I.i.82,
86) – are fully justified. On the evidence before him, Bornwell
believes that fashionable urban living is at odds with human sanity
and integrity.

I am not proposing that Bornwell be taken as Shirley's moral
mouthpiece in the play as whole. His view of events is restricted, his
understanding incomplete. His decision to mimic Aretina's
behaviour – to 'Repent in sack and prodigality', as he terms it
(I.i.290) – amounts to a tactical ploy too shallow to qualify as moral
wisdom. But in the opening confrontation with Aretina, Bornwell's
arguments are cogent and persuasive, all the more so because they
bear the stamp of personal conviction. That these arguments are

placed near the beginning of the play is, I believe, Shirley's way of
providing a vantage point from which prodigal indulgence can be
seen for what it is.

The structural pattern which I have been outlining is in part the
product of social forces which converged on the city of London during the reign of Charles I. In 1632 the king issued one in a series of
Stuart proclamations designed to prevent the rural gentry from
abandoning their estates in order to set up fashionable London re-
sidences, and listing among the consequences of current practice the
expenditure of large sums of money 'in excess of apparel provided
from foreign parts, to the enriching of other nations and unnecessary
consumption of a great part of the treasure of his realm, and in other
delights and expenses'.[25] This proclamation seems to have had about
as much effect as attempts to restrict the economic behaviour of a
privileged class by law normally do. What is important here is that, in
the London of 1632, conspicuous consumption was a social problem
of such magnitude that not even the king could ignore it.

The dimensions of the problem have been studied by Lawrence
Stone, who argues that conspicuous consumers fell into roughly four
overlapping but distinguishable categories. The first group, represented in *The Lady of Pleasure* by the presence of Lord Unready,
consisted of noblemen engaged in service to the crown and hence
required by tradition to maintain a level of 'pomp and circumstance'
consistent with their offices. The second group, of whom Haircut is a
humble example, was composed of persons willing to risk 'the cost of
attendance at Court in the hope of office'. Nearly everyone in the play
would qualify for membership in 'the third and largest group', made
up of 'those attracted to the pleasures and vanities of London, who
entered into a round of dissipation which in time inevitably under-
mined both health and fortune'. The fourth group, represented in
the play only by Bornwell, and imperfectly even then, 'were those
who stuck to the old country ways under the new conditions'. These
conservative gentlemen would need to spend lavishly on servants,
retainers and household provisions if the standards of country hospitality were to be maintained, and thus they could ruin themselves
by encountering the town, which required a second and unrelated
mode of expenditure.[26] Bornwell, who has sold his country estate in
order to accommodate Aretina's desire for urban life, remains tem-
peramentally if not economically a member of this final group.

Shirley's attention to the pattern of prodigality would suggest that,
in *The Lady of Pleasure*, he is a shrewd observer of London life, just

as surely as Dekker is in *The Shoemaker's Holiday*, Middleton in *A Chaste Maid in Cheapside*, Jonson in *Bartholomew Fair*, or Massinger in *The City Madam*. But the London Shirley observes is a rather different one, as might be expected from a playwright who held the title – however temporary or nominal – of 'one of the Valets of the Chamber of Queen Henrietta Maria'. The wide gap which separates *The Lady of Pleasure* from its antecedents in this specialised genre can be underscored by observing that nobody in Shirley's play belongs to a profession (let alone a trade), and hence there is no such thing as an honest day's work. Dekker's world is filled with people of both sexes who make things, ranging from garments to garlands; Middleton's London is centred in Goldsmith's Row and includes, aside from Yellowhammer himself, an assortment of watermen, comfit-makers, nurses, and other employees of the commercial world. Jonson's characters, though inhabiting the holiday world of the fair, are if anything more busily occupied in searching for bargains or guarding their purses or selling their products than they would be on an ordinary working day. And for Massinger, the social and moral standing of apprentices, artisans, merchants and whores is largely dependent on the kind and quality of the work they do. In *The Lady of Pleasure* the closest approximation to productive work is, as Aretina remarks, the effort required in having one's portrait painted:

> It does conclude
> A lady's morning work: we rise, make fine,
> Sit for our picture, and 'tis time to dine. (I.i.321–3)

Shirley's contribution to the comedy of London life rests primarily on his ability to observe and record the behaviour of a segment of society for whom consumption was a business not confined to recreational hours but spread out conspicuously to fill the entire day.

Where, then, does Shirley stand in relation to the world he creates in *The Lady of Pleasure*? Is he presenting us with an ironic vision of a society gone astray? Or is he, like Aretina, rather too easily taken in by the glamour of a circle he has entered as an outsider? Is he too eager to court his audience of would-be conspicuous consumers with a favourable reflection of themselves? These questions are not easily answered, partly because Shirley has neither Dekker's benevolent optimism nor Jonson's satirical swagger. What he has instead is a reticence which is even harder to interpret than Middleton's habitual detachment. 'I will say nothing positive', Shirley writes in the Prologue to *The Cardinal*; 'you may / Think what you please'.[27] I believe,

on the evidence provided by the structure of *The Lady of Pleasure*
itself, that Shirley was keenly aware of the self-indulgent vanity of
the society he created and of the audience he sought to entertain.
This view is consistent with the arguments he gives to Bornwell in
the opening scene. It is also consistent with Lord Unready's shocked
rejection of the proposal that he might sell his armorial bearings
(V.i.134–6); here at last is a stand taken on principle, in defiance of
the ethic of prodigality, and we are meant to respond with admiration. That Shirley is willing to heap scorn on the comic *arriviste*
characters – Sentlove, Kickshaw, Haircut and Littleworth – is readily deduced from the humiliations he prepares for them in the final
act. But with characters drawn from the nobility or gentry he is – like
Massinger – less candid, more insecure. In this sense Shirley was not
a courageous artist; or, to put the matter more charitably, his was the
tightrope-walker's courage, not the lion-tamer's.

Theme

The one crucial event in *The Lady of Pleasure*, which occurs offstage
during Act IV, is the adulterous coupling of Aretina and Alexander
Kickshaw. It is in relation to this act of infidelity that the implicit
values or overt pronouncements of each principal character need to
be assessed. And without claiming for Shirley a greatness that is
beyond his reach, it is only fair to observe that his treatment of infidelity in this play is remarkable in at least three respects: in its
resistance to the established conventions for dealing with infidelity in
the drama; in its presentation of the theme from a point of view which
allows the woman's side of the story to be told; and in its development
of the subject as a private matter with specific emotional consequences rather than as a public scandal.

The quickest way of calling to mind the range of assumptions
about infidelity which can be expected in Jacobean drama would be
to listen to the characters in *Othello*. The men of Shakespeare's
Venice – Brabantio, Cassio, Iago and Othello himself – become
eloquent partisans whenever the subject is introduced. The women
say nothing. Nothing, that is, until the quietly intimate undressing
scene which precedes the catastrophe. Here we are allowed to
overhear Desdemona and Emilia in casual conversation. The subject
is one that of course would preoccupy them. 'O, these men, these
men!' Desdemona begins:

Dost thou in conscience think – tell me, Emilia –

That there be women do abuse their husbands
In such gross kind?

Emilia responds, cryptically, 'There be some such, no question'; but
Desdemona presses forward, insisting on a personal answer.

Desdemona. Wouldst thou do such a deed for all the world?
Emilia. The world's a huge thing; it is a great price for a small vice. . . .
Marry, I would not do such a thing for a joint-ring, nor for
measures of lawn, nor for gowns, petticoats, nor caps, nor any petty
exhibition; but for all the whole world – 'Ud's pity! who would not
make her husband a cuckold to make him a monarch?
(IV.iii.58–75)

Still unconvinced, Desdemona disagrees in principle: 'Beshrew me if
I would do such a wrong / For the whole world' (IV.iii.77–8).

The radical division of opinion represented by Desdemona's absolute 'no' and Emilia's provisional 'yes' is in general characteristic of
attitudes taken towards infidelity in Jacobean drama. The absolute
'no', based overtly on idealistic perceptions of the meaning of chastity and linked indirectly to patterns of sexual paternalism, is the
standard invoked by Jacobean tragic heroes in assessing the
behaviour of their wives. Frankford's desire, in *A Woman Killed with
Kindness*, to recall the impossible past 'that I might take her / As
spotless as an angel in my arms'[28] is a paradigm case of masculine
idealism. Similar attitudes are expressed, often less attractively, by
many tragic husbands who fear betrayal: Sforza in Massinger's *The
Duke of Milan*, Leantio in Middleton's *Women Beware Women*, and
Caraffa in Ford's *Love's Sacrifice* have in common a sexual idealism
too fragile for the experience they encounter. Husbands who count-
enance infidelity with a provisional 'yes' are by definition excluded
from tragic action and relegated to satire. The most famous instance
is Allwit in *A Chaste Maid in Cheapside*, for whom being a cuckold is
'The happiest state that ever man was born to!'[29] Most of the cuck-
olds in Jacobean satire fall short of such amicable adjustment; but the
deflation of stature and esteem which accompanies cuckoldry is implied nonetheless by means of Harebrain's vapid cheerfulness in *A
Mad World, My Masters*, Pietro's impotent posturings in *The Malcontent* or even Camillo's drunken resignation in *The White Devil*.

If the concern over infidelity seems obsessive by modern standards
or the polarisation of attitudes artificial, it should be remembered
that sixteenth- and seventeenth-century laws and customs allowed
for detailed chaperoning of what went on in the bedrooms of the

nation. To judge by surviving evidence from the county of Essex, any
irregular sexual practice was likely to provoke a hearing in the
ecclesiastical courts.[30] Persons found guilty of adultery were subjected to shame punishments such as those listed by William Harrison: 'carting, ducking, and doing of open penance in sheets, in
churches and marketsteads'.[31] Although Harrison finds these modes
of rebuke too lenient ('For what great smart is it to be turned out of an
hot sheet into a cold . . .?' he asks), the threat of humiliation must
have been real enough for anyone who valued public opinion. Married women had more to fear from exposure for adultery than men,
since legal conventions permitted a husband to repudiate an unfaithful wife and protected him in the event that he chose to vindicate his
honour by killing her.[32]

The social context which clarifies the meaning of infidelity in the
drama can be illustrated by referring to the story of Frances Coke, the
younger daughter of Sir Edward Coke and Lady Elizabeth Hatton.
In G. R. Hibbard's lively account of the principal events, Frances
Coke is described as 'a very beautiful girl of fifteen' who was married
in 1617, for all the wrong dynastic reasons, to Sir John Villiers, the
elder brother of the Duke of Buckingham. Unable to endure a husband whose domestic routine included 'periodic fits of insanity', she
abandoned him in favour of a secluded and adulterous life with Sir
Robert Howard. In consequence, she was put on trial in 1627 and
assigned the shame punishment of 'open penance in sheets', to use
Harrison's phrase – a punishment she was able to evade thanks to
personal ingenuity and the collusion of her lover. In the first instance
she escaped the pursuit of her arresting officers by exchanging
clothes with a pageboy. The law, having been made an ass, would
show the persistence of a mule: in 1634, after a lapse of seven years,
Frances Coke was arrested and imprisoned for her failure to perform
penance as ordered. This time a friend of her lover's provided another male disguise, a bribe for the prison officer, and a safe escort to
France. Only after receiving the king's pardon, some six years later,
was she able to return to England.[33]

Aretina's position in *The Lady of Pleasure* is unlike that of Frances
Coke in all respects but one: like her contemporary in real life,
Aretina is playing a very dangerous game. As modern readers, we are
free to applaud her courage or to cringe at her folly, but we are not at
liberty to regard her act of sexual indulgence as a casual and relatively
harmless diversion. In fact, Aretina goes to great lengths to prevent
the public consequences of infidelity, only to find that she is vul-

nerable to the private consequences instead.

From the beginning Aretina is a restless married woman who has come to London looking for adventure and (by implication) trouble. She challenges her husband's authority and asserts her personal free-dom in words that recall Emilia's argument in *Othello* and anticipate the sentiments that would be spoken one day by Nora Helmer and Hedda Gabler:

> I take it great injustice
> To have my pleasures circumscribed and taught me.
> A narrow-minded husband is a thief
> To his own fame, and his preferment too.   (I.i.143–6)

Clearly, Aretina is deliberately seeking pleasures other than the domestic comforts of marriage. She is not actively seeking adultery, but when she meets a man (Alexander Kickshaw) both attractive enough to please her erotic tastes and shallow enough to be readily controlled, she decides that she will try him. And it is here, in her decision, that she stands apart from the passive Anne Frankfords and befuddled Mistress Harebrains of dramatic tradition. Although he disapproves of her decision, Shirley has enough respect for Aretina to treat her as a moral agent: as a person responsible for her actions.

Having settled on Kickshaw as her choice, Aretina directs all of her energies toward ensuring absolute circumspection. This she accom-plishes through the connivance of Madam Decoy, whose pro-fessional credit is dependent on the same code of secrecy which ap-plies to espionage agents in hostile territory. Thus, Aretina gives Decoy her instructions in a confidential whisper (III.ii.13.1), and adds the solemn warning: 'He must not / Have the least knowledge of my name or person' (III.ii.25–6). Decoy's performance borders on the spectacular: Kickshaw is blindfolded and brought to a darkened room where Decoy persuades him, with the rhetoric of gold pieces, to enter an offstage chamber and make love to someone he believes to be a witch in one of her more attractive metamorphoses. In every tech-nical point, Aretina has achieved her purpose; scandal has been avoided, her husband is none the wiser, and her sexual partner is prevented by his ignorance from betraying her.

Shirley's real achievement in writing the part of Aretina rests on his understanding of how she would behave on the morning after this ambivalent encounter. The occasion of her next appearance is Frederick's transformation into a clothes-horse, which she handles with approval and poise. Then Kickshaw enters, also dressed in new

clothes, and Aretina must admit, 'Now he looks brave and lovely'
(IV.ii.143). After an appropriately brief social conversation, she can
reassure herself: 'I am confident he knows me not, and I were worse
than mad to be my own betrayer' (IV.ii.172–3). The need for circumspection, still uppermost in Aretina's mind, continues to govern
every nuance of her social behaviour.

Her husband is the first to notice that Aretina's bearing is unchar-
acteristically 'melancholy' (IV.ii.181). And in private conversation
between husband and wife, Aretina strikes a philosophical key which
has not been hers before. She distinguishes between 'True beauty'
which pertains to the soul and superficial charm 'That touches but
our sense' (IV.ii.194–9), and although she is overtly using the distinction to praise Celestina, her mood suggests that she is introspec-
tively concerned with her own recent actions. Shirley avoids the
stereotypical alternatives which men prepare for unfaithful wives:
Aretina does not melt into guilty incoherence, nor does she turn into
a brazen strumpet of limitless appetite. Instead, she remains what she
was – a morally cogent human being – though her sense of self now
includes a new and disturbing set of experiences.

Careful as she has been to avert public shame, Aretina cannot fore-
stall private humiliation. In her next encounter with Kickshaw she
has the opportunity of speaking with him privately, and what she
learns is devastating to her pride. Not only does Kickshaw swagger
impertinently at the thought of continuing to exploit his new source
of revenue, but he remains convinced that he has slept with 'an old
witch, a strange ill-favoured hag' (V.ii.146), 'a most insatiate, abominable devil with a tail thus long' (V.ii.157–8). To hear herself described – however callously or unwittingly – in these terms is enough
to reduce Aretina to tears. It is in this condition that her husband
finds her in the final scene, at which point the two of them withdraw
for 'ten minutes' (V.iii.10) and return publicly reconciled. For the
first time Aretina takes a submissive stance in relation to Bornwell: 'I
throw my own will off', she announces, 'And now in all things obey
yours' (V.iii.176–7). This resolution, though morally satisfying to
the orthodox, is dramatically specious for reasons I shall hold in
reversion for the moment, since they have more to do with
Bornwell's character than with Aretina's.

I have chosen to concentrate on Shirley's treatment of one character in the adulterous triangle – the unfaithful wife – because it is in the
sensitive revelation of Aretina's nature that he is at his best.
Kickshaw, as I have repeatedly implied, is a fairly stupid fop who

fancies himself a genuine libertine. The part could be flamboyantly arresting if played by the right actor, but hardly more than that. With Bornwell Shirley has created problems that require better solutions than he has given them, particularly in the final scene of the play.

From the outset Bornwell has been an attractive figure: a husband whose heart is in the country but who is willing to tolerate the city for his wife's sake, a man of settled habits who is willing to risk adventure if that is what society requires. The action of the play has made him a cuckold. But the consequences of this deeply personal affront, both for Bornwell's own estimate of himself and for the relationship between husband and wife, Shirley chooses to ignore. At Aretina's tearful request Bornwell follows her offstage, and on their return his rhetorical stance is too pompous to be genuinely reassuring. 'Dearer now / Than ever to my bosom', he says to Aretina, 'thou shalt please / Me best to live at thy own choice' (V.iii.179–81). Are we to assume that Aretina has told him the whole truth, and that he feels the injury no more deeply than this? Or must we believe that Aretina, though presenting herself as 'A penitent' (V.iii.176), has been prudently selective in her confession? The play provides no adequate answers to these questions; the truth is that we can never know.[34] If Shirley took special pains to insist on the emotional complexity of Aretina's experience, he seems to have glossed over the corresponding emotions in the case of Bornwell for the purpose of concluding the play on a note of domestic tranquillity. And the price for achieving this purpose is a heavy one. Just where the audience is expecting a confrontation which will resolve at last the conflict between Aretina's assertion of liberty and Bornwell's insistence on responsibility, Shirley remains enigmatically silent. There is a point at which reticence becomes evasion, and Shirley is dangerously close to it; what appears to be simply a technical fault in dramatic construction is also a failure of nerve.

In complementary opposition to the adulterous meeting between Aretina and Kickshaw, Shirley presents the Platonic relationship between Celestina and Lord Unready. In the early scenes, the contrast between Aretina and Celestina is handled with considerable adroitness. Both women are engaged in the game of indulging in prodigality while keeping appearances unruffled. As the widow of someone called Bellamour, Celestina has a freedom from personal obligations which she enjoys exploiting perhaps beyond the limits of good taste but never farther than modesty permits. While Aretina is growing impatient with the restrictions of married life, Celestina is expertly

avoiding the 'new marriage fetters' (II.ii.47) which any number of
suitors would wish to impose. When Lord Unready appears we learn
that he too has suffered bereavement; the death of someone called
Bella Maria has deprived him of domestic bliss but not of an ideal of
human perfection which he continues to worship.

All that remains is to bring these two lovelorn aristocrats together –
a procedure which Shirley manages at exceeding length. Their first
meeting begins with exchanges of mutual praise that border on idola-
try, and appears to be moving quickly towards a seduction, when
Lord Unready abruptly announces that he has withstood temptation
and remains true to Bella Maria. Celestina now reports that, had her
seducer been in earnest, she would have rewarded his 'wanton flame'
not with compliance but with 'scorn' (IV.iii.175). Their second encounter follows a similar pattern: Lord Unready proposes that
Celestina become his mistress in 'the now court Platonic way'
(V.iii.54), she appears to accept and then scoffs at his offer, he
becomes petulant, she rebukes him, and at length both agree to a
stand-off in which they will celebrate one another 'with chaste
thoughts' (V.iii.159) as if nothing whatever had occurred. It is hard
to believe that Shirley had in mind in these scenes anything more
than an extended allusion to the courtly cult of Platonic love,[35] for in
any other terms the relationship is a shambles. True, nobody wants
to praise a fugitive and cloistered virtue, but this is the opposite
extreme. It is difficult to credit as ideal chastity a pattern of behaviour
which Swinburne described in another context as 'obscene
abstinence'.[36]

Still, if Shirley failed in the noble attempt to dramatise the highest
reaches of moral idealism, he failed in distinguished company. What
remains valuable in *The Lady of Pleasure* is the sensitive interpretation of imperfect humanity, especially in the character of Aretina.
And here the interpretation is a sensitive one, because Shirley has
gone beneath the surfaces of historical custom and literary convention to reveal what is fundamentally an act of betrayal which im-
pinges partly on another person but principally on the self.

Language

The most vigorous attack on Shirley's abilities as a poet is tucked
away, almost as a digression, in an essay entitled 'Variation in
Shakespeare and Others' by C. S. Lewis.[37] The attack depends on a
subtle argument about the poetic habits of Elizabethan and later
dramatists, all of whom, Lewis claims, relied on the 'method of vari-

ation'. As opposed to the method of construction, by means of which a poet such as Milton builds a logical sequence of ideas and images to a point of apparently inevitable completion, the method of variation allows the poet greater freedom and flexibility. He can bring together a dozen different images, all of them experimentally related to a particular idea, none of them presented as definitive. The master of this second technique is Shakespeare, but 'it is shared by all the Elizabethan dramatists'.

The method of variation is especially attractive to playwrights in that it allows the actor to speak, even in moments of great rhetorical splendour, with an apparently unrehearsed tentativeness, as if the character's own sensibility (and not the poet's craft) were proposing the multifarious perceptions of experience. Among the examples which Lewis draws from Marlowe, Jonson, Middleton, Ford and Shakespeare is the following speech from *Antony and Cleopatra*:

> His legs bestrid the ocean: his reared arm
> Crested the world: his voice was propertied
> As all the tunèd spheres, and that to friends;
> But when he meant to quail and shake the orb,
> He was as rattling thunder. For his bounty,
> There was no winter in't: an autumn 'twas
> That grew the more by reaping: his delights
> Were dolphin-like . . . .   (V.ii.82–9)

The coherence of this speech depends on Cleopatra's feeling for Antony, and is hence beyond question. And the poetic technique, to use Lewis's metaphor, is like the darting of a swallow: the music of the spheres, the rattling thunder, the autumn harvest and the dolphin are all genuine glimpses though none of these alternatives offers a point of rest from which one might compose a full portrait.

In Shirley's verse, Lewis argues, all the 'peculiar vices' of this method are 'painfully visible'. These vices consist of imaginative infertility, implied by Shirley's 'unfailing' reliance on the single resource of variation, and dramatic immobility, the result of Shirley's willingness to sacrifice the progressive movement of a scene for 'endless change of language'.

Believing he has observed these vices in the argument between Bornwell and Aretina in the opening scene, Lewis closes his case against Shirley with words that beguile:

> On the strictly dramatic side he has nothing to say that could not have been
> said in six lines. 'Why are you angry?' asks Bornwell. 'Because you stint

me,' retorts the lady. 'I don't. On the contrary I allow you to spend far too much,' says Bornwell. 'Well, I still think you're mean,' says Lady Bornwell. That is the whole scene, as drama. What swells it to its 130 odd lines is pure *variation* on the theme 'you spend too much' put into the mouth of Bornwell. During this the dramatic situation stands still. 'Have you done, Sir?' Lady Bornwell asks at the end of her husband's first speech; at the end of his third she is sill asking, 'Have you concluded your lecture?' The angry husband and the scornful wife remain dramatically immobile and the play ceases to go forward while the waves of variation roll over the audience. In other words, what Shirley has here to say as a dramatist is extremely little; and to convert that little into something that should seem richer he has to call in variation.

These are serious charges, powerfully asserted, and I have quoted them at length because they deserve to be seriously answered.

To begin, Lewis's commentary on the scene between Bornwell and Aretina requires some comment in its own right. His remarks owe their amusing charm to a technique that many experienced lecturers find irresistible: the technique of speeding up the pace of a scene or a plot in the retelling so as to produce a caricature. The effect is the same as that produced by an old piece of newsreel played back at twice the intended speed. In itself this is a harmless diversion, but it provides a very bad basis for judging anything. The same technique could be applied, with hilarious results, to the long expository scene between Prospero and Miranda in *The Tempest* (I.ii.1–185).

Readers who are willing to take the opening scene of *The Lady of Pleasure* at a less breathtaking pace will notice a great many subtleties of dramatic language which caricature cannot reproduce. Before Bornwell enters (I.i.45.1), Aretina has already told her Steward that she is glad to have put behind her the provincial boredom of country living. Bornwell's first words are solicitous: 'How now? What's the matter? . . . Angry, sweet heart?' (ll. 46–7). Aretina's response is beautifully evasive: 'I am angry with myself, / To be so miserably restrained' (ll. 47–8). For the moment her sense of decorum prevents her from admitting that the Steward and Bornwell are the real objects of her anger, and part of the dramatic purpose of the argument as a whole is to show Aretina's genuine dissatisfaction breaking through the surface of well-bred poise.

Bornwell appeals to his own generosity, arguing that Aretina should at least give him credit for his willingness to placate her by moving to the town; but this gets him nowhere, so he rebukes her extravagance in a series of speeches which do depend on rhetorical variation. Among the targets of Bornwell's aversion are the following:

> Your change of gaudy furniture, and pictures
> Of this Italian master and that Dutchman's;
> Your mighty looking-glasses, like artillery,
> Brought home on engines . . .   (ll. 74–7)

The appeal to good taste (in 'gaudy') is intended to nettle Aretina, and the nonchalance about her art collection is deliberately dismissive. But Bornwell remains good-humoured: there is a mock-heroic levity in his inflation of 'looking-glasses' into 'artillery', transported on military 'engines'. As Pope recommends, Bornwell is 'using a vast force to lift a *feather*'.[38]

Aretina's impatience is progressively revealed. She tries the ironic parry – 'I like / Your homily of thrift' (ll. 98–9) – but when this merely provokes further accusations she lets Bornwell know she finds him 'tedious' (l. 133) and 'avaricious' (l. 136). Then she retorts with her own lecture, which includes the reproof of Bornwell, quoted earlier, for behaving as only 'a narrow-minded husband' would (l. 145).

If the actors who play this scene are at all sensitive to what Shirley has given them, they will want to avoid at all cost the suggestion that this is a normal conversation which occurs every other day in the Bornwell household. To give in to caricature in this way would reduce the couple to Dagwood and Blondie, or to 'the angry husband and the scornful wife' of C. S. Lewis's description. What Shirley gives the actors is the chance to develop a series of delicate emotional adjustments between husband and wife – adjustments which occur because of the recent and decisive changes in their pattern of social living. The language he writes for them is not in itself brilliant, but it is full of dramatic possibilities which the actors can exploit and enrich.

I trust that Shirley has been cleared from suspicion on the charge of dramatic immobility. But the question of imaginative infertility remains, and here my defence will be qualified in certain crucial respects. First, however, I should like to offer Shirley the opportunity of defending himself, in the following impressive example of variation spoken by Celestina:

> You two, that have not 'twixt you both the hundredth
> Part of a soul, coarse woollen-witted fellows

Without a nap, with bodies made for burdens;
You that are only stuffings for apparel
(As you were made but engines for your tailors
To frame their clothes upon and get them custom)
Until men see you move, yet then you dare not,
Out of your guilt of being the ignobler beast,
But give a horse the wall (whom you excel
Only in dancing of the brawl, because
The horse was not taught the French way) . . . .
. . . . But I waste time
And stain my breath in talking to such tadpoles.
Go home and wash your tongues in barley-water,
Drink clean tobacco, be not hot i'th' mouth,
And you may 'scape the beadle; so I leave you
To shame and your own garters.   (III.ii.293–319)

This is Shirley at his satiric best: precise yet conversational, inventive but under control. In a series of variations nearly twice as long as that reproduced in the quotation, Celestina is deflating Kickshaw and Littleworth in response to the verbal abuse which they have directed at her. She begins by improvising on a clothing metaphor ('woollen-witted') until she has transformed her assailants into dancing mannequins. She turns the slander of her accusers back on them in the form of foul, unwashed, tobacco-stained breath. And she concludes with a brilliant adaptation of a proverb which recommends hanging in one's own garters as a last resort for fools.[39] The passage as a whole indicates what Shirley owes to his 'acknowledged master, learned JONSON',[40] though in Jonson the fools would have less to fear from a verbal opponent than from the deflating ironies of their own rhetorical habits.

Although Shirley's reliance on variation is not the mechanical and sterile reflex which Lewis's description implies, there are two special respects in which his limited imagination does detract from his ability as a poet. The first of these is a narrowness of range, the result of a virtually exclusive concentration on the social and verbal behaviour of the middle and upper levels of society.[41] Instead of a wide spectrum of languages, ranging as in Jonson from the courtly inanities of Sir Amorous La Foole to the sensual vulgarity of Ursula the pig-woman, Shirley confines himself to the idiom of cultivated speakers of English, and uses their speech as the norm in judging such relatively minor aberrations as pretension (in Haircut's case) or effusion (in Lord Unready's). This constricted verbal register brings with it a second weakness: the inability to provide each character with a distinctively personal style of speaking.[42] Celestina's shrewd wit, in the passage quoted above, is not so much a personal idiom as a particularly agile exercise in a verbal mode which all of the characters in *The Lady of Pleasure* either claim or would like to claim as their own. I am not asserting that all of the characters are equally witty, but rather that all of them would subscribe to the same standard of wit. And though Celestina is a brilliant success by this standard, and Littleworth a dismal failure, there is not in Shirley the close relationship between a character and his or her language which, in the case of greater playwrights, identifies a turn of speech as indelible Mosca or vintage Falstaff.

Shirley's abilities as a poet and playwright are, in the last analysis, those of a highly skilled professional. D. J. Enright's discerning assessment of Shirley is consistent, in large measure, with the arguments I have been advancing:

> Though he had no original genius, the range of his reference is wider than that of later comedy. His is a neat, fluent, easy, and rather colourless style, yet simple rather than insipid. The emotional pressure is never very high, and the metaphorical tension so slack that obviously he wrote in verse only because it was the tradition. Yet this makes for a healthier atmosphere than we find in much of Beaumont and Fletcher; after them we welcome Shirley's lack of pretension. He is concerned with a polite society which has not yet grown altogether complacent about the rest of the world.[43]

No purpose would be served by quarrelling over minor matters of emphasis in this basically sound evaluation. I should like to add only that Shirley's claim on a modern reader's attention rests not exclusively on his literary merits, but also on his performance as a theatrical craftsman. And it is to the theatre of Shirley's day that I now wish to turn.

3. THE PLAY IN PERFORMANCE

The first performance of *The Lady of Pleasure* took place in late October or early November 1635. The play was licensed for the theatre on 15 October, [44] and by 5 or 6 November it had attracted sufficient notice to deserve mention in John Greene's diary. Referring to the party of guests which gathered to celebrate his sister's wedding, Greene wrote as follows: 'wee were at a play, some at cockpit, some at blackfriers. The play at cockpit was Lady of pleasure, at blackfriers the conspiracy'.[45] A month later, on 8 December, Sir

Humphrey Mildmay recorded in his account book the expenditure of
one shilling for admission to the play, and in his diary he added the
following description: 'dined wth Rob[ert] Dowgill wente to the
La[dy] of pleasure & sawe that rare playe came home late Supped'.[46]

Very little can be inferred with confidence from these laconic observations by members of Shirley's audience. Indeed, Greene may
not have been a member of this audience at all, if he was among those
wedding celebrants who chose to see *The Conspiracy* at Blackfriars
rather than Shirley's play at the Cockpit. Still, Greene's notation
confirms one fact and one assumption: it agrees with the title-page of
the quarto (1637) and with the Lord Chamberlain's list (10 August
1639)[47] in assigning *The Lady of Pleasure* to the Cockpit in Drury
Lane, also known as the Phoenix theatre; and it supports the view of
some theatre historians that by 1635 the Cockpit and Blackfriars
were theatrical institutions of virtually equal prestige.[48]

Mildmay's jottings, however cryptic, will reward more detailed
inspection. First, the shilling which Mildmay spent on 8 December
1635 appears to have been the normal minimum price of admission
for a Cavalier gentleman. I doubt that Sir Humphrey would have
been satisfied to pay the absolute minimum of sixpence, if by such
thrift he were to risk the social opprobrium which Shirley attaches to
unsophisticated spectators in the Prologue to *The Example*:

> Nay, he that in the parish never was
> Thought fit to be o' the jury, has a place
> Here, on the bench, for sixpence; and dares sit,
> And boast himself commissioner of wit.[49]

Indeed, in his recorded decade of playgoing, Mildmay never paid
less than a shilling for a performance at a professional theatre.[50] He
often paid exactly a shilling, as he did when he saw 'a pretty & Merry
Co[m]edy att the Cocke' (6 June 1933), or when he visited Blackfriars
to see *The Wits* on one occasion (22 January 1633/4), *The Elder Brother* on another (25 April 1635). Frequently Mildmay paid more than
a shilling: 'a Newe play Called the spartan Lady' (1 May 1634) cost
him a shilling and threepence, a 'base play att the Cocke pitt' (20
March 1633/4) cost him one and six, and an unnamed play at the
Globe (18 July 1633) one shilling and tenpence. When he was 'with
company' Mildmay's expenditures reflected his hospitality, ranging
from about three shillings up to eleven. On these occasions, no doubt,
Mildmay wanted to be thought well of, to be 'held the witty man, /

[Who] censures finely, rules the box, and strikes / With his court nod consent to what he likes'.[51]

When he paid his shilling to see *The Lady of Pleasure*, Mildmay was doing what was typical and unpretentious for a person of his social class and theatrical tastes.[52] And, in attending the theatre between his mid-day meal (when he 'dined') and his evening meal (when he 'Supped'), Mildmay was engaging in perfectly normal behaviour both for himself and countless others. When he described *The Lady of Pleasure* as 'that rare playe', however, Mildmay was breaking with his personal habits: though in the space of a decade he recorded sixty-one theatrical excursions, he seldom confided his judgement to the diary. On three occasions he expressed distaste for a play, and on three others approbation. In the eyes of its first theatrical critic, *The Lady of Pleasure* appears to have been an outstanding achievement.

It is no longer possible to see what Sir Humphrey Mildmay saw or to hear what he heard. Modern readers who wish to recover some rough impression of the nature and quality of Sir Humphrey's experience on the afternoon of 8 December 1635 are at the mercy of historical evidence, especially as it pertains to three principal subjects: the design of the playhouse which Mildmay visited, the talents of the theatrical company engaged in the performance and the staging requirements of the play being performed.

The Theatre

The Cockpit in Drury Lane must have seemed like a second home to James Shirley in 1635. Out of nearly twenty full-length plays he had written by this date, all but one had been produced on the Cockpit stage. In the present context, therefore, anything that can be discovered about the design of the Cockpit serves the double purpose of bringing into focus the first production of *The Lady of Pleasure* while enriching with substance the setting for the playwright's career. Since much of the evidence connected with this playhouse has been the subject of fairly recent enquiry, debate and conjecture, I have chosen to deal separately with these scholarly problems in Appendix A, pp. 189–97. Readers curious about the details of theatre history may wish to consult these pages, and even the not-so-curious will find in the drawing by Inigo Jones (p. 192) – quite possibly a design for the Cockpit in Drury Lane – a visual point of departure for the theatrical imagination. And so, without making the scholarly detours and tentative qualifications which would otherwise be necessary, I propose here to offer as brief and simple a description of the Cockpit as the complexity of the evidence will allow.

The Cockpit in Drury Lane was a relatively small, indoor theatre, with seating capacity for approximately 500 spectators. Most of the spectators were seated in two levels of U-shaped galleries which began on either side of the stage and extended to the back of the auditorium. The space enclosed by the U of the galleries was divided into two roughly equal areas: a rectangular space reserved for the platform-style stage, and a semicircular space known as the 'pit', in which spectators were seated on benches. The most coveted seats were the 'boxes', and these were probably situated in the lower gallery, directly to the left and right of the stage. Distinguished patrons were, in some instances, allowed to sit on stools at the left and right margins of the stage.

As was the case in the other great London theatres of the day, the stage itself was divided into two levels: the main acting area on the platform, and an 'above'. Entrances and exits to and from the platform were routinely made from two doors, at upstage left and upstage right, in the wall separating the stage from the backstage tiring-house. This wall was decorated with hangings, a feature of the stage often put to practical use in scenes requiring a character to withdraw or to be discovered. There may have been a third, centrally located door in the façade between the entrances upstage left and right. Or the company may have used the aperture between two panels of arras at upstage centre when the action of a particular scene required a third point of entry to the platform.

The upper acting level, or the 'above', was most commonly used as an observation post from which one or two characters could view and comment on the action unfolding below. There was certainly a staircase connecting the above and the platform, but it was probably situated backstage, out of the view of the audience. Thus an actor could descend in a few seconds from the observation post above to the platform stage, but he would have to make his descent by a backstage route.

Many small hand-held properties (books, letters, tapers, musical instruments, mirrors, etc.) were carried on stage by the actors who would use them in particular scenes, but large properties would have to be placed in advance by the servants, maids or other minor characters in the cast. The list of large properties required by plays written for the Cockpit is long but fairly conventional: it includes tables, chairs, thrones, beds, banquets, chessboards and coffins. The company's property room no doubt held a supply of these basic items which, with a little ingenuity, could be adapted to the needs of almost any production.

Musical effects or intervals, dancing and masques within plays were frequently called for by playwrights who wrote for the Cockpit. In Shirley's plays alone the musicians of the Cockpit are called upon, at various times, to support the dramatic action with such traditional instruments as lutes, recorders, trumpets, cornets, fiddles, drums, bells and even bagpipes.

In general, the sights and sounds which Sir Humphrey Mildmay would have expected on the afternoon of 8 December 1635 were not radically different from those familiar to an earlier generation of playgoers for whom the Hope, the Fortune and the Globe had set the standard in theatrical taste. But the sheer physical scale of the spectacle had been drastically reduced, and with it had come a change in the style of production. As an indoor playhouse, the Cockpit (like Blackfriars) provided candles to illuminate the action, and this technical change in itself promoted a feeling of intimacy which would have been impossible in broad daylight. And the relative uniformity of the smaller audience, now drawn exclusively from the social group which could afford to squander a shilling or more on an afternoon at the theatre, was bound to exert its influence in such directions as cultural sophistication or smugness. In this new environment, playwrights and actors alike might reach for subtleties of expression and modulations of tone unfamiliar to their Elizabethan predecessors. If this was indeed the case, it should become apparent as the actors take their places on the Cockpit stage.

The Company

From 1625 until 1636 (precisely the years of Shirley's regular association with the Cockpit), the resident company was Queen Henrietta Maria's men – the most famous of a succession of theatrical troupes organised by the Cockpit impresario, Christopher Beeston. Of the actors in Queen Henrietta's company in 1635, at least twelve can be securely identified. Collectively, they possess all of the talents one would expect of a first-class company put together by a shrewd theatrical entrepreneur. The members include the sedate if ageing leading man, the fresh-faced adolescent already admired for his female roles, the former adolescent now being groomed for romantic leads, the veteran comedian who has never been averse to earning a laugh by exploiting his unusually skinny physique, and a sprinkling of character actors who habitually expend their energies on assorted merchants, dukes, old men and servants. In short, Queen Henrietta's men were a repertory company in the best sense of the term: their well-balanced and amply diversified abilities must have been perfectly suited to a play like *The Lady of Pleasure*, which requires stylish collaboration among the actors who play the sixteen speaking roles, and which distributes responsibility rather evenly among the players who take the eight principal parts.

If the company had a star actor, it would be Richard Perkins (*c.* 1585–1650). I qualify his status in this way because, among the virtues attributed to Perkins by his contemporaries is the one which star performers shun: professional modesty. Perkins played Barabas in the Cockpit revival of Marlowe's *The Jew of Malta* (1633); in the Prologue which Heywood wrote for this occasion, Edward Alleyn is described as 'peerless' in his creation of the original Jew for Lord Strange's men; Perkins is awarded the lesser laurel of 'merit' which is said to be consistent with his own view of the matter: 'nor is it his ambition / To exceed or equal [Alleyn], being of condition / More modest'.[53] However surprising, Heywood's assertion should not be lightly dismissed, for his association with Perkins was of long standing, dating back more than thirty years to an earlier generation when Perkins, Heywood and Beeston were all young actors with the Earl of Worcester's men. The earliest known reference to Perkins's career, in Henslowe's *Diary*, is remarkable for its quaint anticipation of a professional friendship: 'Lent unto Richard perkens the 4 of septemb[er] 1602 to bye thing[s] for thomas hewode playe . . . xvˢ'.[54] Probably seventeen years of age, Perkins was obviously very much the apprentice in 1602. But a decade later he had acquired the skills to attract an unprecedented compliment from Webster. Now a member of Queen Anne's men at the Red Bull, Perkins had played in the first staging of *The White Devil*: a generally unsuccessful production, to judge by Webster's grumblings in the preliminary letter 'To the Reader' of the published play. Whatever the causes of Webster's disappointment, the actors' performances were not among them, for he acknowledges their efforts in a note appended to the final scene, concluding his commendation as follows: 'in particular I must remember the well approved industry of my friend Master Perkins, and confess the worth of his action did crown both the beginning and end'.[55]

By 1635, at the age of fifty, Perkins was a veteran performer. His known roles, aside from Barabas, are Sir John Belfare in Shirley's

The Wedding (*c.* 1626), Captain Goodlack in the first part of Heywood's *The Fair Maid of the West* (*c.* 1630), Fitzwater in Davenport's *King John and Matilda* (*c.* 1634), and Hanno in Nabbes's *Hannibal and Scipio* (1635). All of these parts he played for Queen Henrietta's Men, whom he joined in about 1626 and with whom he remained until their dispersion a decade later.[56] In one of them he earned a tribute from Andrew Pennycuicke, a man who claimed to be a fellow actor and whose edition of *King John and Matilda* (1655) informs us that the part of Fitzwater was played by 'M[aster] Perkins, Whose action gave Grace to the Play'.[57]

Of these roles, the one which most clearly concerned Shirley is that of Sir John Belfare in *The Wedding*. Here Perkins played the part of a dignified father, a man who behaves with surprising restraint in his dealings with his marriageable daughter, but who is nevertheless prepared to defend her honour with firmness and vigour. When Belfare makes comfortable allusions to his 'gray hairs' (III.ii),[58] Shirley seems to be indulging in his habit of writing with even the personal appearance of a particular actor in mind. This impression can be confirmed by observing the attitude of candid confidence and whimsical frankness on the Cavalier-style face in the only known portrait of Perkins, reproduced as the frontispiece to this volume.

When Shirley wrote *The Lady of Pleasure* he must have visualised Perkins in one of the principal roles. I believe Sir Thomas Bornwell to have been the only genuinely suitable part. His is the only 'straight' role which could be effectively played by an actor of fifty. As the exceptionally tolerant husband of Aretina, Bornwell combines authority, good humour and restraint in a manner quite reminiscent of Sir John Belfare in *The Wedding*. Since modesty, industry and grace were characteristics apparently within Perkins's command, he would have been eminently qualified (both by experience and by nature) to take on Bornwell's part. It should not be surprising to find such easy compatibility between the player and his role in a company where, as in this case, the working relationship between star actor and leading dramatist extended over approximately nine years.

The outstanding comic among Queen Henrietta's men was William Robbins, evidently a professional thin man, who appears to have been generously assisted by William Sherlock, a professional fat man. In *Historia Histrionica* (1699), James Wright names '*Robins* a Comedian' among 'those of principal Note at the *Cockpit*'.[59] Shirley seems to have placed considerable confidence in his talent, for in *The Wedding* it is Robbins in the role of 'Rawbone, *a thin citizen*' who

remains onstage at the close to speak the Epilogue and ask for the
spectators' applause. Physically emaciated and morally avaricious,
Rawbone repeatedly draws attention to these comic faults, as do
other characters, who refer to him as 'a piece of folly! / A thing made
up of parchment', or little more than 'an anatomy' (I.iii).[60] Robbins's
other known roles include 'Carazie, *an Eunuch*' in *The Renegado*[61]
and Antonio, the title role, in *The Changeling*.[62] William Sherlock
appears in *The Wedding* as 'Lodam, *a fat gentleman*' with a penchant
for obvious lines, like 'I have no stomach to your acquaintance'
(II.iii) or 'love is worse than a Lent to me, and fasting is a thing my
flesh abhors' (III.ii).[63] His other roles include 'Mr Ruffman, *a swag-
gering Gentleman*' in the first part of *The Fair Maid of the West*.[64]

This pair must have played two of the three principal comic roles
in *The Lady of Pleasure*: Sir William Sentlove, Master Haircut and
Sir John Littleworth. Just which is which remains a matter of speculation, but I am tempted – on grounds of girth – to cast Sherlock as
Littleworth. In Act V, after an offstage dunking in the Thames, Littleworth enters *'wet'* (V.ii.57.1) and complains that his 'belly' has
disgorged 'a tun of water, beside wine' (V.ii.61, 64). Sir William
Sentlove, the trickster and ringleader among the comedians, might
well have been Robbins's role.

John Sumner, a regular though not a leading member of the company, would have been the obvious choice for the part of Alexander
Kickshaw. He seems to have played roles demanding sexual char-
isma, like that of Marwood in *The Wedding* or that of Mustapha in
The Renegado. In *The Wedding*, Beauford's jealousy is confirmed by
his assessment of Marwood's masculinity: 'He has a handsome presence and discourse, / Two subtle charms to tempt a woman's frailty'
(II.ii).[65] These qualities are exactly what Kickshaw needs, if
Aretina's behaviour in *The Lady of Pleasure* is to be credible.

Among the adolescent actors of the company, Ezekiel Fenn is the
most likely candidate for one of the female leads. He played the
pathos-laden parts of Sophonisba in *Hannibal and Scipio* (1635) and
Winnifride in a revival of *The Witch of Edmonton* (*c.* 1635). Since
both of these demanding roles were probably acted in the same
season as *The Lady of Pleasure*, we can assume that Fenn was at the
height of his powers as a 'woman actor' when Shirley's play was
staged. At fifteen he was already experienced, and his voice must
have broken late, for he played his first 'mans part' four years later –
an event celebrated by Glapthorne in the 1639 edition of his *Poems*.[66]
Fenn would have played either Celestina or Aretina, but in the ab-

sence of other evidence, it is impossible to be more specific.

The speculative casting I have so far engaged in still leaves plenty of room for such journeymen actors as William Allen, Robert Axen, George Stutville and Anthony Turner. There is also room for Michael Bowyer, who frequently played male romantic leads, but may have left the company before *The Lady of Pleasure* opened.[67] And there is additional room on both sides of the sexual divide for Theophilus Bird, Hugh Clark and John Page, all of whom played women's parts, but all of whom may have been too old for anyone but Madam Decoy by 1635, when they were gradually taking on more and more responsibility as adult male actors. Michael Mohun, a boy actor already well-known by 1637, may have joined the company in time to play one of the female leads.[68] But at this point speculation becomes rainbow-chasing. I propose to abjure the rough magic of conjecture, to return to the reliably substantial pageant of the Cockpit stage, and to watch the playwright as he confronts and solves the problems of staging in a few of the more theatrically demanding scenes from *The Lady of Pleasure*.

The Playwright's Craft

Shirley's ability to create arresting and amusing dramatic action out of domestic situations and social interplay is nowhere better displayed than in the first scene of Act III. What happens in the scene is easy enough to describe: Lord Unready is offered two different sexual proposals, both of which he rejects. The first is a blatan⁺ proposition made by Madam Decoy, who believes that she can now manipulate Aretina into whatever bed she chooses. Lord Unready rejects this as preposterous, pointing out that Aretina is his 'kinswoman' (III.i.57), writes a letter to Aretina warning her of Decoy's intentions, and contrives to have Decoy deliver the letter to Aretina herself. Even while he is dictating the letter, Lord Unready is obliged to listen to Sentlove and Kickshaw as they offer him a seductive description of Celestina. These blandishments Lord Unready brushes aside by appealing to his enduring devotion to Bella Maria. The second proposal is managed with such understated deftness as to disguise, for social purposes, its fundamental similarity to the first.

What Shirley has created here is a highly moral scene, but his method of arriving at this result is elegantly tailored to fit the theatre and its audience. The opening stage direction runs as follows: '*Enter* Lord *unready*; HAIRCUT *preparing his periwig, table, and looking-glass*' (III.i.0.1–2). Even before the scene opens, in the musical interval

between Acts II and III, anonymous hirelings have presumably
placed the specified table and the unspecified but necessary stool or
chair into a reasonably prominent downstage position. The looking-
glass may also have been placed in advance, perhaps by Master Haircut. During the last bars of music, Lord Unready enters by one of the
two doors, crosses to the table and sits. He adjusts the mirror to allow
himself to watch Haircut arranging the wig to best advantage and
completing the application of his cosmetic powers. Conversation
begins, only to be interrupted by the Secretary's arrival at the other
stage door to announce the approach of Madam Decoy. She now
enters and requests a private audience; to oblige her, Lord Unready
asks the Secretary and Haircut to 'Wait i'th' next chamber till I call'
(III.i.13), upon which they go out through the door from which
Decoy has just entered.

The rest of the scene can be managed in precisely the same way,
though embellished with many hand-held properties. The Secretary
must produce – perhaps from a hiding-place in the table – a pen, an
inkwell and a sheet of paper. He must sit while writing the letter
which Lord Unready dictates, and must produce sealing-wax, melt-
ing it no doubt by using the nearest convenient candle. After Sentlove and Kickshaw enter, Lord Unready must produce a miniature of
his dead mistress (Bella Maria) from a pocket in his costume, and
Kickshaw will study the image with affected nonchalance. At the end
of the scene the stage will be cleared, though the table and chair will
no doubt remain in place until the end of the act. Superficially, the
elegant surfaces of Cavalier politeness have been left undisturbed
while negotiations of lust and personal ambition are being played
out.

The scene which follows immediately (III.ii) takes place in the
lodgings of Bornwell and Aretina in the Strand. No changes of scen-
ery are required, but a special problem arises in relation to exits,
entrances and eavesdropping. Near the beginning of the scene,
Aretina extracts promises from Littleworth and Kickshaw to the
effect that they will use their combined wits to humiliate Celestina,
who is at present the Bornwells' guest. But, Aretina specifies, 'Begin
not, till I whisper you' (III.ii.85). Now Bornwell, Celestina, Mariana
and Isabella enter, and a highly social conversation (much of it in
French) ensues. Aretina's Steward and Master Frederick join the
party, and after further badinage, a stage direction reads: '*Ex[eunt]
all but Cel[estina], Alex[ander], and Little[worth]*' (III.ii.201.1). At
this point Aretina says, 'Now, gentlemen' (l. 201); that is, she gives

the promised cue to Kickshaw and Littleworth. The two gentlemen subject Celestina to a round of invective which continues without a halt even after the stage direction, '*Enter* BORNWELL' (III.ii.224.1). Bornwell's two brief lines – 'How's this?' (l. 224) and 'A conspiracy!' (l. 268) – have no effect whatever on some fifty lines of dialogue during which the flyting continues. At last Bornwell addresses Celestina as 'Brave soul!' and vilifies her abusers as a 'brace of horse-leeches' (ll. 283–4). Encouraged by Bornwell, Celestina takes the initiative, gains verbal revenge for some thirty lines, and then asks Bornwell: 'How shall I / Acquit your lady's silence?' (ll. 321–2). After a brief exchange of graceful exit lines between Bornwell and Celestina, Aretina unexpectedly asks, 'Is she gone?' (l. 326).

Here there is confusion in plenty. How is it that Bornwell's presence fails to intrude on the action for fifty lines? Why does Celestina remark on Aretina's silence, if indeed she has been offstage for more than a hundred lines? Even more oddly, how can an absent Aretina suddenly resume her place in the dialogue without the stage direction, '*Enter* ARETINA'?

I believe the answers to these questions lie in the use of the 'above', even though there is no authority for such a notion in the quarto. As soon as the 'above' is allowed its normal function as an observation post, the action of this scene falls readily into place. Aretina, after giving her instructions to Kickshaw and Littleworth, goes out with the general '*Ex[eunt]*' (III.ii.201.1), leaving only Celestina and her two assailants on the platform. By a backstage route, Aretina ascends and reappears silently at the observation point, above. '*Enter* BORNWELL' (III.ii.224.1) means that he appears on the platform, taking a position reasonably distant from the characters involved in the game of insults. From this position his two brief interjections (ll. 224 and 268) can be spoken as asides without interrupting the scene. But when Bornwell cries out 'Brave soul!' (l. 283), he attracts the attention of the other characters on the platform. While Celestina completes her verbal revenge, Bornwell approaches her in order to be quite near her when she enquires, 'How shall I / Acquit your lady's silence?' (ll. 321–2). The reference, of course, is to the silent but visible Aretina at the observation point above. Now Aretina retreats and, retracing her backstage route, descends to the platform level. She enters just as Bornwell and Celestina go out, and hence addresses Littleworth and Kickshaw with the most natural question: 'Is she gone?' (l. 326).

In the two scenes which I have been discussing, indeed in *The*

Lady of Pleasure as a whole, the broad outlines of Shirley's theatre craft are remarkably clean. He allows actions of major significance to be played out on the platform, where the actors' voices and gestures will be most effective. He frequently calls for properties, but most of these are small hand-held articles which not only contribute to the action but also reveal the social circumstances or personal inclinations of his characters. Numerous asides, many of them not clearly marked in the quarto, and frequent references to goings-on in this or that chamber just offstage are among the techniques Shirley uses to build the conspiratorial atmosphere which characterises much of the social and sexual activity in the play.

In selecting particular scenes for analysis I have necessarily slighted others, among them the crucial actions of Act IV, in which Kickshaw is led in '*blind*[*fold*]*ed*' (IV.i.0.2), bribed by Madam Decoy, and bedded by Aretina. When Decoy presses her offer, showing Kickshaw 'a prospect / Of the next chamber' and asking him to 'observe / That bed' (IV.i.84–90), I believe that the action has moved to upstage centre, where Decoy is enticing her confused client to enter Aretina's bedroom by going out through the gap between the hangings. If this is the case, then it is another instance of Shirley's shrewdness: if this unusual exit (upstage centre) is used at all, it is fitting that it should be used, here, and used only once.

To follow Madam Decoy a single step further would violate the rules of circumspection imposed not only by Aretina but by the playwright as well. I shall resist, and I shall conclude by gathering a few indications of the quality of Shirley's theatrical style in *The Lady of Pleasure*. Something of Shirley's taste in this matter can be inferred from his address to the reader prefixed to *The Grateful Servant*. In response to adverse criticism from Blackfriars partisans, Shirley takes a stand which he hopes will 'do the comedians justice, amongst whom, some are held comparable with the best that are, and have been in the world, and most of them deserving a name in the file of those that are eminent for graceful and unaffected action'.[69]

Just what actions will qualify as free of affectation is always open to question, especially in the theatre; but it is fair to assume that, in the relatively small, indoor, artificially lighted Cockpit playhouse, an actor like Richard Perkins, whose background included the Hope and the Red Bull, would reduce the volume of his voice and the scale of his gestures in accordance with the modesty of his nature and the dimensions of his new environment. In doing so, Perkins would have increased his attractiveness in the eyes of a playwright who designed each scene with a special alertness to social nuance. An acknowledged runner-up in his re-creation of Marlowe's towering passions, Perkins may well have been 'comparable with the best that are' when the script required subtle adjustments within an intricately balanced network of social relationships.

'Graceful . . . action', in Shirley's terms, was undoubtedly very considerable praise. A playwright who repeatedly places his characters into dance-like formations, and who thinks of a Lord as unready until he is armed with his periwig, is admitting a taste for elegance. And actors who deal in mirrors and miniatures rather than tankards and targets will need to be graceful in both bearing and speech. As the leading playwright of Queen Henrietta's men in 1635, Shirley knew the resources of his theatre, the talents of his actors, and the tastes of his audience. In response to these external influences, he created the 'graceful and unaffected action' of *The Lady of Pleasure*: 'that rare playe' by which he earned, in its first production, the admiration of Sir Humphrey Mildmay, and for which he is awarded, even today, 'a name in the file of those that are eminent' for ingeniously crafted comedy of social artifice.[70]

4. THE TEXT

This edition of *The Lady of Pleasure* is based on the only early text, the quarto of 1637, which appeared under the following title-page:

THE | LADY OF | PLEASURE. | A | COMEDIE, | As it was Acted by her Ma- | jesties Servants, at the private | House in *Drury* Lane. | [rule] Written by *James Shirly*. | [rule, ornament, rule] *LONDON*, | Printed by *Tho. Cotes*, for *Andrew Crooke*, | and *William Cooke*. | *1637*.

I have collated twenty-five copies of Q, and these are identified, along with the abbreviations used in referring to them, in Appendix B, p. 198.

Authority for publication was recorded in the Stationers' Register on 13 April 1637 as follows:

Andrew Crooke and William Cooke. Entred for their Copies under the hands of THOMAS HERBERT Deputy to Sir HENRY HERBERT and Master Downes warden two Playes called. *The Lady of pleasure.* and *The young Admirall* by James Shirley. . . . . xii d.[71]

The publishing partnership of Crooke and Cooke has been inves-
tigated by Allan H. Stevenson, who points out that Cooke had been
selling Shirley's plays in London since 1632, that Crooke was a new
partner as of 13 April 1637, and that Crooke is known to have been
operating a bookshop in Dublin by 1640.[72] Since Shirley himself was
employed at the Werburgh Street theatre in Dublin between 1636
and 1640, it would appear that Crooke and Cooke were entering into
a 'contract or agreement', in Stevenson's words, 'covering the publication of Shirley's plays during the time that he should be in
Ireland'.

The Printer

When he printed *The Lady of Pleasure* in 1637, Thomas Cotes (*c.*
1581–1641) was at the zenith of a busy and vigorous career. Having
served his apprenticeship in the Jaggard printing house (1597–1606),
Cotes was by 1627 in a position of sufficient means and stature to
acquire from 'Dorathye Jaggard widowe' the printing rights for
twenty-four titles including 'her parte in SHACKSPHEERE *playes*.'[73]
This transaction was doubtless a major step on the road to becoming
a master printer, for in 1634 a note in the Stationers' Register includes the information that 'Thomas Coates succeeded Master Jaggard, an ancient Erection'[74] and the Second Star Chamber Decree
regulating printing, dated 11 July 1637, places Thomas Cotes twelfth
in a list of twenty master printers entitled to operate one or more
presses.[75]

In many of his official ventures after 1627 Thomas Cotes was sec-
onded by his brother Richard, who appears to have been the junior
partner.[76] This collaboration generated enough prosperity and
gained enough recognition to allow for the operation of two presses:
the 'ancient Erection' in the Barbican acquired from the Jaggards
and the press in Parish Clerks' Hall for which Thomas Cotes, as
Parish Clerk of St Giles Cripplegate, assumed responsibility in or
before 1636.[77]

The image of Thomas Cotes which emerges from these scattered
references is that of an enterprising self-made man who, after humble
beginnings, rose to a position of great esteem in his profession. Such
an impression is hardly challenged by admitting that, on 26 March
1610, Cotes was assessed a fine of seven pence 'for keepinge a prentise
unpresented contrary to order';[78] rebukes of this kind are entirely
typical in the careers of rising men in any establishment, and this one
was no doubt long forgotten by the time that Cotes, a thriving master

craftsman in his fifties, undertook to print *The Lady of Pleasure* in 1637.[79]

The Printing Process

The manuscript copy which Cotes acquired was probably a fair copy prepared for the press by the author himself, or at least under close authorial supervision. Copy originating in the playhouse can be ruled out, because Q bears none of the traces of the prompter's annotations: i.e., actors' real names, crisp imperative stage directions, anticipated entrances, and so on. Where Q does provide detailed stage directions, they suggest the author rather than the prompter at work, as in the provision that '*While Haircut is busy about his hair, Sentlove goes to Celestina*' (IV.iii.11.1–2). In the playhouse this series of actions would require two commands rather than one, namely, 'Haircut, attend to milord's periwig' and 'Sentlove, go to Celestina'. The tone of the printed stage direction suggests that someone with a vivid theatrical imagination prepared the copy, perhaps with the memory of the production by Queen Henrietta's men in mind; on both counts, Shirley is an obvious candidate. Stage directions elsewhere may be counted as evidence in favour of this line of argument, especially the declarative assertion '*They dance*' (II.ii.269.1), or the synoptic description '*Enter* Lord *unready*; HAIRCUT *preparing his periwig, table, and looking-glass*' (III.i.0.1–2). Add to this the absence of cues (such as 'hautboys') even where music is manifestly required (II.ii.269, IV.i.17, V.iii.214) or the occasional misattribution of lines in the speech headings (which a prompter would assiduously correct), and the case against playhouse copy may be closed. I know of no persuasive reason to doubt that Shirley prepared the manuscript copy himself (or supervised its preparation), and passed along his fair copy to Crooke and Cooke, who in turn supplied it to Cotes.

Precisely what happened to the copy in the Cotes establishment is a more difficult riddle to solve, but a few details can be asserted as fact. Collation has shown that considerable attention was given to press correction in sheets C to F inclusive, and again in sheets K and A, but none at all in sheets B, G, H and I.[80] The printing in G, H and I is, if anything, sloppier than in the rest of the play, especially as regards accidentals and technical errors which one might reasonably expect the corrector to discover. Thus it is apparent that press correction stopped after sheet F, and was resumed only for the final half-gathering (K) and the preliminary pages (A).

Analysis of running titles reveals that only one skeleton forme was used from sheets B to I inclusive. The same running title (with a distinctively bent tail on the long *s* of *Pleasure*) was used in every inner forme (at sigs. B4, C4, D4, E4, F4, G2, H2, I2, K2), and in every outer forme (at sigs. B3, C3, D3, E3, F1, G1, H1, I1) except for the final half-gathering (K). This pattern confirms that only one skeleton forme was used, and leads to the following supplementary inferences: (1) that the skeleton forme was regularly kept in the same position from the time printing began until F (inner) had been completed; (2) that it was inverted end-for-end for the printing of F (outer) and remained in this position until sheet I had been completed; (3) that the inner forme of F was printed before the outer; and (4) that some stoppage of work intervened between the printing of F (inner) and F (outer). In connection with this last inference, I should add that gatherings B–F are printed with 38 lines to a page, gatherings G–I with 39 lines. If the stoppage of work took place after F (inner) had been printed and the type for F (outer) was already standing, then both the inversion of the skeleton forme and the enlarging of the page to 39 lines would have happened when work was resumed.

Beginning with gathering C, the typesetting of Q seems to have been governed by a space-saving economy bordering on parsimony. The compositor frequently saved a line by placing the stage direction calling for a character to enter in the righthand margin, opposite a line of dialogue, rather than allowing it a line of its own in the centre of the page. When dealing with a line of verse divided among several speakers, the compositor's tendency was to crowd it into a single line of type, speech headings and all. In sixteen instances this gave him a longer line than the page would accommodate, so he carried over the extra words or syllables to the line directly above (or in exceptional cases, below), placing them near the righthand margin and marking them off from the normally placed dialogue with a single bracket. Such economies were not unusual in the Cotes establishment; *Hyde Park* and *The Young Admiral* (both printed in 1637) bear similar though fewer marks of the desire to crowd the page with as many lines as possible. By contrast, *The Humorous Courtier* (printed by Cotes in 1640) is not so tightly compressed: all entrances are centred, and a reasonable amount of white space per page is tolerated. Since the frequency of space-saving techniques in *The Lady of Pleasure* does not vary radically from gathering to gathering, from inner to outer forme, or within the pages of a forme, I do not believe that the crowded appearance of Q constitutes evidence of cast-off copy.

The manuscript copy was probably very lightly punctuated, leaving the compositor often at the mercy of his fallible discretion. If so, this would explain why the punctuation of Q is erratic by modern standards, and at best informal by seventeenth-century norms. The most striking instance of discretion gone awry is recorded in the collation line at IV.ii.157. The ten-syllable line in Q ('When you please ile attend you; *Littleworth*') has been cobbled together by reading a speech heading as if it belonged to the dialogue. Here a misreading of punctuation (or lack of punctuation in the copy) leads to mislineation, and the obvious error is relatively easy to correct. In several other instances the lineation of Q is whimsical enough to invite suspicion or even readjustment (as recorded in the collations). And in many passages (notably IV.ii.220–21 and V.i.6–8) I have assumed that the punctuation of Q represents the compositor's imperfect attempt to make sense of dialogue left unpunctuated in the manuscript.

Without making heavy bibliographical weather out of small bits of evidence, I wish to state my belief that the printing of *The Lady of Pleasure* could not have proceeded in conformity with the model proposed for seventeenth-century play quartos by the *avant garde* of scientific bibliography: i.e., by two or more compositors working simultaneously to set up type forme by forme.[81] I have been unable to detect signs of cast-off copy, and my best efforts to distinguish the work of multiple compositors have been thwarted.[82] Still, having taken to heart D. F. McKenzie's warnings about the human fallibility, or laziness or unpredictability of printers and their establishments,[83] I am content without conformity to a model. Thomas Cotes was a busy man in 1637, and *The Lady of Pleasure* had to compete for his attention with books as monumental as the *Sermons Preached by that Reverend and Learned Divine Richard Clerke* (clearly the prestige book of the Cotes enterprise in 1637) or as ephemeral as *An Elegie Upon my Deare Brother, the Jonathan of my Heart, Mr John Wheeler* by Francis Quarles, to say nothing of *Hyde Park* and *The Young Admiral*. If printing had to be interrupted, if the skeleton forme was inverted, if press correction was done imperfectly, if pages of type were at times uncomfortably crowded, these were no doubt occurrences for which the causes are to be sought in human nature.

The press corrections in Q deserve closer scrutiny than I have so far implied. They can be readily divided into two classes: typographical and substantive corrections. The first class includes turned letters, failure to capitalise at the beginning of a line, spelling errors caused by omitted letters, and so on. Such typographical errors will

be found in the uncorrected state of all of the formes which contain
evidence of stop-press correction. Substantive corrections, however,
occur exclusively in gatherings E (inner), F (inner), and F (outer).
The most striking example is the change from 'Where all the yeare is'
to 'Though all the yeare were' (III.i.133), but a glance at Appendix B
will reveal other specimens which imply a scrutiny of the printed
page well beyond the merely typographical.

Before proposing a tentative hypothesis to account for the uneven
proofreading which characterises Q, I wish to report one more event
which occurred in the Cotes establishment, though it happened three
years later. In 1640 Cotes printed a quarto by Thomas Heywood
entitled *The Exemplary Lives and Memorable Acts of Nine the Most
Worthy Women of the World: Three Jewes, Three Gentiles, Three
Christians*. On the last page (sig. 2F4v) someone inserted the following apology: 'Excusing the Compositor, who received this Coppy in a
difficult and unacquainted hand, and the Corrector who could not
bee alwayes ready in regard of some necessary imployments, I in-
treate the generous Reader to take notice of these Errata following,
and to rectifie them in his reading after this manner.' The list which
follows includes corrections of precisely the kind that belong to the
second (substantive) class. And I would surmise that the note of
apology, whether written by Cotes or by Heywood, represents a fairly heated conversation between these two seasoned professionals in
which sloppy manuscript copy and careless proofreading were the
gauntlets thrown down on either side.

What remains to be said about the printing of Q is offered quite
frankly as conjecture. Shirley, though residing in Dublin from 1636
to 1640, is known to have planned a trip to London, probably in 1637,
to attend to what he called his '*affairs in England*'.[84] If he in fact made
this journey, he may have arrived in London when *The Lady of
Pleasure* was in press.[85] Suppose that he entered the Cotes printing
house to find his affairs advanced as far as the inner forme of gathering E. Suppose that he found the standard of proofreading in previous gatherings – as done by the 'Corrector' – inadequate, and that he
insisted on reading proofs for E (inner) and F himself. Suppose further that this procedure was bothersome enough to cause numerous
stop-press corrections and a suspension of printing between F
(inner) and F (outer), after which the return passage to Ireland removed Shirley from direct contact with the press. At this point I can
imagine Thomas Cotes breathing a sigh of relief and deciding that
The Lady of Pleasure would be subjected to no more press correction.

Cosmetic touches in the preliminary and closing pages, perhaps, but the rest (G, H and I) could fend for itself.

The foregoing narrative is a fanciful view of what might have been, and I should hasten to add that it is not the ground on which my text is built. The press corrections in Q have influenced my text, but in a much more conservative way. Most obviously, where the choice is between Qa (the uncorrected quarto) and Qb (the corrected quarto), I have taken Qb as the basis for my own reading. In addition, I have emended rather more liberally in those formes in which no evidence of press correction is apparent. This last rule applies to E (outer) – which may well have been printed before E (inner) – as well as to gatherings G, H and I. All of my own emendations will be found identified by the phrase '*This ed.*', and where my choices are at all controversial, I have defended them with argument in the notes. My aim throughout has been to offer the best possible reading of Shirley's intentions, without reproducing the errors which Thomas Cotes, through human weakness of whatever kind, placed between the author and his readers.

Previous Modern Editions

The nine previous editors of *The Lady of Pleasure* are identified in the table of abbreviations at the beginning of this book. I am particularly grateful to the first and last of these editors, though for widely divergent reasons. Gifford's text appears in what is the first and still the only complete edition of Shirley. It betrays throughout both the virtues and the vices of nineteenth-century editorial practice: emendations ranging from the inspired to the capricious, rigorously standardised punctuation and grammar, stage directions based on an appetite for melodrama, and gentlemanly disregard for documentation. I have often adopted Gifford's readings, sometimes with admiration (as at III.ii.40), but have rejected them whenever their purpose was to replace Shirley's Cavalier doublet with a Victorian waistcoat. My collations include only a few samples of the many fanciful emendations by Gifford which deserve oblivion.

The edition by Marilyn D. Papousek, though I have consulted and cited it as an unpublished PhD. thesis, has now been very slightly revised and published as *A Critical Edition of James Shirley's 'The Lady of Pleasure'*, edited by Marilyn J. Thorssen (New York, 1980). Despite the change in the editor's name, the work remains fundamentally the same, and I have therefore referred throughout to the earlier version. Papousek's text is conservative in the sense that it

retains the spellings of Q and restores many readings which earlier
editors had emended. Among the ironies of this respectful procedure
is the production of a text which repeats a significant number of
printer's errors and various uncorrected readings because it assigns
to Q an authority in excess of its merits. Still, the complete and
carefully documented apparatus of Papousek's edition has been useful to me in ways that are difficult to specify, and for which I should
like to record my thanks.

The remaining editions appear in anthologies of various kinds,
ranging from Gosse's virtual reprint of Gifford in the Mermaid series
to Harrier's old-spelling presentation of the copy of Q in the Folger
Shakespeare Library. Each anthologised version was prepared by an
intelligent reader who left some evidence, by way of emendation or
gloss, of his interpretation. Instead of estimating the varying degrees
of fidelity to Q, or the relative perspicacity of the commentary in each
case, I shall refer the reader to the notes which accompany the text in
this edition, where the influence of each previous editor will become
apparent.

The Present Edition

Since I have already disclosed my view of the copy-text (Q) and
admitted my willingness to emend it, where bibliographical argument and common sense will permit, all that remains is to give some
account of the manner in which *The Lady of Pleasure* is here presented. The conventions of dress, so to speak, will be familiar to readers
of other volumes in the Revels series. Spelling and punctuation are
modern, except in those rare instances where meaning or metre
would be distorted by modern dress. The stage directions of Q are
faithfully reproduced, though not their peculiar spellings or typographical features, and all additions to the stage directions are placed
inside square brackets. Whenever Q calls for a character to enter by
placing a stage direction in the righthand margin, I have centred the
stage direction; only the first instance of this practice (I.i.316.1) is
recorded in the collations. The division into acts is taken over directly from Q. Scene divisions (not marked in Q) are those of Gifford and
subsequent editors for Acts I–IV. Unlike previous editors, I have
also divided Act V into scenes, for reasons explained where the first
such division occurs (V.ii.0.1n.). The press corrections in Q are
listed systematically in Appendix B (pp. 198–200) and are therefore
not recorded in the collation lines, except if they have a bearing on a
particular textual argument.

Like many early printed plays, Q uses a capital letter at the beginning of each line of type, whether in verse or prose, and this makes
the problem of deciding where the prose passages begin and end a
notoriously difficult one. The passages of dialogue in French
(III.ii.86–106, 117–20, 128) are certainly prose; in transcribing them
I have silently modernised archaic spellings (such as *plustost* at
III.ii.98), but I have refrained from correcting slips in grammar, and
I have retained the italics of Q. The English prose passages have been
harder to identify, particularly since Shirley's verse is metrically flex-
ible and heavily dependent on the rhythms of ordinary speech. As a
rule of thumb I have assigned verse and prose respectively to particular moods: thus, verse is appropriate to the emotional tension of
V.i, prose to the revelry of V.ii, and verse again to the formality of
V.iii. It would follow that Celestina's natural idiom should be verse,
and Madam Decoy's prose; and this is in general true, though both of
them overstep this division where the mood created by the dramatic
situation requires. But my rule of thumb can hardly be described as a
principle, and I have often been thrown on the mercy of the Master of
Philosophy in *Le Bourgeois gentilhomme*: 'Tout ce qui n'est point
prose est vers: et tout ce qui n'est point vers est prose', he reminds
Monsieur Jourdain. 'Il faut bien que ce soit l'un ou l'autre.'

One special contributor to the present edition remains anonymous. The copy of Q in the Library of Congress contains annotations
in ink in a seventeenth-century hand, conspicuously on the page
which lists the *dramatis personae* (sig. A1v), but also in many scattered places throughout. Wherever these annotations have been useful or suggestive, I have called attention to them in the notes and
collation lines by using the abbreviation 'Con. MS'.

The anonymous annotator clearly knew the play inside-out. His
descriptions of the characters are shrewd and to the point: Bornwell
is 'the indulgent husband of Aretina', Sentlove and Kickshaw are
'ffantastick Gallants' and Madam Decoy is 'an impudent bawd'.
Occasionally he goes deeper than such simple identifications of particular humours, as in his remark that Aretina is 'so affected with prodigalitie she onely studies her owne ruine'. The annotator had some
sense of the play in performance, for he directed Celestina to reward
the insubordination of her Steward with 'a box / [on the] Ear' (sig.
C2v; see note to I.ii.97.S.D.), and he anticipated Gifford in correcting the speech headings at II.ii.154 and III.i.89. But many of his
annotations were the result of close textual scrutiny, as in the change
from 'when' to 'what' in IV.ii.201, or from 'rich' to 'riches' in V.i.54.

In this last instance I have cited 'Con. MS' as the sole authority for
my own reading.

I am inclined to believe that the person who produced these annotations was preparing *The Lady of Pleasure* for a second edition
which never, in fact, appeared. This assumption would be consistent
with the annotator's desire to dress up the *dramatis personae* with
character descriptions that could be easily grasped, and with his attention to textual correctness. I do not believe, on the evidence of
comparison with surviving autograph manuscripts,[86] that the annotations are in Shirley's hand. I have therefore treated them with the
respect they deserve, as the work of a contemporary of Shirley's who
knew how to read a play with intelligent comprehension of the whole
and with an observant eye for detail.

Among the joys of editing, I would assign a very high rank to the
accidental discovery which happens unexpectedly while one is looking for something else. This was my experience when, following up a
line of enquiry now forgotten, I stumbled across a memorable saying
in William Rowley's *A New Wonder, A Woman Never Vext* (1632),
sig. F2v: 'Spoy'le not a good Text with a false Comment.' In preparing the explanatory glosses for the present edition I have tried to live
up to this exacting standard, but I will resist recommending the same
attitude to readers of *The Lady of Pleasure* who will, I trust, give
greater scope to playfulness than prudence.

NOTES TO INTRODUCTION

1 *Athenæ Oxoniensis*, 3rd ed. (London, 1817), III, 737–40.
2 The first scholarly biography is by Nason, pp. 1–162, and it remains valuable for its presentation of all Shirley documents known in 1915. New
   documentary evidence is reported in Ray Livingstone Armstrong's brief
   but elegant profile of Shirley in the Introduction to *The Poems of James
   Shirley* (New York, 1941), pp. xiii–xvii; in Bentley's judicious treatment
   of the playwright's career (V, 1064–72); and in Georges Bas's compendi-
   ous doctoral thesis, *James Shirley (1596–1666): Dramaturge caroléen*
   (Lille, 1973), pp. 1–66. My own account relies on all of these works, and on
   the more specialised studies cited below.
3 Nason, p. 17.
4 These are handsomely reproduced in Nason, opposite pp. 139 and 151. I
   can find no trace of the mole in the oil portrait which hangs in the Bodleian
   Library and which Nason presents as a frontispiece.
5 See J. P. Feil, 'James Shirley's Years of Service', *R.E.S.*, n.s. VIII (1957),
   413–16.
6 See Albert C. Baugh, 'Some New Facts about Shirley', *Modern Language
   Review*, XVII (1922), 234.

7 Arber, III, 618.
8 See Albert C. Baugh, 'Further Facts about James Shirley', *R.E.S.*, VI
   (1931), 62–3.
9 Nason, p. 160.
10 Baugh, 'Further Facts', p. 64.
11 See Georges Bas, 'James Shirley, pasteur dans le Hertfordshire', *Études
   anglaises*, XV (1962), 267.
12 Herbert, pp. 54–5.
13 Allan H. Stevenson, 'Shirley's Years in Ireland', *R.E.S.*, XX (1944), 20,
   28.
14 Prynne had included, in *Histriomastix: The Players Scourge, or Actors
   Tragaedie* (London, 1633), sig. 2F2v, an attack on the practice of 'effeminate Dancing on the Stage', adding that women who participate in such
   entertainments are '*Whores or persons more infamous, (for such are all those
   females in Saint* Chrysostomes *judgement, who dare dance publikely on a
   Theater)*'. By the time these words reached print, the queen had made a
   celebrated personal appearance as a dancer in Walter Montagu's *The
   Shepherd's Paradise* (see Bentley, IV, 917–20). For this indiscreet coin-
   cidence Prynne suffered imprisonment, the loss of his ears, and the brand
   of S.L. (seditious libeller) on his cheeks. For a cogent account of Prynne's
   attack and its consequences, see Jonas A. Barish, *The Antitheatrical Pre-
   judice* (Berkeley, California, 1981), pp. 83–8.
15 See Bentley, V, 1154–63.
16 See the Introduction to *Poems*, ed. Armstrong, p. xv.
17 See Georges Bas, 'Two Misrepresented Biographical Documents
   Concerning James Shirley', *R.E.S.*, n.s. XXVII (1976), 307–9.
18 Bentley, V, 1071.
19 *Wks*, VI, 396–7.
20 Nason, pp. 159–60.
21 'Excerpta Quaedam per A. W. Adolescentem', British Library Add. MS
   22608, fol. 101v. This and subsequent quotations from Wright's manuscript are taken from the transcription by Arthur C. Kirsch in 'A Caroline
   Commentary on the Drama', *Modern Philology*, LXVI (1968–9), 256–9.
   Wright's commonplace book is discussed and dated not earlier than 1639
   by James G. McManaway in 'Excerpta Quaedam per A. W. Adolescentem', *Studies in Honor of Dewitt T. Starnes*, ed. Thomas P. Harrison *et al.*
   (Austin, Texas, 1967), pp. 117–26.
22 Of indirect relevance to the structure of the play is Shirley's procedure of
   writing, evidently, with no specific narrative or dramatic sources in mind.
   Forsythe nominates Fletcher's *The Noble Gentleman* and Davenant's *The
   Just Italian* as plays which seem to have influenced *The Lady of Pleasure*
   (p. 372), but the strongest claim to be made for them is consignment to the
   dubious rank of analogues. That Shirley's imagination was a virtual
   storehouse of situations, characters and phrases drawn from the dramatic
   repertoire of his day is beyond question. But the raw material which went
   into the making of *The Lady of Pleasure* is the social world of Caroline
   London (see Papousek, pp. 66–9).
23 The symbolic nature of food in Jonson has been discussed by Jonas A.
   Barish, who remarks on the one hand that in *Bartholomew Fair* 'the ubiquitous word "belly" focuses our attention on the center of appetite, the

stomach' (*Ben Jonson and the Language of Prose Comedy*, Cambridge, Mass., 1960, p. 227), and observes elsewhere that 'Jonsonian cuisine' can appeal to the sophisticated palate as well, notably in *The Alchemist* where the menu includes 'the dolphin's milk butter in which Sir Epicure Mammon's shrimps will swim' ('Feasting and Judging in Jonsonian Comedy', *Renaissance Drama*, n.s. V, 1972, 6).

24 See III.i.o.1 and the note at this point, in which my decision to christen Lord Unready is explained.

25 The text of the proclamation is quoted by Papousek, as Appendix A of her edition (pp. 278–81).

26 *The Crisis of the Aristocracy, 1558–1641* (Oxford, 1965), pp. 186–8.

27 *Wks*, V, 275.

28 Heywood, *A Woman Killed with Kindness*, ed. R. W. Van Fossen (London, 1961), xiii.61–2.

29 Middleton, *A Chaste Maid in Cheapside*, ed. R. B. Parker (London, 1969), I.ii.21.

30 See F. G. Emmison, *Elizabethan Life: Morals and the Church Courts* (Chelmsford, Essex, 1973), pp. 1–2: 'nearly 10,000 men and women were summoned on sexual charges by the Elizabethan Essex spiritual courts', a number which amounts to about one in seven of the adult population. For their concern with regulating sexual conduct, the church courts 'became known in vulgar parlance throughout England as the Bawdy Courts'.

31 *The Description of England*, ed. Georges Edelen (Ithaca, New York, 1968), p. 189.

32 See Keith Thomas, 'The Double Standard', *Journal of the History of Ideas*, XX (1959), 200–1; and Van Fossen's Introduction to *A Woman Killed with Kindness*, pp. xxx–xxxi.

33 See G. R. Hibbard, 'Love, Marriage and Money in Shakespeare's Theatre and Shakespeare's England', *The Elizabethan Theatre*, VI (1975), 140–2.

34 On this point I am in substantial agreement with Nathan Franklin Cogan's analysis of Bornwell's character in 'The London Comedies of James Shirley, 1625–1635: The Dramatic Context of *The Lady of Pleasure*' (Ph.D. thesis, University of California, Berkeley, 1971), pp. 213–15.

35 See G. F. Sensabaugh, 'Platonic Love in Shirley's *The Lady of Pleasure*', *A Tribute to George Coffin Taylor*, ed. Arnold Williams (Chapel Hill, North Carolina, 1952), pp. 168–77.

36 Swinburne uses this phrase, in *Essays and Studies*, 3rd ed. (London, 1888), pp. 287–8, to characterise the relationship between Fernando and Bianca in Ford's *Love's Sacrifice*.

37 The essay appears in *Rehabilitations and Other Essays* (Oxford, 1939), pp. 161–80.

38 See the Postscript to the *Odyssey*, in *The Poems of Alexander Pope*, ed. John Butt *et al.* (New Haven, 1939–69), X, 387.

39 Tilley, G 42. See also III.ii.319n.

40 See the Dedication to *The Grateful Servant* (Shirley, *Wks*, II, 3).

41 See Richard Morton, 'Deception and Social Dislocation: An Aspect of James Shirley's Drama', *Renaissance Drama*, IX (1966), 245.

42 See Juliet McGrath, 'James Shirley's Uses of *Language*', *Studies in English Literature, 1500–1900*, VI (1966), 332: 'only rarely are linguistic

extremes displayed, and the language spoken by the majority of the characters seems to have a pronounced sameness almost regardless of the character who is speaking'.

43 'Elizabethan and Jacobean Comedy', in *The Age of Shakespeare*, vol. II
of *A Guide to English Literature*, ed. Boris Ford (Harmondsworth,
Middlesex, 1955), p. 427.

44 '*The Lady of Pleasure*, by James Shirley, licensed' (Herbert, p. 37).

45 Bentley, V, 1125.

46 Bentley, II, 677.

47 Bentley, I, 330–1.

48 See Markward, p. 166; Bentley, I, 224–6; King, p. 146; and Andrew Gurr,
The Shakespearean Stage, 1574–1642 (Cambridge, 1970), p. 43.

49 Shirley, *Wks*, III, 282.

50 See the records printed in Bentley, II, 674–80. Two expenditures of sixpence each do not qualify as exceptions: the first pertains to a masque
performed at Whitehall (18 Feb. 1633/4), the second 'To a Playe of Warre'
(16 Nov. 1643) which took place after the closing of the theatres. Neither
of these events is necessarily comparable to attendance at a professional
theatre.

51 Prologue to *The Example* (Shirley, *Wks*, III, 282).

52 For an account of the audience of which Mildmay was but one member,
see Clifford Leech, 'The Caroline Audience,' *Modern Language Review*,
XXXVI (1941), 304–19.

53 Marlowe, *Plays*, p. 178.

54 *Henslowe's Diary*, ed. R. A. Foakes and R. T. Rickert (Cambridge, 1961),
p. 213.

55 *The White Devil*, ed. John Russell Brown (London, 1960), p. 187. Brown
infers that only if Perkins were playing the part of Flamineo could he be
described as crowning 'both the beginning and end', since Bracciano dies
long before the conclusion (see Brown's Introduction, p. xxiii).

56 See Bentley, II, 526–8.

57 See Bentley, II, 528.

58 Shirley, *Wks*, I, 415.

59 Bentley, II, 693.

60 Shirley, *Wks*, I, 366, 372, 375.

61 Massinger, *Plays*, II, 12.

62 Bentley, II, 401, 548.

63 Shirley, *Wks*, I, 366, 393, 409.

64 Bentley, II, 572–3.

65 Shirley, *Wks*, I, 385.

66 Bentley, II, 433–4.

67 See Bentley, II, 386–7.

68 See Bentley, II, 511–12.

69 Shirley, *Wks*, II, 5.

70 To judge by the fate of *The Lady of Pleasure*, Shirley has been less well
remembered in theatrical than in literary circles. Although several of his
plays were revived on the Restoration stage, *The Lady of Pleasure* has left
no record of being among them. Selected incidents involving Aretina,
Decoy and Bornwell were pilfered by William Taverner and melted down
to compose *The Artful Husband* (1717), but Shirley's play had effectively

disappeared. I have been able to trace only two modern revivals, both of them experimental. Between 22 and 26 June 1976, the London Academy of Music and Dramatic Art, under the direction of David Ryal, performed *The Lady of Pleasure* at the Cockpit Theatre, Gateforth Street, London. This was the first production in a special season for which C. Walter Hodges had devised a conjectural reconstruction of the stage at the Cockpit in Drury Lane. At the University of Toronto, the Graduate Centre for the Study of Drama performed the play in their Studio Theatre on Glen Morris Street from 6 to 16 December 1978. Directed by Dorothy Kelleher, this production was staged in order to test and vindicate Shirley's talents as a comic writer. In the spirit of this intention, the programme took as its epigraph the proverb quoted by Littleworth: 'Fools are a family over all the world' (IV.ii.102). I am grateful to T. J. King and Dorothy Kelleher for private communications about the London and Toronto productions respectively.

71 Arber, IV, 381. *Hyde Park* was also registered on this date by the same publishers.

72 'Shirley's Publishers: The Partnership of Crooke and Cooke', *The Library*, 4th series, XXV (1945), 140–61.

73 Arber, IV, 182.

74 Arber, III, 700.

75 Arber, IV, 532.

76 See, for example, the entry in the Stationers' Register for 8 December 1630, which identifies the brothers respectively as 'master Cotes' and 'Richard Cotes' (Arber, IV, 244).

77 See James Christie, *Some Account of the Parish Clerks, More Especially of the Ancient Fraternity (Bretherne and Sisterne), of S. Nicholas* (London, 1893), pp. 187–8: 'In the old Hall also stood the printing press, set up in 1626. In the previous year an Act had been obtained under the seal of the Court of High Commission, to set up a press in the Hall, the printer to be appointed being always a person approved by the Archbishop of Canterbury and the Bishop of London. . . . In 1636, Thomas Cotes, Parish Clerk of Cripplegate Without, was the Company's printer, and on his death in 1641 Richard Cotes succeeded.'

78 William A. Jackson, ed., *Records of the Court of the Stationers' Company, 1602 to 1640* (London, 1957), p. 445.

79 I have deleted from this account of Cotes's career the details of his domestic life: the birth of eleven children, seven of whom died in infancy, and the death of his wife Margaret on 27 October 1627. The appropriate records are cited by William E. Miller in 'Printers and Stationers in the Parish of St Giles Cripplegate 1561–1640', *S.B.*, XIX (1966), 24.

80 See Appendix B, pp. 198–200.

81 See, for example, Robert K. Turner, Jr, 'The Printing of *A King and No King* Q1', *S.B.*, XVIII (1965), 255: 'As an increasing number of Elizabethan play quartos are subjected to bibliographical analysis, it begins to appear that these books were more often than not composed by formes'; and MacD. P. Jackson, 'Compositorial Practices in Tourneur's *The Atheist's Tragedy*', *S.B.*, XXXII (1979), 211: 'Careful inspection and measurement of the headlines reveals that two skeletons were used . . . . This implies normal two-skeleton printing.'

82 These efforts include the study of spelling frequencies in such cases as *would/wod, do/doe,* and *-y/-ie*; analysis of variations in speech headings; and observation of the placement of stage directions. Similarly, the specimens of foul case and damaged type which I have traced do not lead to the conclusion that typesetting proceeded forme by forme.

83 See 'Printers of the Mind: Some Notes on Bibliographical Theories and Printing-House Practices', *S.B.*, XXII (1969), 1–6, 16–41.

84 The phrase is from the Dedication of *The Royal Master* to the Earl of Kildare (Shirley, *Wks*, IV, 103): '*Be pleased now, my most honourable lord, since my affairs in England hasten my departure, and prevent my personal attendance, that something of me may be honoured to wait upon you in my absence; this poem.*' The chronology of events connected with Shirley's period in Ireland has been thoroughly studied by Allan H. Stevenson, who asserts, in 'James Shirley and the Actors of the First Irish Theater', *Modern Philology*, XL (1942), 151, that 'we are reasonably certain that Shirley left Ireland for a time in the spring of 1637 to attend to his "Affaires in England," as he promises us in the dedication to *The royall master*'.

85 The scenario proposed here is, thus far, identical to the one outlined by Papousek, pp. 9–10.

86 Namely, the collection entitled 'Verses and Poems, by James Shirley' in the Bodleian Library (MS Rawl. poet. 88) and the revisions to the manuscript of *The Court Secret* in the Worcester College Library, Oxford (MS 120.D).

THE LADY OF PLEASURE

PERSONS OF THE COMEDY

Lord.
SIR THOMAS BORNWELL.
SIR WILLIAM SENTLOVE.
MR ALEXANDER KICKSHAW.
MR JOHN LITTLEWORTH.   5
MR HAIRCUT.
MR FREDERICK.
Steward *to the Lady Aretina.*
Steward *to the Lady Celestina.*
Secretary.   10
Servants, etc.

ARETINA, *Sir Thomas Bornwell's Lady.*
CELESTINA, *a young widow.*
ISABELLA.

3. SENTLOVE] *Q;* Scentlove *Gifford.*

---

1. Lord] identified in the present ed. as 'Lord Unready'; see III.i.o.1n.

2. *Bornwell*] 'the indulgent husband of Aretina' (Con. MS). For a discussion of the annotations in the Library of Congress copy of Q, see Introduction, pp. 43–4.

3–4. *Sentlove . . . Kickshaw*] 'ffantastick Gallants' (Con. MS). I retain the spelling of Sentlove's name in Q (rather than following Gifford) in order to preserve the pun on 'sent' and 'scent'. Sentlove's character is designed according to the Fool's adage in *Lear*, I.v.19–20, i.e., with his 'eyes of either side's nose, that what a man cannot smell out he may spy into'. Kickshaw's name (derived from *quelque chose*) identifies him as 'something dainty or elegant, but unsubstantial', i.e., 'a fantastical frivolous person' (*O.E.D.*).

5. *Littleworth*] 'Serv[an]t to ye Lord but disgui[s]de' (Con. MS).

6. *Haircut*] 'Suitor to Celestina' (Con. MS).

7. *Frederick*] 'Nephew to Aretina' (Con. MS).

12. *Aretina*] 'so affected with prodigalitie she onely studies her owne ruine' (Con. MS). If, as appears likely, Shirley intended *Aretina* to be taken as a feminine version of 'Aretino', then the name itself would suggest a lascivious flavour. Pietro Aretino's reputation as a pornographic writer and illustrator is alluded to by Lady Politic Would-be in *Volpone*, III.iv.96–7 (Jonson, *Wks*, V, 74): 'But, for a desperate wit, there's ARETINE! / Onely, his pictures are a little obscene'.

13. *Celestina*] 'the like' (Con. MS). The name is probably derived from the Spanish novel in dialogue form, attributed to Fernando de Rojas and translated by James Mabbe as *The Spanish Bawd, Represented in Celestina: Or, the Tragicke-Comedy of Calisto and Melibea* (1631). In borrowing the name, Shirley gives his character a salacious tone by association; but in other respects, there is no similarity between the Spanish Celestina and Shirley's.

MARIANA.   15
MADAM DECOY.
[Gentlewoman, *a servant to the Lady Celestina.*]

SCENE: THE STRAND

17.] *not in Q; Gentlewoman Gifford.*

14–15. *Isabella, Mariana*] 'Two Ladyes associates of Celestina' (Con. MS).
16. *Decoy*] 'an impudent bawd' (Con. MS).
18. *Strand*] frequently referred to in the drama of the period as a fashionable residential district; cf. I.ii.79n.

C

[THE EPISTLE]

To the right honourable, Richard, Lord Lovelace, of Hurley.

My Lord,

I cannot want encouragement to present a poem to your lordship, while you possess so noble a breast, in which so many 5
seeds of honour (to the example and glory of your name) obtained before your years a happy maturity. This comedy, fortunate in the scene, and one that may challenge a place in the first form of the author's compositions, most humbly addresseth itself to your honour; if it meet your gracious acceptance, 10
and that you repent not to be a patron, your lordship will only crown the imagination, and forever by this favour oblige,

My Lord,
The most humble services
of your honourer, 15
James Shirley.

Epistle] dedicatory letter.

1. *Richard ... Lovelace*] If the intended patron was indeed Richard Lovelace (1568?–1634), created Baron Lovelace of Hurley in 1627, then Shirley could not have known of his death on 22 April 1634, some eighteen months before the play was first performed, and more than three years before its publication. But Shirley may well have meant his son and successor as Baron of Hurley, John (1616–70), since he praises his patron for precocious moral development (ll. 5–7); only in that case he got his Christian name wrong. For the careers of both barons, see *The Complete Peerage*, ed. Doubleday and de Walden (1910–40), VIII, 229–32.

7–8. *fortunate ... scene*] i.e., successfully performed on stage. For an account of the first production, see Introduction, pp. 23–5.

9. *first form*] highest rank.

11–16. *your ... Shirley*] a difficult and elegant parallel construction, in which the patron is visualised as simultaneously *crowning* the imagination of the author and *obliging* his continued service. In this context, *only* has the force of 'uniquely' or 'pre-eminently' (*O.E.D.*, adv., 3).

The First Act.

Enter ARETINA *and her* Steward.

Steward. Be patient, madam, you may have your pleasure.
Aretina. 'Tis that I came to town for: I would not
    Endure again the country conversation
    To be the lady of six shires! The men
    So near the primitive making, they retain   5
    A sense of nothing but the earth, their brains
    And barren heads standing as much in want
    Of ploughing as their ground! To hear a fellow
    Make himself merry (and his horse) with whistling
    Sellinger's round! To observe with what solemnity   10
    They keep their wakes, and throw for pewter candlesticks,
    How they become the morris, with whose bells

---

10. *Sellinger's round*] an extremely popular country dance, the score for which is printed in William Chappell, *Old English Popular Music* (1893), I, 256–7. The tune was also known by the alternate title, 'The Beginning of the World', on the grounds that it was the first piece of music performed by the planets. Cf. Heywood, *A Woman Killed with Kindness*, ed. Van Fossen (1961), ii.31–2, 47–8.

11. *throw . . . candlesticks*] probably a game played at the rustic festivals here described as 'wakes'. One would imagine that throwing some projectile (either for distance or accuracy) was the competitive activity, and that the candlesticks were the prize. But I have been able to locate no evidence to support this conjecture.

12. *morris*] a country folk-dance 'the chief characteristic of which', according to E. K. Chambers (*The Mediaeval Stage*, 1903, I, 195) 'is that the performers wear bells which jingle at every step. Judging by the evidence of account books, as well as by the allusions of contemporary writers, the morris was remarkably popular in the sixteenth and seventeenth centuries.'

They ring all into Whitsun ales, and sweat
Through twenty scarfs and napkins, till the hobbyhorse
Tire and the Maid Marian, dissolved to a jelly,   15
Be kept for spoon meat!
Steward. These, with your pardon, are no argument
To make the country life appear so hateful,
At least to your particular, who enjoyed

---

13. *Whitsun ales*] a reference to the traditional summer festival, variously celebrated at the beginning of May or at Whitsuntide (seven weeks after Easter). Here the holiday is seen in its bibitory aspect, as opposed to the theatrical aspect suggested by the phrase 'Whitsun pastorals' in *Wint.*, IV.iv.134. Cf. E. K. Chambers, *The Mediaeval Stage* (1903), I, 179: 'In many places, even during the Middle Ages, and still more afterwards, the summer feast dropped out or degenerated. It became a mere beer-swilling, an "ale." And so we find in the sixteenth century a "king-ale" or a "Robin Hood's ale," and in modern times a "Whitsun-ale".'

14. *scarfs . . . napkins*] articles of costume worn by morris-dancers. In *The Gypsies Metamorphos'd*, ll. 738–9 (Jonson, *Wks*, VII, 589), Clod comments as follows on the dancing gypsies: 'They should be Morris dancers by theire gingle, but they have no Napkins.' In *The Knight of the Burning Pestle*, ed. Doebler (1967), IV.i.419–20, Rafe encourages his London auditors to imitate the dress of morris-dancers 'With bells on legs and napkins clean unto your shoulders tied, / With scarfs and garters as you please'.

hobbyhorse] 'An important feature' of the morris dance, the hobbyhorse 'was formed by a man inside a frame fitted with the head and tail of a horse, and with trappings reaching to the ground and hiding the feet of the actor, who pranced and curvetted about' (*Shakespeare's England*, II, 438). Not one of the dancers proper, the hobbyhorse appears to have held the position of a mascot; see *Every Man Out of his Humour*, II.i.40–41 (Jonson, *Wks*, III, 460): 'Sbloud, you shall see him turne morris-dancer, he ha's got him bels, a good sute, and a hobby-horse.'

15. *Maid Marian*] According to E. K. Chambers (*The Mediaeval Stage*, 1903, I, 196), morris-dancers 'were generally accompanied by grotesque personages, . . . one of these was a woman, or a man dressed in woman's clothes, to whom literary writers at least continued to give the name of Maid Marian'. In the context of the morris, Maid Marian seems to have lost her traditional association with Robin Hood, and to have developed an affinity to the hobbyhorse; see *A Very Woman*, III.i.127–8 (Massinger, *Plays*, IV, 245); 'How like an everlasting Morris-dance it looks; / Nothing but Hobby-horse, and Maid-marrian.'

16. *spoon meat*] soft food suitable for small children (*O.E.D.*). Cf. Jonson, *Epicoene*, IV.v.137–8 (*Wks*, V, 239): 'He has no employment for his armes, but to eate spoone-meat'; Middleton, *A Chaste Maid in Cheapside*, ed. Parker (1969), II.ii.29: 'Wipe her, and give her spoon-meat'; and Massinger, *A New Way to Pay Old Debts*, I.ii.55 (*Plays*, II, 307): 'But will you never tast but spoonemeat more?'

A blessing in that calm (would you be pleased   20
To think so) and the pleasure of a kingdom.
While your own will commanded what should move
Delights, your husband's love and power joined
To give your life more harmony, you lived there
Secure and innocent, beloved of all,   25
Praised for your hospitality, and prayed for;
You might be envied, but malice knew
Not where you dwelt. I would not prophesy,
But leave to your own apprehension
What may succeed your change.
Aretina.   You do imagine,   30
No doubt, you have talked wisely and confuted
London past all defence. Your master should
Do well to send you back into the country
With title of Superintendent Bailie.
Steward. How, madam?   35
Aretina. Even so, sir.
Steward. I am a gentleman, though now your servant.
Aretina. A country gentleman, by your affection to converse
      with stubble. His tenants will advance your wit, and
      plump it so with beef and bag-pudding.   40
Steward. You may say your pleasure; it becomes not me
      dispute.
Aretina. Complain to the lord of the soil, your master.
Steward. Y'are a woman of an ungoverned passion, and I pity
      you.   45

Enter SIR THOMAS BORNWELL.

Bornwell. How now? What's the matter?

---

34. Bailie] *Q subst.; bailiff Gifford.*   37–41.] *verse in Q, divided* servant. | A
. . . gentleman, / By . . . stuble, / His . . . so / With . . . bag-pudding. / You
. . . pleasure, / It.   46. How now?] *Gifford;* How how? *Q.*

---

34. *Superintendent Bailie*] a mock-heroic title, conferring nothing more
than the status of the bailiff, i.e., 'the steward of a landholder, who manages
his estate; one who superintends the husbandry of a farm for its owner or
tenant' (*O.E.D.*, 3). *Bailie*, according to *O.E.D.*, is an obsolete equivalent of
'bailiff'. I do not follow Gifford in adopting the modern word for fear of
spoiling the tone of Aretina's reproach.
    40. *bag-pudding*] a pudding boiled in a bag (*O.E.D.*); i.e., sausage.

Steward.   Nothing, sir.

Bornwell. Angry, sweet heart?   [*Exit* Steward.]

Aretina.   I am angry with myself,
To be so miserably restrained in things
Wherein it doth concern your love and honour
To see me satisfied.

Bornwell.   In what, Aretina,   50
Dost thou accuse me? Have I not obeyed
All thy desires: against mine own opinion
Quitted the country, and removed the hope
Of our return by sale of that fair lordship
We lived in? changed a calm and retired life   55
For this wild town, composed of noise and charge?

Aretina. What charge more than is necessary for
A lady of my birth and education?

Bornwell. I am not ignorant how much nobility
Flows in your blood: your kinsmen great and powerful   60
I'th' state. But with this lose not your memory
Of being my wife. I shall be studious,
Madam, to give the dignity of your birth
All the best ornaments which become my fortune;
But would not flatter it to ruin both   65
And be the fable of the town, to teach
Other men loss of wit by mine, employed
To serve your vast expenses.

Aretina.   Am I then
Brought in the balance? So sir.

Bornwell.   Though you weigh
Me in a partial scale, my heart is honest   70
And must take liberty to think you have
Obeyed no modest counsel to affect,
Nay study ways of pride and costly ceremony:
Your change of gaudy furniture, and pictures
Of this Italian master and that Dutchman's;   75

50–1. Aretina, / Dost] *Gifford; Aretina?* / Dost *Q*.   55. retired] *Gifford;*
retire *Q*.   57–8. necessary for / A] *Gifford;* necessarie, / For a *Q*.   72.
affect] *Gifford;* effect *Q*.

75.] Under the direct or indirect patronage of Charles I, many continental
painters were temporarily resident in London between 1625 and 1640; see M.

Your mighty looking-glasses, like artillery,
Brought home on engines; the superfluous plate,
Antic and novel, vanities of tires,
Fourscore pound suppers for my lord your kinsman,
Banquets for t'other lady, aunt, and cousins;   80
And perfumes that exceed all train of servants,
To stifle us at home, and show abroad
More motley than the French or the Venetian
About your coach, whose rude postillion
Must pester every narrow lane, till passengers   85
And tradesmen curse your choking up their stalls,
And common cries pursue your ladyship
For hindering o' their market.

Aretina.   Have you done, sir?

Bornwell. I could accuse the gaiety of your wardrobe

---

77. home] *Gifford;* whom *Q.*   78. Antic] *Knowland;* Anticke *Q;* Antique
Gifford.   81. all train] *Q;* all: train *Gifford.*

Whinney and O. Millar, *English Art, 1625–1714* (1957), pp. 4–14, 60–74. A
lady of Aretina's pretensions might be expected to purchase paintings by
these artists, since she employs a 'Belgic gentleman' (II.i.25) to make her
portrait.

   77. *engines*] machinery (*O.E.D.*), here designating the pieces of furniture on
which Aretina's mirrors are mounted.

   78. *Antic*] I follow Knowland in printing the archaic *antic* rather than the
modern *antique* for two reasons: (1) to preserve the pun on two alternate
meanings, namely 'ancient' and 'outlandish'; (2) to ensure that the first
syllable will be accented, in keeping with the rhythm of the line as a whole. Cf.
I.i.121, II.i.72.

   tires] ornamental clothing, especially headdresses (*O.E.D.*).

   81–84.] The passage is confusing, even when heavily repunctuated;
Bornwell seems to be alleging that Aretina's retinue displays more variegated
colour (motley) than its counterparts in France or Venice would. To judge by
the accounts of travellers, this claim does fit the French (who dressed extrava-
gantly), but not the Venetians (who dressed conservatively). See Thomas
Coryat, *Coryat's Crudities* (1905), I, 398: 'For whereas they [the Venetians]
have but one colour, we use many more then are in the Rain-bow, all the most
light, garish, and unseemly colours that are in the world. . . . For we weare
more phantasticall fashions then any Nation under the Sunne doth, the
French onely excepted.' Moryson (IV, 218–28) confirms these distinctions:
'All the Gentlemen [in Venice], not one excepted, weare blacke cloth gownes'
and avoid 'those mixed colours which we so highly esteeme'. In France, however, 'Gentlemen weare mixed and light colours . . . with great inconstancy in
the fashion.' By 1635 most Englishmen would have been more conversant
with French than with Venetian fashion.

And prodigal embroideries, under which   90
Rich satins, plushes, cloth of silver, dare
Not show their own complexions; your jewels,
Able to burn out the spectators' eyes
And show like bonfires on you by the tapers;
Something might here be spared, with safety of   95
Your birth and honour, since the truest wealth
Shines from the soul, and draws up just admirers.
I could urge something more –

Aretina.   Pray do, I like
Your homily of thrift.

Bornwell.   I could wish, madam,
You would not game so much.

Aretina.   A gamester too?   100

Bornwell. But are not come to that repentance, yet,
Should teach you skill enough to raise your profit.
You look not through the subtlety of cards
And mysteries of dice, nor can you save
Charge with the box, buy petticoats and pearls   105
And keep your family by the precious income.
Nor do I wish you should. My poorest servant
Shall not upbraid my tables, nor his hire
Purchased beneath my honour. You make play

---

95. with safety] *Con. MS, Gifford;* which safely *Q.*   101. repentance] *Q;*
acquaintance *Gifford.*

---

91. *plushes*] 'Plush was an expensive silk fabric with nap longer and softer
than velvet' (Linthicum, p. 121).

cloth of silver] fabric made by one of a variety of methods of interweaving
silver with silk or wool (Linthicum, p. 114).

92. *own complexions*] i.e., individual qualities.

94. *by . . . tapers*] i.e., by virtue of the candle-light which they reflect.

95. *with safety*] This is the first of many instances in which the person who
annotated the Con. copy of Q corrected a dubious passage. Whenever Con.
MS anticipates an editor (in this case Gifford), I give double credit in the
collation line.

105. *box*] the 'bank' in a gaming establishment. Bornwell might be para-
phrasing Cotton's advice to the apprentice gamester: 'if you be not careful and
vigilant, the Box-keeper shall score you up double or treble Boxes, and
though you have lost your money, dun you as severely for it, as if it were the
justest debt in the World' (sig. B6–6v). Cf. Middleton, *A Chaste Maid in
Cheapside*, ed. Parker (1969), V.i.168: 'whoe'er games, the box is sure a
winner'.

Not a pastime but a tyranny, and vex   110
    Yourself and my estate by't.
Aretina.   Good, proceed.
Bornwell. Another game you have, which consumes more
    Your fame than purse: your revels in the night,
    Your meetings called the ball, to which appear,
    As to the court of pleasure, all your gallants   115
    And ladies thither bound by a subpoena
    Of Venus, and small Cupid's high displeasure.
    'Tis but the family of love translated
    Into more costly sin. There was a play on't,
    And had the poet not been bribed to a modest   120
    Expression of your antic gambols in't,
    Some darks had been discovered, and the deeds too;
    In time he may repent and make some blush
    To see the second part danced on the stage.
    My thoughts acquit you for dishonouring me   125
    By any foul act, but the virtuous know

---

114. *the ball*] the name of a social club to which Aretina allegedly belongs.
The activities of such a society are treated satirically in Shirley's *The Ball*
(1632), a play to which the dramatist alludes in ll. 119–22.

118. *family . . . love*] a puritan sect often ridiculed for hypocrisy and suspected of sexually irregular practices. It is alluded to in *Eastward Ho*, V.ii.33,
and glossed as follows by Herford and Simpson (Jonson, *Wks*, IX, 674): 'A
sect founded by David George or Joriszoon, an Anabaptist of Delft, who
claimed to be the restorer of the kingdom of Israel. He died in 1556, and was
succeeded by "Harry Nicholas". . . . In 1580 Elizabeth issued a proclamation
to suppress it.' Cf. Tourneur, *The Atheist's Tragedy*, ed. Ribner (1964),
I.iv.56. In Middleton's *The Family of Love* (*Works*, ed. Bullen, 1885–6, III,
11–120), Mistress Purge, a new member of the sect, implies something of its
character when she admits that 'we fructify best i'th' dark' (III.iii.22).

119–22.] The play referred to is *The Ball*, performed with some contro-
versy by Queen Henrietta Maria's men at the Cockpit in 1632. Herbert made
the following entry for 18 November 1632, two days after issuing a licence for
performance: 'In the play of *The Ball*, written by Sherley, and acted by the
Queenes players, ther were divers personated so naturally, both of lords and
others of the court, that I took it ill, and would have forbidden the play, but
that Biston [Christopher Beeston, the manager] promiste many things which
I found faulte withall should be left out, and that he would not suffer it to be
done by the poett any more, who deserves to be punisht' (Herbert, p. 19). In
Bornwell's fictional version of the incident, Aretina is one of the people whose
outlandish behaviour (*antic gambols*) is 'personated so naturally' as to cause
trouble for the playwright. But for censorship (here caricatured as bribery),
the poet might have exposed the secret stains (*darks*) on Aretina's character.

124.] This putative *second part* was never written.

    'Tis not enough to clear ourselves, but the
    Suspicions of our shame.

Aretina.   Have you concluded
    Your lecture?

Bornwell.   I ha' done, and howsoever
    My language may appear to you, it carries   130
    No other than my fair and just intent
    To your delights, without curb to their modest
    And noble freedom.

Aretina.   I'll not be so tedious
    In my reply, but without art or elegance
    Assure you I keep still my first opinion;   135
    And though you veil your avaricious meaning
    With handsome names of modesty and thrift,
    I find you would entrench and wound the liberty
    I was born with. Were my desires unprivileged
    By example, while my judgement thought 'em fit   140
    You ought not to oppose; but when the practice
    And tract of every honourable lady
    Authorise me, I take it great injustice
    To have my pleasures circumscribed and taught me.
    A narrow-minded husband is a thief   145
    To his own fame, and his preferment too;
    He shuts his parts and fortunes from the world,
    While from the popular vote and knowledge, men
    Rise to employment in the state.

Bornwell.   I have
    No great ambition to buy preferment   150
    At so dear rate.

Aretina.   Nor I to sell my honour
    By living poor and sparingly; I was not
    Bred in that ebb of fortune, and my fate
    Shall not compel me to't.

Bornwell.   I know not, madam,
    But you pursue these ways.

---

130. may] *Gifford;* my *Q.*   142. tract] *Q;* track *Gifford.*

---

   142. *tract*] a conflation of the relevant meanings of 'trace' (sb.) and 'track'
(sb.); precedent (*O.E.D.*).
   147. *parts*] abilities; cf. II.ii.185n.

Aretina.   What ways?   155
Bornwell. In the strict sense of honesty, I dare
  Make oath they are innocent.
Aretina.   Do not divert,
  By busy troubling of your brain, those thoughts
  That should preserve 'em.
Bornwell. How was that?   160
Aretina. 'Tis English.
Bornwell. But carries some unkind sense.

                Enter MADAM DECOY.

Decoy. Good morrow my sweet madam.
Aretina. Decoy, welcome. This visit is a favour.
Decoy. Alas sweet madam, I cannot stay; I came but to present   165
  my service to your ladyship. I could not pass by your door,
  but I must take the boldness to tender my respects.
Aretina. You oblige me, madam, but I must not dispense so
  with your absence.
Decoy. Alas, the coach, madam, stays for me at the door.   170
Aretina. Thou shalt command mine; prithee sweet Decoy.
Decoy. I would wait on you, madam, but I have many visits to
  make this morning. I beseech –
Aretina. So you will promise to dine with me.
Decoy. I shall present a guest.   175
Aretina. Why then good morrow, madam.
Decoy. A happy day shine on your ladyship.   *Exit.*

                Enter Steward.

Aretina. What's your news, sir?
Steward.   Madam, two gentlemen –
Aretina. What gentlemen? Have they no names?
Steward.   They are
  The gentleman with his own head of hair   180

---

157. Make oath] *Q; Make my oath Knowland.*   165–77.] *verse in Q, divided*
came / But . . . Ladiship; / I . . . take / The . . . respects. / You . . . must / Not
. . . absence. / Alas . . . doore. / Thou . . . *Decoy.* / I . . . many / Visits . . .
beseech. / So . . . shall / Present . . . Madam. / A.   167. take] *Q; make
Schelling.*

---

155. *But*] except; otherwise than (Abbott, § 122).
157–9.] The antecedent of *'em* is *ways* (l. 155).

Whom you commended for his horsemanship
In Hyde Park, and becoming the saddle
The tother day.

Aretina.   What circumstance is this
To know him by?

Steward.   His name's at my tongue's end.
He liked the fashion of your pearl chain, madam,   185
And borrowed it for his jeweller to take
A copy by it.

Bornwell.   What cheating gallant's this?

Steward. That never walks without a lady's busk
And plays with fans? Mr Alexander Kickshaw.
I thought I should remember him.

Aretina.   What's the other?   190

Steward. What an unlucky memory I have!
The gallant that still danceth in the street,
And wears a gross of ribbon in his hat,
That carries oringado in his pocket,
And sugar-plums to sweeten his discourse,   195
That studies compliment, defies all wit
On black, and censures plays that are not bawdy –

---

182. the] *Q;* so the *conj. Gifford.*   197. On] *Q;* In *Gifford.*

---

182. *Hyde Park*] already a fashionable meeting-place for the gentry, as Shirley's comedy, *Hyde Park* (1632), demonstrates. Sugden describes its attractions as follows: 'Early in the reign of Charles I the Ring, or Tour, was formed: it was a circular drive about 90 yards in diameter, and lay some 150 yards N. of the E. end of the Serpentine. It was used for horse, foot, and coach-races, and soon became a fashionable resort; and cakes and cream were provided for the visitors at the Cake House.'

188. *busk*] 'stays of wood or whalebone' worn underneath a lady's bodice, and fastened to her corset-like undergarment with ribbons called buskpoints. 'Ladies gave their busk-points to their lovers, who wore them about their wrists or in other conspicuous places, and made sonnets to them, much to the envy of less fortunate suitors' (Linthicum, p. 178).

193. *gross*] twelve dozen (*O.E.D.*).

194. *oringado*] candied orange-peel; variant of orangeado (*O.E.D.*).

195. *sugar-plums*] sweetmeats or comfits made of boiled sugar (*O.E.D.*).

196. *compliment*] the observance of ceremony or courtesy in social relations (Onions). Cf. Shirley's *Love Tricks: Or the School of Complement*, III.v (*Wks*, I, 47), in which the character Gasparo runs a 'Complement-school' which he describes also as 'A school of generous education'; in this academy, instruction in social behaviour proceeds along highly conventional and formal lines.

defies] looks down upon; snobbisly rejects. Cf. II.i.125n.

  Mr John Littleworth.
Aretina.   They are welcome. But
  Pray entertain them a small time, lest I
  Be unprovided.
Bornwell.   Did they ask for me?   200
Steward. No, sir.
Bornwell.   It matters not, they must be welcome.
Aretina. Fie, how's this hair disordered! Here's a curl
  Straddles most impiously. I must to my closet. *Exit.*
Bornwell. [*To Steward*] Wait on 'em; my lady will return again.
               [*Exit* Steward.]

  I have to such a height fulfilled her humour   205
  All application's dangerous. These gallants
  Must be received or she will fall into
  A tempest, and the house be shook with names
  Of all her kindred; 'tis a servitude
  I may in time shake off.   210

    Enter ALEXANDER *and* LITTLEWORTH.

Alexander and Littleworth. Save you, Sir Thomas.
Bornwell.   Save you, gentlemen.
Alexander. I kiss your hand.
Bornwell.   What day is it abroad?
Littleworth. The morning rises from your lady's eye;
  If she look clear, we take the happy omen
  Of a fair day.
Bornwell.   She'll instantly appear,   215
  To the discredit of your compliment;
  But you express your wit thus.
Alexander.   And you modesty,
  Not to affect the praises of your own.
Bornwell. Leaving this subject, what game's now on foot?

---

203. Straddles] *Con. MS, Gifford;* Straddle *Q.* 206. application's] *Gifford;*
applications *Q.* 211–12. Save . . . gentlemen. / I] *lineation as in Schelling;*
Thomas. / Save . . . hand. / What *Q.*

---

 197. *On black*] not adequately explained. F. D. Hoeniger proposes that to
defy 'all wit on black' is to find fault with everyone's wit, to reject all true wit,
to blacken wit with malice. The context would support this reading, but I
have been unable to find further evidence.
 200. *unprovided*] i.e., not properly dressed and made up for the occasion.

What exercise carries the general vote   220
O'th' town now? Nothing moves without your
     knowledge.
Alexander. The cocking now has all the noise; I'll have
A hundred pieces of one battle. O,
These birds of Mars!
Littleworth.   Venus is Mars his bird too.
Alexander. Why, and the pretty doves are Venus's   225
To show that kisses draw the chariot.
Littleworth. I am for that skirmish.
Littleworth.   When shall we have
More booths and bagpipes upon Banstead downs?
No mighty race is expected – but my lady returns.

Enter ARETINA.

Aretina. Fair morning to you, gentlemen. You went   230
Not late to bed by your early visit.
You do me honour.
Alexander.   It becomes our service.
Aretina. What new abroad? You hold precious intelligence.

220–1. vote / O'th' town now? Nothing] *Gifford subst.; * vote? / Oth' towne now
nothing *Q.* 223. of] *Q;* on *Gifford.* 225. Venus's] *Gifford; Venusses*
Q. 230–1. gentlemen. You went / Not] *lineation of this ed.;* gentlemen, /
You went not *Q.*

---

222. *The cocking . . . noise*] Cf. Cotton, sig. O7v: 'Cocking is a sport or
pastime so full of delight and pleasure, that I know not any Game in that
respect is to be preferred before it, and since the *Fighting-Cock* hath gain'd so
great an estimation among the Gentry, in respect to this noble recreation I
shall here propose it before all the other Games of which I have afore suc-
cinctly discoursed.'
223. *pieces*] gold coins worth twenty-two shillings each (*O.E.D.*).
Mars his] Mars's (Abbot, § 217).
225–6.] Cf. Webster, *The Duchess of Malfi*, ed. Brown (1964), III.ii.21–2:
'Venus had two soft doves / To draw her chariot.' Webster, like Shirley, is
exploiting the traditional association between the doves and kisses; in the
Webster passage, Antonio has just kissed the Duchess once, and is using the
metaphor to ask for a second kiss.
228. *Banstead downs*] the hills near Epsom, fourteen miles south-south-
west of London. After the discovery of mineral springs here in 1618, the
downs became a resort and favoured site for country fairs. The annual races
on the downs appear to have begun when James I was residing at Nonesuch,
the tradition becoming a permanent institution after 1730 (see *Encyclopaedia
Britannica*, 11th ed., under *Epsom*).

Littleworth. All tongues are so much busy with your praise
    They have not time to frame other discourse.   235
    Will please you madam taste a sugar-plum?
Bornwell. What does the goldsmith think the pearl is worth
    You borrowed of my lady?
Alexander.   'Tis a rich one.
Bornwell. She has many other toys whose fashion you
    Will like extremely; you have no intention   240
    To buy any of her jewels?
Alexander.   Understand me –
Bornwell. You had rather sell, perhaps. But leaving this,
    I hope you'll dine with us.
Alexander.   I came a purpose.
Aretina. And where were you last night?
Alexander.   I madam? Where
    I slept not; it had been sin, where so much   245
    Delight and beauty was to keep me waking.
    There is a lady, madam, will be worth
    Your free society: my conversation
    Ne'er knew so elegant and brave a soul
    With most incomparable flesh and blood,   250
    So spirited, so courtly, speaks the languages,
    Sings, dances, plays o'th' lute to admiration,
    Is fair and paints not, games too, keeps a table,
    And talks most witty satire; has a wit
    Of a clean Mercury.
Littleworth.   Is she married?
Alexander.   No.   255
Aretina. A virgin?
Alexander.   Neither.
Littleworth.   What? A widow? Something

---

236. Will] *Q;* Wilt *Gifford;* Will't *Gosse.*   madam . . . sugar-plum?]
Gifford; Madam? . . . Sugerplum. *Q.*   243. a] *Q;* o' *Gifford.*   251. courtly,
speaks] *Baskervill;* Courtly speakes *Q;* courtly! speaks *Gifford.*

---

    236. *sugar-plum*] See l. 195n.
    243. *a*] on (Abbott, § 140).
    255. *clean Mercury*] In his role as patron of thieves and tricksters, Mercury
exhibits the qualities of adroitness and cunning; see Shakespeare's Thersites
in *Troil,* II.iii.11–13: 'Mercury, lose all the serpentine craft of thy caduceus, if
ye take not that little, little, less than little wit from them that they have.' In
this context, *clean* signifies 'clever' (*O.E.D.,* adj., 8).

Of this wide commendation might have been
Excused. This such a prodigy?

Alexander.   Repent
Before I name her. She did never see
Yet full sixteen, an age in the opinion   260
Of wise men not contemptible; she has
Mourned out her year, too, for the honest knight
That had compassion of her youth and died
So timely. Such a widow is not common,
And now she shines more fresh and tempting   265
Than any natural virgin.

Aretina.   What's her name?

Alexander. She was christened Celestina, by her husband
The Lady Bellamour. This ring was hers.

Bornwell. You borrowed it to copy out the posy.

Alexander. Are they not pretty rubies? 'Twas a grace   270
She was pleased to show me, that I might have
One made of the same fashion, for I love
All pretty forms.

Aretina.   And is she glorious?

Alexander. She is full of jewels, madam, but I am
Most taken with the bravery of her mind,   275
Although her garments have all grace and ornament.

Aretina. You have been high in praises.

Alexander.   I come short,
No flattery can reach her.

Bornwell.   [*Aside*] Now my lady
Is troubled as she feared to be eclipsed;
This news will cost me somewhat.

Aretina.   You deserve   280
Her favour for this noble character.

Alexander. And I possess it, by my stars' benevolence.

Aretina. You must bring us acquainted.

271–2. have / One made] *lineation of this ed.;* have one / Made *Q.*   283. Ay,
pray] *This ed.;* I pray *Q.*

---

269. *posy*] 'motto inscribed on the inside of a finger-ring' (Onions).
273. *glorious*] 'splendid in beauty or richness of adornment' (*O.E.D.*).
275. *bravery*] 'splendour' (Onions).
279. *as*] as if.
283. *Ay, pray*] The emendation of this ed. is based on the observation that
the compositor elsewhere failed to distinguish between *I* and *Ay*, as in sig.

Bornwell.   Ay, pray do sir.
    I long to see her too. Madam, I have
    Thought upon't and corrected my opinion;   285
    Pursue what ways of pleasure your desires
    Incline you to; not only with my state,
    But with my person I will follow you.
    I see the folly of my thrift, and will
    Repent in sack and prodigality   290
    To your own heart's content.
Aretina.   But do not mock.
Bornwell. Take me to your embraces, gentlemen,
    And tutor me.
Littleworth.   And will you kiss the ladies?
Bornwell. And sing and dance. I long to see this beauty.
    I would fain lose a hundred pounds at dice now.   295
    [*To Aretina*] Thou shalt have another gown and petticoat;
    Tomorrow will you sell my running horses?
    We have no Greek wine in the house, I think;
    Pray send one of our footmen to the merchant,
    And throw the hogsheads of March beer into   300
    The kennel to make room for sack and claret.
    What think you to be drunk yet before dinner?
    We will have constant music, and maintain

---

288. person I] *Q;* person; I *Gifford.*   301. sack] *Gifford;* Sackes *Q.*

C4v, where 'I forsooth' (Q) becomes 'Ay, forsooth' (II.i.64) in this and other
edd. In the present instance, *I* is a logically possible but dramatically inferior
reading; since Bornwell is concurring with Aretina's request, *Ay* is the more
likely of the two.

    290. *sack*] 'the generic name for Spanish and Canary wines, . . . popular
with all classes' (*Shakespeare's England*, II, 136).

    296. *petticoat*] a woman's underskirt, worn underneath gown and kirtle,
and fastened to the bodice. Though technically an undergarment, the petticoat was often visible during such normal activities as walking or dancing;
consequently, it was 'made of material as rich and ornamental as the wearer
could afford' (Linthicum, p. 187).

    298. *Greek wine*] a socially desirable beverage, to judge by Overreach's
hospitality in *A New Way to Pay Old Debts*, III.ii.168–9 (Massinger, *Plays*,
II, 338): 'May it please my Lord / To taste a glasse of Greeke wine first.'

    300. *March beer*] known for its potency, and so named because it was
brewed in March (*O.E.D.*).

    301. *kennel*] a gutter for draining off water and other liquids (*O.E.D.*).

Them and their fiddles in fantastic liveries.
I'll tune my voice to catches. I must have   305
My dining-room enlarged, to invite ambassadors;
We'll feast the parish in the fields, and teach
The military men new discipline,
Who shall charge all their new artillery
With oranges and lemons, boy, to play   310
All dinner upon our capons.
Alexander.   He's exalted.
Bornwell. I will do anything to please my lady,
Let that suffice, and kiss o'th' same condition.
I am converted; do not you dispute,
But patiently allow the miracle.   315
Aretina. I am glad to hear you, sir, in so good tune.

Enter Servant.

Servant. Madam, the painter.
Aretina.   I am to sit this morning.
Bornwell. Do, while I give new directions to my steward.
Alexander. With your favour, we'll wait on you; sitting's but
A melancholy exercise without   320
Some company to discourse.
Aretina.   It does conclude
A lady's morning work: we rise, make fine,
Sit for our picture, and 'tis time to dine.
Littleworth. Praying's forgot.
Alexander.   'Tis out of fashion.   *Exeunt.*

310. boy, to] *Con. MS, Gifford;* boy to *Q.*   316.1] *S.D. set in righthand
margin opposite l.* 315 *in Q.*

307–11.] In attempting to make sense of this passage, one should bear in
mind that Bornwell is constructing a deliberately bizarre fantasy. Thus, he
visualises oranges and lemons harmlessly shot at capons – i.e., castrated cocks
or, figuratively, coxcombs (*O.E.D.*).

311. *exalted*] elated, rapturously excited (*O.E.D.*).

315. *miracle*] See III.i.115–16n.

316.1] In many subsequent instances, Q places stage directions calling for
characters to enter in the righthand margin rather than centrally on a separate
line. Further examples of this practice will not be collated.

ACT I, SCENE ii

Enter CELESTINA *and her* Steward.

Celestina. Fie, what an air this room has.
Steward.   'Tis perfumed.
Celestina. With some cheap stuff. Is it your wisdom's thrift
    To infect my nostrils thus? Or is't to favour
    The gout in your worship's hand you are afraid
    To exercise your pen in your account book?   5
    Or do you doubt my credit to discharge
    Your bills?
Steward.   Madam, I hope you have not found
    My duty, with the guilt of sloth or jealousy,
    Unapt to your command.
Celestina.   You can extenuate
    Your faults with language, sir, but I expect   10
    To be obeyed. What hangings have we here?
Steward. They are arras, madam.
Celestina.   Impudence, I know't.
    I will have fresher and more rich, not wrought
    With faces that may scandalise a Christian,
    With Jewish stories stuffed with corn and camels;   15
    You had best wrap all my chambers in wild Irish,
    And make a nursery of monsters here
    To fright the ladies come to visit me.

---

4. hand you] *Gifford subst.;* hand? You *Q.*   18. come] *Gifford;* comes *Q.*

---

11. *hangings*] 'hangings of tapestry or arras work . . . invariably covered the walls of the chief rooms in the large houses' (*Shakespeare's England*, II, 4). King discusses the theatrical function of the hangings at the Cockpit theatre, especially their importance in staging discovery scenes (pp. 160–4); for further comment, see Appendix A, pp. 194–5.

12. *arras*] 'rich tapestry fabric, in which figures and scenes are woven in colour' (*O.E.D.*).

15.]Celestina is alluding to such Old Testament narratives as the story in which Joseph interprets Pharaoh's dreams (Gen. xli.1–37). Cf. Gifford.

16. *wild Irish*] The phrase generally refers to the native (non-English) inhabitants of Ireland, as in Ford's *Perkin Warbeck*, ed. Ure (1968), III.ii.III.1–3: '*enter . . . four wild* Irish *in trowses, long-haired, and accordingly habited*'. Here it refers elliptically to Irish frieze, a coarse woollen cloth, which Sugden describes as 'almost the only manufacture' of Ireland.

Steward. Madam, I hope –
Celestina.   I say I will have other,
    Good master steward, of a finer loom.   20
    Some silk and silver, if your worship please
    To let me be at so much cost. I'll have
    Stories to fit the seasons of the year,
    And change as often as I please.
Steward.   You shall, madam.
Celestina. I am bound to your consent, forsooth; and is   25
    My coach brought home?
Steward.   This morning I expect it.
Celestina. The inside, as I gave direction,
    Of crimson plush?
Steward.   Of crimson camel plush.
Celestina. Ten thousand moths consume't! Shall I ride
      through
    The streets in penance, wrapped up round in hair-cloth?   30
    Sell't to an alderman; 'twill serve his wife
    To go a-feasting to their country house,
    Or fetch a merchant's nurse-child, and come home
    Laden with fruit and cheesecakes. I despise it.
Steward. The nails adorn it, madam, set in method   35
    And pretty forms.
Celestina.   But single gilt, I warrant.
Steward. No, madam.
Celestina.   Another solecism. [*Aside*] O fie,
    This fellow will bring me to a consumption
    With fretting at his ignorance! [*To Steward*] Some lady
    Had rather never pray, than go to church in't.   40
    The nails not double gilt? To market with't;

27. direction] *Q;* directions *Gosse.*   41. with't] *Gifford;* wo't *Q.*

---

28. *plush*] See I.i.91n.
  camel] probably an adj. form of cameline, a fabric made (or thought to be made) of camel's hair (*O.E.D.*).
  33. *nurse-child*] It was customary, as Stone observes, for 'infants of the landed, upper bourgeois and professional classes in the sixteenth and seventeenth centuries [to be] sent out to hired wet-nurses for the first twelve to eighteen months' (p. 107).
  36. *single gilt*] covered with only one thin layer of gold (*O.E.D.*), as opposed to the two layers implied by 'double gilt' (l. 41).

       'Twill hackney out to Mile-end, or convey
       Your city tumblers to be drunk with cream
       And prunes at Islington.
Steward.   Good madam, hear me.
Celestina. I'll rather be beholding to my aunt,   45
       The countess, for her mourning coach, than be
       Disparaged so. Shall any juggling tradesman
       Be at charge to shoe his running horse with gold,
       And shall my coach nails be but single gilt?
       How dare these knaves abuse me so?
Steward.   Vouchsafe   50
       To hear me speak.
Celestina.   Is my sedan yet finished?
       And liveries for my men-mules, according
       As I gave charge?
Steward.   Yes madam, it is finished,
       But without tilting plumes at the four corners;
       The scarlet's pure, but not embroiderèd.   55
Celestina. What mischief were it to your conscience
       Were my coach lined with tissue, and my harness
       Covered with needlework? If my sedan

---

42. *Mile-end*] a rural hamlet, located exactly one mile beyond Aldgate, the eastern extremity of the city of London in the seventeenth century (Sugden). In *2H4* Shallow remembers practising archery 'at Mile-end Green' (III.ii.262).

43. *tumblers*] variously glossed as 'courtesans' (Neilson), 'common women' (Schelling), 'prostitutes' (Baskervill) and 'harlots' (Spencer). *O.E.D.* lends no support to such a notion, listing the primary meaning as 'acrobats' and the secondary meaning as 'street ruffians'. However, the sexual significance does seem inescapable in 'tumbler' (V.ii.25) and in Ophelia's use of 'tumbled' in *Ham.*, IV.v.62–3: 'Quoth she, "Before you tumbled me, / You promised me to wed".'

44. *Islington*] A rustic village north of London (not yet a suburb), Islington was in the seventeenth century 'a favourite place for outings with the citizens, and the many dairies there supplied them with cream and cakes' (Sugden).

48. *shoe . . . gold*] Gifford notes the allusion to a comic song in *Hyde Park*, IV.iii (Shirley, *Wks*, II, 513), which contains the line: '*Nor Toby with his golden shoes*'. Since the song also names such horses as '*Herring Shotten*' and '*Jilian Thrust*', I suspect that Shirley is using poor Toby as an emblem of equestrian absurdity; Celestina, at least, seems aware of the pretensions of the horse's owner.

52. *men-mules*] footmen responsible for bearing the sedan chair (Papousek).

54. *tilting plumes*] See l. 92n.

     Had all the story of the prodigal
     Embroid",rèd with pearl?

Steward.   Alas, good madam,   60
     I know 'tis your own cost; I am but your steward,
     And would discharge my duty the best way.
     You have been pleased to hear me: 'tis not for
     My profit that I manage your estate
     And save expense, but for your honour, madam.   65

Celestina. How sir, my honour?

Steward.   Though you hear it not,
     Men's tongues are liberal in your character
     Since you began to live thus high; I know
     Your fame is precious to you.

Celestina.   I were best
     Make you my governor; audacious varlet,   70
     How dare you interpose your doting counsel?
     Mind your affairs with more obedience,
     Or I shall ease you of an office, sir.
     Must I be limited to please your honour,
     Or for the vulgar breath confine my pleasures?   75
     I will pursue 'em in what shapes I fancy:
     Here, and abroad, my entertainments shall
     Be oftener and more rich. Who shall control me?
     I live i'th' Strand, whither few ladies come
     To live and purchase more than fame. I will   80
     Be hospitable, then, and spare no cost
     That may engage all generous report

74–5. honour, / . . . pleasures?] *Gifford;* honour? / . . . pleasures, *Q;* honour? / . . . pleasures? *Knowland.*

---

59. *story . . . prodigal*] Here Celestina alludes to the parable of the prodigal son (Luke xv. 11–24), who 'wasted his substance with riotous living', repented, and was rescued from indigence by his forgiving father. If such a didactic narrative seems an inappropraate decoration for Celestina's sedan, one should remember Falstaff's chamber in the Garter Inn (*Wiv.*, IV.v.6–7), 'painted about with the story of the Prodigal, fresh and new'.

79. *Strand*] The London street near the shore of the Thames, running parallel to the river from Charing Cross to Temple Bar. Sugden remarks that the Strand became, in Jacobean times, 'the fashionable residential quarter' of the city, 'the West End of those days'. This evaluation is borne out by numerous references in the drama, such as Clerimont's observation in *Epicoene*, I.iii.34–6 (Jonson, *Wks*, V, 174), that Sir Amorous La Foole 'invites his guests to 'hem, aloud, out of his windore, as they ride by in coaches. He has a lodging in the *Strand* for the purpose.'

To trumpet forth my bounty and my bravery
Till the court envy and remove. I'll have
My house the academy of wits, who shall   85
Exalt it with rich sack and sturgeon,
Write panegyrics of my feasts, and praise
The method of my witty superfluities;
The horses shall be taught, with frequent waiting
Upon my gates, to stop in their career   90
Toward Charing Cross, spite of the coachman's fury,
And not a tilter but shall strike his plume
When he sails by my window; my balcony
Shall be the courtier's idol, and more gazed at
Than all the pageantry at Temple Bar   95
By country clients.
Steward.   Sure my lady's mad.
Celestina. [*Striking him*] Take that for your ill manners.
Steward.   Thank you madam.
I would there were less quicksilver in your fingers. *Exit.*

86. Exalt it with] *F.D. Hoeniger;* Exalt with *Q;* Exalt their genius with *conj. Gifford.*

---

86. *Exalt . . . with*] Both metre and meaning would suggest that something is missing from the line in Q, but Gifford's guess is no more than that. The solution proposed by F. D. Hoeniger strikes me as irresistible. *Exalt it* now means 'extol my house', the antecedent of *it* being Celestina's house (l. 85). The parallel acts of praise alluded to in the rest of this clause (ll. 87–8) add strong contextual support.

91. *Charing Cross*] a landmark at the southwestern extremity of the Strand (cf. l. 79n.), between London and Westminster. The actual cross was erected by Edward I, in 1290, to commemorate Queen Elinor. By Shirley's time it had fallen into disrepair; it was eventually condemned (1643), demolished (1647), and replaced by an equestrian statue of Charles I (Sugden).

92. *tilter*] contestant in a joust, i.e., one who tilts; metaphorically, a gallant, as implied in Hotspur's use of the verb form in *1H4*, II.iii.87–8: 'This is no world / To play with mammets and to tilt with lips.'

plume] large feather attached to one's hat or other headdress (*O.E.D.*).

95. *Temple Bar*] a gate, at the western end of Fleet Street, marking the limit of the jurisdiction of the city of London; see Sugden, who believes the *pageantry* referred to by Celestina to be 'the traitors' heads exposed there, which people used to come to see'.

97. S.D.] Con. MS records the following in the lefthand margin: 'him a box / Ear'. Since the margins have been trimmed, part of the annotation has been cut away; the missing words can be supplied on the model of *2H6*, I.iii.136.1: '*She gives the Duchess a box on the ear.*'

98. *quicksilver*] capacity for quickness of motion, comparable to that of the metal mercury (*O.E.D.*, 2).

Celestina. There's more than simple honesty in a servant
        Required to his full duty; none should dare   100
        But with a look, much less a saucy language,
        Check at their mistress' pleasure. I'm resolved
        To pay for some delight, my estate will bear it,
        I'll rein it shorter when I please.

                    Enter Steward.

Steward.   A gentleman
        Desires to speak with your ladyship.
Celestina.   His name?   105
Steward. He says you know him not; he seems to be
        Of quality.
Celestina.   Admit him.

            Enter HAIRCUT.   [*Exit* Steward.]

                    Sir, with me?
Haircut. Madam, I know not how you may receive
        This boldness from me, but my fair intents,
        Known, will incline you to be charitable.   110
Celestina. No doubt, sir.
Haircut.   He must live obscurely, madam,
        That hath not heard what virtues you possess;
        And I, a poor admirer of your fame,
        Am come to kiss your hand.
Celestina.   That all your business?
Haircut. Though it were worth much travel, I have more
        In my ambition.
Celestina.   Speak it freely, sir.
Haircut. You are a widow.
Celestina.   So.
Haircut.   And I a bachelor.
Celestina. You come a-wooing, sir, and would perhaps
        Show me a way to reconcile these two.
Haircut. And bless my stars for such a happiness.   120
Celestina. I like you, sir, the better, that you do not
        Wander about but shoot home to the meaning;
        'Tis a confidence will make a man
        Know sooner what to trust to. But I never

119. these] *Qb;* thee *Qa;* the *Gifford.*

Saw you before, and I believe you come not   125
With hope to find me desperate upon marriage.
If maids, out of their ignorance of what
Men are, refuse these offers, widows may
Out of their knowledge be allowed some coyness.
And yet I know not how much happiness   130
A peremptory answer may deprive me of;
You may be some young lord, and though I see not
Your footmen and your groom, they may not be
Far off, in conference with your horse. Please you
To instruct me with your title, against which   135
I would not willingly offend.

Haircut.   I am
A gentleman, my name is Haircut, madam.

Celestina. Sweet Mr Haircut, are you a courtier?

Haircut. Yes.

Celestina.   I did think so by your confidence.
Not to detain you, sir, with circumstance,   140
I was not so unhappy in my husband
But that 'tis possible I may be a wife
Again; but I must tell you, he that wins
My affection shall deserve me.

Haircut.   I will hope,
If you can love, I sha' not present, madam,   145
An object to displease you in my person;
And when time and your patience shall possess you
With further knowledge of me, and the truth
Of my devotion, you will not repent
The offer of my service.

Celestina.   You say well.   150
How long do you imagine you can love, sir?

128. Men are, refuse] *Gifford;* Men, are refuse *Q.*

127–9.] In asserting her right to *coyness*, Celestina is inverting the popular
stereotype of the widow: 'it was generally assumed that young widows, suddenly deprived of regular sexual satisfaction by the loss of a husband, were
likely to be driven by lust in their search for a replacement. A proverb that
goes back at least to the Elizabethan period, and probably much further, has it
that "He that wooeth a widow must go stiff before". Suitors of widows were
expected to make aggressive sexual advances, unlike suitors of virgins, who
in upper-class circles were virtually untouchable before marriage' (Stone,
p. 281).

Is it a quotidian, or will it hold
But every other day?

Haircut.   You are pleasant, madam.

Celestina. Does't take you with a burning at the first,
 Or with a cold fit? For you gentlemen   155
 Have both your summer and your winter service.

Haircut. I am ignorant what you mean, but I shall never
 Be cold in my affection to such beauty.

Celestina. And 'twill be somewhat long ere I be warm in't.

Haircut. If you vouchsafe me so much honour, madam,   160
 That I may wait on you sometimes, I sha' not
 Despair to see a change.

Celestina.   But now I know
 Your mind, you shall not need to tell it when
 You come again; I shall remember it.

Haircut. You make me fortunate.

     Enter Steward.

Steward.   Madam, your kinswomen,   165
 The Lady Novice and her sister, are
 New lighted from their coach.

Celestina.   I did expect 'em;
 They partly are my pupils, I'll attend 'em.

Haircut. Madam, I have been too great a trespasser
 Upon your patience; I'll take my leave.   170
 You have affairs, and I have some employment
 Calls me to court. I shall present again
 A servant to you.

Celestina.   Sir, you may present,

        Exit HA[IRCUT].

But not give fire, I hope. Now to the ladies:
 This recreation's past; the next must be   175
 To read to them some court philosophy.   *Exeunt.*

---

152. *quotidian*] daily occurrence, i.e., analogous to the quotidian fever,
which recurs daily (*O.E.D.*).

156. *summer . . . winter*] hot and cold states of the affected love-fever which
Celestina is attributing to Haircut.

172. *present*] formally offer myself; the reflexive is implied (*O.E.D.*, vb.,
II.2).

173–4. *present . . . fire*] Celestina is punning on two meanings of *present*: (1)
to formally introduce oneself, and (2) to aim a firearm so as to be ready to

shoot. In the second context, *give fire* means 'discharge the weapon' (*O.E.D.*); cf. Peacham, *The Compleat Gentleman* (1634), sig. R3v: 'whensoever you skirmish you shall use no more of direction then. *1. Make Ready. 2. Present. 3. Give fire.*

'The first importeth all the *Postures* unto presenting: The second to stand ready to give Fire, but not to execute it before the command be given.'

The Second Act.

Enter SIR THOMAS BORNWELL.

Bornwell. 'Tis a strange humour I have undertaken
    To dance, and play, and spend as fast as she does;
    But I am resolved: it may do good upon her
    And fright her into thrift. Nay, I'll endeavour
    To make her jealous too; if this do not   5
    Allay her gambolling, she's past a woman
    And only a miracle must tame her.

Enter Steward.

Steward. 'Tis Mr Frederick, my lady's nephew.
Bornwell. What of him?
Steward. Is come from the university.   10
Bornwell. By whose directions?
Steward. It seems my lady's.
Bornwell. Let me speak with him before he see his aunt. [*Aside*]
    I do not like it.

Enter MR FREDERICK.

    Mr Frederick, welcome! I expected not   15
    So soon your presence. What's the hasty cause?
Frederick. These letters from my tutor will acquaint you.
Steward. Welcome home, sweet Mr Frederick.

1. *Bornwell.*] *S.H. not in Q.*   8–14.] *verse in Q, divided* him? / Is . . . directions? / It . . . him / Before.   13. see] *Q;* sees *Gosse.*

1. *humour*]' fancy, whim, caprice' (Onions, sb., 5).
6. *gambolling*] frolicsome behaviour (*O.E.D.*); cf. I.i.121.
7. *miracle*] See III.i.115–16n.

Frederick.   Where's my aunt?

Steward. She's busy about her painting, in her closet;
    The outlandish man of art is copying out   20
    Her countenance.

Frederick.   She is sitting for her picture.

Steward. Yes sir, and when 'tis drawn, she will be hanged
    Next the French cardinal in the dining-room;
    But when she hears you're come, she will dismiss
    The Belgic gentleman to entertain   25
    Your worship.

Frederick.   Change of air has made you witty.

                                [*Exit* Steward.]

Bornwell. Your tutor gives you a handsome character,
    Frederick, and is sorry your aunt's pleasure
    Commands you from your studies. But I hope
    You have no quarrel to the liberal arts.   30
    Learning is an addition beyond
    Nobility of birth; honour of blood
    Without the ornament of knowledge is
    A glorious ignorance.

Frederick. I never knew more sweet and happy hours   35
    Than I employed upon my books. I heard

---

20. *outlandish*] foreign, alien, with a possible pun on the secondary sense of 'bizarre, uncouth' (*O.E.D.*).

23. *French Cardinal*] doubtless Cardinal Richelieu, chief minister to Louis XIII for eighteen years (1624–42). He is referred to as 'the French Cardinal' and 'the *Infante* Cardinal' in the letters of James Howell; see especially the description in a letter to Lord Herbert of Cherbury, from Paris, dated 1 April 1641 (*Familiar Letters*, ed. Jacobs, 1890, p. 353): 'Certainly he is a rare Man, and of a transcedent reach, and they are rather Miracles than Exploits that he hath done, tho' those Miracles be of a sanguine dye (the colour of his habit), steep'd in blood.'

25. *Belgic gentleman*] Since 'Belgia' or 'Belgium' could refer to the Netherlands in general (Sugden), it is unlikely that Shirley intends a more specific national identity here. Sugden reads Shirley's phrase as a 'reference to Rubens and Vandyke' on the grounds that both were active in England *c.* 1635. I do not think Shirley is alluding to a particular 'outlandish' painter, but he is doubtless reflecting contemporary interest in the work of Van Dyck, whose influence is described by M. Whinney and O. Millar as 'the most important single factor in the development of portrait painting in this country' (*English Art, 1625–1714*, 1957, p. 60). Cf. I.i.75n.

34. *glorious*] ostentatious, vainglorious (*O.E.D.*).

36. *heard*] attended lectures in (*O.E.D.*, 'hear', 5).

A part of my philosophy, and was so
Delighted with the harmony of nature,
I could have wasted my whole life upon't.

Bornwell. 'Tis pity a rash indulgence should corrupt   40
So fair a genius. [*Aside*] She's here; I'll observe. [*Retires.*]

Enter ARETINA, ALEXANDER, LITTLEWORTH, Steward.

Frederick. My most loved aunt.
Aretina.   Support me, I shall faint!
Littleworth. What ails your ladyship?
Aretina.   Is that Frederick,
     In black?
Alexander.   Yes madam, but the doublet's satin.
Aretina. The boy's undone.
Frederick.   Madam, you appear troubled.   45
Aretina. Have I not cause? Was not I trusted with
     Thy education, boy, and have they sent thee
     Home like a very scholar?
Alexander.   'Twas ill done,
     Howe'er they used him in the university,
     To send him to his friends thus.
Frederick.   Why sir, black   50
     (For 'tis the colour that offends your eyesight)
     Is not within my reading any blemish;

---

41. *genius*] natural capacity, including temper of mind (*O.E.D.*). In the
seventeenth century the word does not imply exceptional ability.

41. Retires] Bornwell must observe the action unobtrusively until his next
speech (ll.106–10) and the exit following it. Since the Cockpit was equipped
with an upper level (see Appendix A, p. 194), characteristically used as
'an observation post for characters who comment on, or converse with, characters in the main playing area' (King, p. 159), I am tempted to suppose that
Bornwell withdraws to the above at this point. If so, he must go out through
one of the rear exists as Aretina's party enters, make his ascent by means of the
backstage staircase, and reappear above to watch the scene unfold.

44. *doublet's satin*] The doublet, a close-fitting garment for the upper body
with detachable sleeves, 'harmonized in colour with the remainder of the
costume but often was of different material' (Linthicum, p. 197). Frederick's
doublet is black, like the rest of his academic garb, but is made of the expensive and highly desirable 'glossy silk' referred to as satin (Linthicum, pp.
122–3).

48. *very*] 'veritable, real, true' (Onions).

Sables are no disgrace in heraldry.

Alexander. 'Tis coming from the college thus that makes it
    Dishonourable. While you ware it for   55
    Your father, it was commendable; or were
    Your aunt dead, you might mourn and justify.

Aretina. What luck I did not send him into France;
    They would have given him generous education,
    Taught him another garb: to wear his lock   60
    And shape as gaudy as the summer, how
    To dance and wag his feather *à la mode*,
    To compliment and cringe, to talk – not modestly,
    Like 'Ay, forsooth' and 'No, forsooth,' or blush
    And look so like a chaplain. There he might   65
    Have learned a brazen confidence, and observed

---

55. ware] *Q;* wore *Gifford.*   63. talk – not] *This ed.;* talke not *Q.*   64. or
blush] *This ed.;* to blush *Q.*

53.] Sable (or black) is one of the seven heraldic colours; it is associated with
the planet Saturn and with diamonds. On the evidence of G. Legh's *The
Accidens of Armory* (1563), sig. B6v–7, the colour is indeed no disgrace:
'although it doe represente moornynge [mourning] , yet it is honorable, and
woorthye to be borne in armes, so that it be born orderlye'. A sable field
signifies 'constancie, divine doctrine, and heavines for losse of frendes'.

55. *ware*] wore.

57. *justify*] probably a metaphorical use of the legal meaning of the word: 'to
show adequate grounds for (that with which one is charged)' (*O.E.D.*, 7a).
Used in this sense, the verb can be intransitive, though in common usage it
does require an object. The grammatical obscurity of the line does make
emendation tempting but, I think, not compellingly so. It is possible that the
compositor misread 'justlie' in the copy; if so, 'and justly' could have the
perfectly normal meaning of 'and with good reason'. The compositor may
even have been one of those professional bores who falls back on the jargon of
his trade whenever he is unsure of himself: he erroneously printed 'justifie'
elsewhere instead of 'justice' (II.ii.61), as evidently required by the copy (see
Appendix B, p. 199).

61. *shape*] almost equivalent to fashion, according to Onions, who cites
Ado, III.ii.30–3: 'or in the shape of two countries at once, as a German from
the waist downward, all slops, and a Spaniard from the hip upward, no
doublet'.

63. *compliment*] See I.i.196n.

64. *or blush*] The reading of Q seems to have arisen because of the
compositor's natural tendency to produce a series of infinitives: 'to wear' (l.
60), 'to dance' (l. 62), 'To compliment', 'to talk' (l. 63), and at last 'to blush'.
The meaning requires, however, that blushing *not* be one of the activities
which Frederick might have learned in France.

So well the custom of the country that
He might by this time have invented fashions
For us, and been a benefit to the kingdom,
Preserved our tailors in their wits, and saved   70
The charge of sending into foreign courts
For pride and antic fashions. Observe
In what a posture he does hold his hat, now.
Frederick. Madam, with your pardon, you have practised
Another dialect than was taught me when   75
I was commended to your care and breeding.
I understand not this. Latin or Greek
Are more familiar to my apprehension,
Logic was not so hard in my first lectures
As your strange language.
Aretina.   Some strong waters, O!   80
Littleworth. Comfits will be as comfortable to your stomach,
        madam.
Aretina. I fear he's spoiled forever: he did name
Logic, and may for aught I know be gone
So far to understand it. I did always
Suspect they would corrupt him in the college.   85
Will your Greek saws and sentences discharge
The mercer, or is Latin a fit language

---

67. *the . . . country*] an allusion to a highly popular play, so entitled, by
Fletcher and Massinger; cf. Dryden's remark, 'There is more Baudry in one
Play of *Fletcher's* call'd *The Custom of the Country*, than in all ours together'
(Bentley, III, 324–8). The reputation of the play alluded to increases the
likelihood that both *custom* and *country* are intended as indecent puns (see
Partridge).

68–72.] The sentiment of this passage is remarkably close to that expressed
by Peacham in *The Truth of our Times* (1638), sig. E1-1v: 'I have much won-
dered why our *English* above other nations should so much doat upon new
fashions, but more I wonder at our want of wit, that wee cannot invent them
our selves, but when one is growne stale runne presently over into *France*, to
seeke a new, making that noble and flourishing Kingdome the magazin of our
fooleries: and for this purpose many of our Tailors lye leger there, and Ladies
post over their gentlemen Ushers, to accoutre them and themselves as you
see.' If Peacham were writing today, he would be able to make roughly the
same point about fashions in literary criticism.

72. *antic*] grotesque, ludicrous, marked by bizzare incongruity (*O.E.D.*).

80. *strong waters*] alcoholic spirits, as in *aqua fortis* (*O.E.D.*).

81. *Comfits*] sweetmeats made of fruit preserved in sugar; sugar-plums
(*O.E.D.*). Cf. I.i.195n.

87–8. is . . . in] Evidently Frederick thinks it is; see III.ii.126–7.

To court a mistress in? Mr Alexander,
If you have any charity, let me
Commend him to your breeding. I suspect   90
I must employ my doctor first, to purge
The university that lies in's head;
It alters his complexion.

Alexander.   If you dare,
Trust me to serve him.

Aretina.   Mr Littleworth,
Be you joined in commission.

Littleworth.   I will teach him   95
Postures and rudiments.

Aretina.   I have no patience
To see him in this shape, it turns my stomach;
When he has cast his academic skin
He shall be yours. I am bound in conscience
To see him bred; his own state shall maintain   100
The charge while he's my ward. [*To Frederick*] Come
    hither, sir.

Frederick. [*To Steward*] What does my aunt mean to do with
    me?

Steward. To make you a fine gentleman, and translate you
Out of your learned language, sir, into
The present Goth and Vandal, which is French.   105

Bornwell. [*Aside*] Into what mischief will this humour ebb?
She will undo the boy, I see him ruined;
My patience is not manly, but I must
Use strategem to reduce her; open ways
Give me no hope.   *Exit.*

Steward. [*To Aretina*] You shall be obeyed, madam.   110
                    Exeunt [*all but Frederick and Steward*].

Frederick. Mr Steward, are you sure we do not dream?
Was't not my aunt you talked to?

Steward.   One that loves you
Dear as her life. These clothes do not become you,
You must have better, sir –

Frederick.   These are not old.

---

97. *shape*] See l. 61n.

100. *state*] private means, estate (*O.E.D.*, sb., V.3).

105. *Goth ... Vandal*] barbarian languages which replaced Latin after the
fall of Rome.

Steward. More suitable to the town and time. We keep   115
        No Lent here, nor is't my lady's pleasure you
        Should fast from anything you have a mind to
        (Unless it be your learning, which she would have you
        Forget with all convenient speed that may be,
        For the credit of your noble family).   120
        The case is altered since we lived i'th' country:
        We do not invite the poor o'th' parish
        To dinner, keep a table for the tenants,
        Our kitchen does not smell of beef, the cellar
        Defies the price of malt and hops, the footmen   125
        And coachdrivers may be drunk like gentlemen
        With wine, nor will three fiddlers upon holidays
        With aid of bagpipes (that called in the country
        To dance and plough the hall up with their hobnails)
        Now make my lady merry. We do feed   130

122. not invite] *Q;* not now invite *conj. Gifford.*

---

121. *The . . . altered*] an allusion to the Jonson play, so entitled; proverbial (Tilley, C 111).

122-4. *We . . . beef*] The Steward is lamenting the decline in standards of 'good lordship', as described by Stone, p. 125: 'The practice of open-handed hospitality, shown not only to members of the extended family but to any friend or even to casual passers-by of gentlemanly status, was one which dated back at least to the days of Beowulf. It was certainly an ideal to which everyone paid respect at least up to 1640. . . . There was, of course, more to this ideal than personal honour defined by generosity demonstrated by open-handed support of kin relatives, clients and allies, for it extended to a whole way of life, including the retaining of hordes of largely idle servants and the keeping of an open table for all comers. . . . The decline of these habits of the late sixteenth and early seventeenth centuries was evidence of a lessening preoccupation with the preservation of connections with the inner circle of kin as well as with the outer layer of retainers and supporters. It involved a major reorientation of consumption patterns, caused by the growth of a more inward-looking, more private and more urbanized life-style for the aristocratic family. It was characterized by the withdrawel of the family from the great hall to the private dining-room and by the increasing habit of residing for long periods in London to enjoy the "season".'

125. *Defies*] looks down upon; snobbishly rejects. The context (ll. 124-7) implies that even low-ranking retainers, who in the country would enjoy traditional ale ('malt and hops'), are now served wine instead. For a statement of normal practice, see Moryson, IV, 176: 'Clownes and vulgar men only use large drinking of Beere or Ale, how much soever it is esteemed excellent drinke even among strangers, but Gentlemen garrawse [carouse] onely in Wine.'

    Like princes, and feast nothing but princes.

    And are these robes fit to be seen amongst 'em?

Frederick. My lady keeps a court, then. Is Sir Thomas

    Affected with this state and cost?

Steward.   He was not,

    But is converted. And I hope you wo' not   135

    Persist in heresy, but take a course

    Of riot to content your friends. You shall

    Want nothing, if you can be proud and spend it

    For my lady's honour. [*Giving him a purse*] Here are a

        hundred

    Pieces will serve you till you have new clothes.   140

    I will present you with a nag of mine –

    Poor tender of my service, please you accept;

    My lady's smile more than rewards me for it.

    I must provide fit servants to attend you,

    Monsieurs for horse and foot.

Frederick.   I shall submit,   145

    If this be my aunt's pleasure, and be ruled.

    My eyes are opened with this purse already,

    And sack will help to inspire me; I must spend it.

Steward. What else, sir?

Frederick.   I'll begin with you: to encourage

    You to have still a special care of me,   150

    There is five pieces [*Gives him gold.*], not for your nag.

Steward. No sir, I hope it is not.

Frederick.   Buy a beaver

    For thy own block. I shall be ruled – who does

---

131. nothing but] *Q;* nothing else but *conj. Gifford.*

---

    134. *Affected*] favourably impressed (*O.E.D.*).

    135 *wo' not*] contraction for 'woll not', equivalent to 'will not' (*O.E.D.*).

    140 *Pieces*] See I.i.223n.

    142. *tender*] an offering or gift (*O.E.D.*, sb.2, 2).

    151. *pieces*] See I.i.223n.

    152. *beaver*] hat made from the pelt of the beaver. Buying a beaver was costly in Jacobean times, when prices ranged from £3 to £6; in Caroline England the velvet hat was replacing the beaver as the favourite headgear among the gentry (Linthicum, pp. 228–9).

    153. *block*] 'The block was the mould on which the hat was shaped, but here the head is evidently intended' (Gosse); both literal and figurative senses are confirmed by *O.E.D.*

Command the wine-cellar?

Steward.   Who command but you, sir?

Frederick. I'll try to drink a health or two – my aunt's   155
   Or anybody's – and if that foundation
   Stagger me not too much, I will commence
   In all the arts of London.

Steward.   If you find, sir,
   The operation of the wine exalt
   Your blood to the desire of any female   160
   Delight, I know your aunt wo' not deny
   Any of her chambermaids to practise on,
   She loves you but too well.

Frederick.   I know not how
   I may be for that exercise. Farewell Aristotle,
   Prithee commend me to the library   165
   At Westminster, my bones I bequeath thither,
   And to the learnèd worms that mean to visit 'em.
   I will compose myself; I begin to think
   I have lost time indeed. Come, to the wine-cellar!

         Exit [FREDERICK *with* Steward].

ACT II, SCENE ii

Enter CELESTINA, MARIANA, ISABELLA.

Mariana. But shall we not, madam, expose ourselves
   To censure for this freedom?

Celestina.   Let them answer
   That dare mistake us. Shall we be so much
   Cowards to be frighted from our pleasure
   Because men have malicious tongues and show   5
   What miserable souls they have? No cousin,
   We hold our life and fortunes upon no

---

154. command] *Q;* commands *Gifford.*   0.1. MARIANA] *Gifford; Mardana Q.*

  159–60. *exalt ... blood*] stimulate your (sexual) appetite. Cf. I.i.311n.
  161. *wo' not*] See l. 135n.
  165–6. *library . . . Westminster*] probably, as Papousek believes, an ironic reference to Poets' Corner in Westminster Abbey, 'where England's most famous authors were buried, or put to rest in their final "bookshelves"'.

Man's charity; if they dare show so little
Discretion to traduce our fames, we will
Be guilty of so much wit to laugh at 'em.   10
Isabella. 'Tis a becoming fortitude.
Celestina.   My stars
Are yet kind to me, for in a happy minute
Be't spoke, I'm not in love, and men shall never
Make my heart lean with sighing, nor with tears
Draw on my eyes the infamy of spectacles.   15
'Tis the chief principle to keep your heart
Under your own obedience: jest, but love not.
I say my prayers, yet can wear good clothes
And only satisfy my tailor for 'em.
I wo' not lose my privilege.   20
Mariana. And yet they say your entertainments are
(Give me your pardon, madam) to proclaim
Yourself a widow and to get a husband.
Celestina. As if a lady of my years, some beauty,
Left by her husband rich, that had mourned for him   25
A twelvemonth too, could live so obscure i'th' town
That gallants would not know her and invite
Themselves without her chargeable proclamations!
Then we are worse than citizens. No widow
Left wealthy can be throughly warm in mourning,   30
But some one noble blood or lusty kindred
Claps in, with his gilt coach and Flandrian trotters,
And hurries her away to be a countess.

---

18. Prayers, yet can] *Gifford;* prayers yet, can *Q.*   31. some one noble] *Q;*
some one of noble *conj. Knowland.*

---

9. *traduce*] malign, besmirch.

15. *spectacles*] objects put on public display (*O.E.D.*, sb.1, 2).

17. *jest . . . not*] perhaps an adaptation of the proverb: 'Play with me and
hurt me not, jest with me and shame me not' (Tilley, P 400).

20. *wo' not*] See II.i.135n.

28. *chargeable*] expensive (Neilson).

proclamations] public declarations.

30. *throughly*] equivalent to, and more common than, 'thoroughly'
(Onions).

32. *Flandrian trotters*] Flemish horses; cf. *The Witty Fair One*, III.v (Shirley, *Wks*, I, 324), where Brains expresses a wish for 'twenty horse in the
stable, beside a caroch and six Flanders mares'.

    Courtiers have spies, and great ones with large titles
    (Cold in their own estates) would warm themselves   35
    At a rich city bonfire.
Isabella.   Most true, madam.
Celestina. No matter for corruption of the blood:
    Some undone courtier made her husband rich,
    And this new lord receives it back again.
    Admit it were my policy, and that   40
    My entertainments pointed to acquaint me
    With many suitors that I might be safe
    And make the best election: could you blame me?
Mariana. Madam, 'tis wisdom.
Celestina.   But I should be
    In my thoughts miserable to be fond   45
    Of leaving the sweet freedom I possess
    And court myself into new marriage fetters.
    I now observe men's several wits and windings,
    And can laugh at their follies.
Mariana.   You have given
    A most ingenious satisfaction.   50
Celestina. One thing I'll tell you more, and this I give you
    Worthy your imitation from my practice:
    You see me merry, full of song and dancing,
    Pleasant in language, apt to all delights
    That crown a public meeting, but you cannot   55
    Accuse me of being prodigal of my favours
    To any of my guests. I do not summon

---

34. large] *Gifford;* lharge *Qb;* charge *Qa;* charged *conj. Harrier.*

34–6. *great ones . . . bonfire*] Impoverished members of the gentry are pic-
tured here as anxious to marry into middle-class fortunes; this indeed is the
assumption Overreach makes about Lovell in *A New Way to Pay Old Debts*,
III.ii.103–4 (Massinger, *Wks*, II, 336): 'my wealth / Shall weigh his titles
downe, and make you equalls'.
37.] Adulteration of the noble blood-line is of no concern (to those cold
gentlemen who covet new middle-class warmth).
38–9.] The *new lord* simply regains his due when he marries a wealthy
middle-class widow; after all, her previous husband made his fortune by
ruining a nobleman (see Spencer). The assumptions made here about class
antagonism are shared by Massinger in *A New Way to Pay Old Debts* and *The
City Madam*; see the discussion by L. C. Knights in *Drama and Society in the
Age of Jonson* (1937), pp. 273–92.

(By any wink) a gentleman to follow me
To my withdrawing chamber; I hear all
Their pleas in court; nor can they boast abroad　　　　60
(And do me justice) after a salute
They have much conversation with my lip.
I hold the kissing of my hand a courtesy,
And he that loves me must, upon the strength
Of that, expect till I renew his favour.　　　　65
Some ladies are so expensive in their graces
To those that honour 'em, and so prodigal,
That in a little time they have nothing but
The naked sin left to reward their servants;
Whereas a thrift in our rewards will keep　　　　70
Men long in their devotion, and preserve
Our selves in stock, to encourage those that honour us.

Isabella. This is an art worthy a lady's practice.

Celestina. It takes not from the freedom of our mirth,
But seems to advance it, when we can possess　　　　75
Our pleasures with security of our honour;
And that preserved, I welcome all the joys
My fancy can let in. In this I have given
The copy of my mind, nor do I blush
You understand it.

Isabella.　　　　　　You have honoured us.　　　　80

Enter Celestina's Gentlewoman.

Gentlewoman. Madam, Sir William Sentlove's come to wait on
　　you.

Celestina. There's one would be a client; make excuse
　　For a few minutes.

　　　　　　　　　　　[*Exit* Gentlewoman.]

Mariana.　　　　　　One that comes a-wooing?

---

60. *in court*] publicly.

65. *expect*] wait (Onions).

66. *expensive*] eager to expend, lavish (*O.E.D.*).

72. *in stock*] literally 'possessed of capital' (*O.E.D.*) in keeping with the
metaphor of 'prodigal' expenditure in the preceding lines.

78. *fancy*] 'amorous inclination' (Onions).

79. *copy*] possibly a pun: (1) fulness, abundance, copiousness; (2) the pattern or original from which copies can be made (*O.E.D.*).

82. *client*] a retainer, one who pays court (*O.E.D.*); i.e., a suitor.

Celestina. Such a thing he would seem, but in his guiltiness
          Of little land, his expectation is not   85
          So valiant as it might be. He wears clothes,
          And feeds with noblemen – to some I hear
          No better than a wanton emissary
          Or scout for Venus' wild-fowl, which made tame,
          He thinks no shame to stand court sentinel   90
          In hope of the reversion.
Mariana.   I have heard
          That some of them are often my lord's tasters;
          The first fruits they condition for, and will
          Exact as fees for the promotion.
Celestina. Let them agree; there's no account shall lie   95
          For me among their traffic.

                    Enter Gentlewo[man].

Gentlewoman.   Mr Haircut, madam,
          Is new come in to tender you his service.
Celestina. Let him discourse a little with Sir William.
                                        Exit [Gentlewoman].

---

86. wears clothes] *Q subst.;* wears rich clothes *Gifford.*

---

89. *Venus' wild-fowl*] young women who have not yet been captured ('made tame') by the court.

90. *stand . . . sentinel*] act the pander's role. In *The Revenger's Tragedy*, ed. Foakes (1966), I.ii.187–8, the bastard Spurio claims to have been born 'In such a whisp'ring and withdrawing hour, / When base male-bawds kept sentinel at stair-head'.

91. *reversion*] 'prospect of possessing a thing at some future time' (Onions). A posittion closely resembling Sentlove's is delightfully described by Maquerelle in Marston's *The Malcontent*, ed. Hunter (1975), V.v.30–3: 'in truth, he [Marshal Make-room] hath all things in reversion: he has his mistress in reversion, his clothes in reversion, his wit in reversion; and, indeed, is a suitor to me for my dog in reversion.'

92–4.] Among a lord's pimps may be those who, before providing satisfaction, insist on sampling the merchandise themselves.

92. *tasters*] domestic officers who taste in advance whatever is served to their master in order to ensure its quality and freedom from poison (*O.E.D.*).

93. *condition*] bargain (*O.E.D.*).

94. *promotion*] 'i.e., their efforts in furthering the affair' (Spencer).

95–6.] Let them strike whatever bargain they wish; I have no part in their arrangements.

95. *agree*] come to terms; reach a contract (*O.E.D.*).

96. *traffic*] business, occupation (Onions).

Mariana. What is this gentleman, Mr Haircut, madam?
        I note him very gallant and much courted   100
        By gentlemen of quality.
Celestina.   I know not,
        More than a trim gay man. He has some great office,
        Sure, by his confident behaviour.
        He would be entertained under the title
        Of servant to me, and I must confess   105
        He is the sweetest of all men that visit me.
Isabella. How mean you, madam?
Celestina.   He is full of powder:
        He will save much in perfume for my chamber,
        Were he but constant here. [*To Gentlewoman, offstage*]
            Give 'em access.

            Enter SIR WILL[IAM] SENTLOVE, MR HAIRCUT.

Sentlove. Madam, the humblest of your servants is   110
        Exalted to a happiness, if you smile
        Upon my visit.
Haircut.   I must beg your charity
        Upon my rudeness, madam; I shall give
        That day up lost to any happiness
        When I forget to tender you my service.   115
Celestina. You practise courtship, gentlemen.
Sentlove.   But cannot
        Find where with more desert to exercise it.
        [*Noticing Mariana*] What lady's this, I pray?
Celestina.   A kinswoman
        Of mine, Sir William.

---

105. *servant*] lover (Neilson), especially in the fashionable Platonic sense;
see V.iii.54n.

107. *He . . . powder*] Cosmetic powders were in liberal use, partly to offset
the results of infrequent bathing (see Stone, pp. 485–6). In Ford's *Love's
Sacrifice* (1633), sig. D2v, the lady Fiormonda is said to 'powder her haire'; as
his name implies, this may be Haircut's practice. Celestina may be further
suggesting that Haircut's abundance of powder is a treatment for venereal
disease; see Beaumont, *The Knight of the Burning Pestle*, ed. Doebler (1967),
III.i.374–7: 'This giant train'd me to his loathsome den / Under pretense of
killing of the itch, / And all my body with a powder strew'd, / That smarts and
stings.'

116. *courtship*] 'courtliness' (Spencer), with a secondary suggestion of dip-
lomacy and flattery (*O.E.D.*, 4).

Sentlove.   I am more her servant.

Celestina. [*To Haircut*] You came from court now, I presume.

Haircut.   'Tis, madam,   120
    The sphere I move in, and my destiny
    Was kind to place me there where I enjoy
    All blessings that a mortal can possess
    That lives not in your presence; and I should
    Fix my ambition, when you would vouchsafe   125
    Me so much honour, to accept from me
    An humble entertainment there.

Celestina.   But by
    What name shall I be known? in what degree
    Shall I be of kindred to you?

Haircut.   How mean you, madam?

Celestina. Perhaps you'll call me sister – I shall take it   130
    A special preferment – or it may be
    I may pass under title of your mistress,
    If I seem rich and fair enough to engage
    Your confidence to own me.

Haircut.   I would hope.

Celestina. But 'tis not come to that yet; you will, sir,   135
    Excuse my mirth.

Haircut.   Sweet madam.

Celestina.   Shall I take
    Boldness to ask what place you hold in court?
    'Tis an uncivil curiosity,
    But you'll have mercy to a woman's question.

Haircut. My present condition, madam, carries   140
    Honour and profit, though not to be named
    With that employment I expect i'th' state
    (Which shall discharge the first maturity

120–59.] During the dialogue between Haircut and Celestina, Sentlove draws the other two women aside, engaging them in conversation which cannot be heard by the audience until l. 160. Indeed, the remainder of this scene derives its atmosphere from a dance-like pairing-off and regrouping of couples, or groups of three and four, culminating in the literal dance at l. 269.1.

132. *mistress*] a woman who is the object of a man's devotion, especially in the fashionable Platonic sense; see V.iii.54n.

134. *own*] acknowledge or recognise as your own (*O.E.D.*, vb., 3).

143. *discharge . . . maturity*] be paid (like a debt) on the first day it falls due

  Upon your knowledge); until then, I beg
  You allow a modest silence.
Celestina.   I am charmed, sir; 145
  And if you 'scape ambassador, you cannot
  Reach a preferment wherein I'm against you.
  But where's Sir William Sentlove?
Haircut.   Give him leave
  To follow his nose, madam; while he hunts
  In view, he'll soon be at a fault.
Celestina.   You know him. 150
Haircut. Know Sentlove? Not a page but can decipher him.
  The waiting-women know him to a scruple:
  He's called the blistermaker of the town.
Celestina. What's that?
Haircut.   The laundry ladies can resolve you,
  And you may guess: an arrant Epicure 155
  As this day lives, born to a pretty wit,
  A knight – but no gentleman. I must
  Be plain to you; your ladyship may have
  Use of this knowledge, but conceal the author.
Sentlove. [*To Mariana*] I kiss your fairest hand.

---

154. *Haircut.*] *Con. MS, Gifford subst.; Is. Q.* 157. knight – but] *Baskervill subst.;* Knight but *Q.*

(*O.E.D.*); figuratively, a highly pompous way of saying that Celestina will be the first to know of his advancement.

 146. *'scape ambassador*] escape (by moving even higher than) the title of ambassador.

 149–50. *while . . . fault*] When he relies on his eyesight, he soon loses track of the quarry. *O.E.D.* defines *in view* as 'within sight of, near enough to see', and *at a fault* as 'off the scent or track', citing this example. In seventeenth-century hunting parlance, *view* may also refer to the footprints of a deer.

 152. *scruple*] literally, a unit of weight equivalent to 1/24 of an ounce, or slightly more than a gram; hence, figuratively, 'a very small quantity or amount,' an infinitesimal fragment (*O.E.D.*, sb.1, 1 and 4).

 153. *blistermaker*] Spencer may be wide of the mark in seeing an allusion to the Spanish fly (also called 'blister-fly'), but his conclusion makes intuitive sense: '*i.e.*, he is a pimp'.

 154. S.H.] All edd. follow Gifford in assigning this speech to Haircut rather than Isabella; Con. MS corroborates editorial practice.

 laundry ladies] whores. 'Laundress' was among the many euphemisms for 'whore' or 'bawd'. The Bawd in Massinger's *The Unnatural Combat*, IV.ii.135 (*Plays*, II, 258), says with mock innocence: 'I am his Nurse and Landresse'.

 155. *arrant Epicure*] thorough-going sensualist (Onions).

Mariana.   You make a difference; 160
   Pray, reconcile 'em to an equal whiteness.
Sentlove. You wound my meaning, lady.
Celestina.   Nay, Sir William
   Has the art of compliment.
Sentlove.   Madam, you honour me
   'Bove my desert of language.
Celestina. [*Aside to Sentlove*] Will you please
   To enrich me with your knowledge of that gentleman. 165
Sentlove. Do you not know him, madam?
Celestina.   What is he?
Sentlove. A camphire ball. You shall know more hereafter;
   He shall tell you himself and save my character.
   Till then, you see he's proud.
Celestina.   One thing, gentlemen,
   I observe in your behaviour which is rare   170
   In two that court one mistress; you preserve
   A noble friendship. There's no gum within
   Your hearts, you cannot fret or show an envy
   Of one another's hope. Some would not govern
   Their passions with that temper.
Sentlove.   The whole world 175
   Sha' not divorce our friendship. Mr Haircut –
   Would I had lives to serve him; he is lost
   To goodness does not honour him.
Haircut.   My knight!
Celestina. This is right playing at court shuttlecock.

Enter Gentlew[oman].

---

   167. *camphire ball*] piece of aromatic, volatile, crystalline substance, now
commonly spelled 'camphor'; 'it is used in pharmacy, and was formerly in
repute as an antaphrodisiac' and as a measure for counteracting venereal disease (*O.E.D.*). Cf. Massinger, *The Guardian*, III.i.19–22 (*Plays*, IV, 149):
'And kill this letcherous Itch with drinking Water, / . . . Then bathe my self,
night by night, in marble dew, / And use no Soap but Camphir-Balls'.
   168. *save my character*] save me the trouble of sketching his character. Cf.
Cor., V.iv.26: 'I paint him in the character.'
   172–3. *There's . . . fret*] Gifford claims to detect an allusion to *1H4*,
II.ii.1–2: 'I have removed Falstaff's horse, and he frets like a gummed velvet.'
Celestina is telling the rival suitors that their hearts, not having been stiffened
(with gum), are immune to the chafing which causes gummed velvet to wear.
Cf. Marston, *The Malcontent*, ed. Hunter (1975), I.ii.13–14: 'I'll come among
you . . . as gum into taffeta, to fret, to fret'.
   178. *does not*] who (understood) does not (Abbott, § 244).

Gentlewoman. Madam, there is a gentleman desires   180
     To speak w'ee, one Sir Thomas Bornwell.
Celestina.   Bornwell?
Gentlewoman. He says he is a stranger to your ladyship.
Sentlove. I know him.
Haircut.   Your neighbour, madam.
Sentlove.   Husband to
     The lady that so revels in the Strand.
Haircut. He had good parts, they say, but cannot help   185
     His lady's bias.
Celestina.   They have both much fame
     I'th' town for several merits. Pray, admit him.
                              [*Exit* Gentlewoman.]
Haircut. What comes he for?

                    Enter SIR THOMAS [BORNWELL].

Bornwell. Your pardon, noble lady, that I have
     Presumed, a stranger to your knowledge.
Celestina.   Sir,   190
     Your worth was here before you, and your person
     Cannot be here ingrateful.   [*Kisses Bornwell*.]
Bornwell.   'Tis the bounty

---

183. madam. Husband to / The] *lineation as in Neilson;* Madam. / Husband to
the *Q*.   192. ingrateful] *Q subst.;* ungrateful *Gifford*.

---

179. *court shuttlecock*] The game of shuttlecock, a precursor of badminton,
is played by the Ward and Sordido in *Women Beware Women*, ed. Mulryne
(1975), II.ii.79.1–2, where the following gloss is supplied: 'The game's object
was to keep the shuttlecock in the air as long as possible, either with one's own
racquet or by hitting it to and fro between two players'. Figuratively, the
game often represents frivolous, inconsequential and perhaps effeminate activity, as in Marston's *Sophonisba*, I.ii.20–2 (*Works*, ed. Bullen, 1887, II,
243): 'We things call'd women, only made for show / And pleasure, created to
bear children / And play at shuttlecock'. Thus, Haircut and Sentlove are
playing the game of reciprocal courtly compliment.
     181. *w'ee*] obsolete contraction for 'with you' (*O.E.D.*).
     185. *parts*] personal attributes or abilities (Onions); cf. *Wiv.*, II.ii.97–8:
'Setting the attraction of my good parts aside, I have no other charms.'
     185–6. *cannot . . . bias*] is unable to prevent his wife's errant behaviour. The
metaphor is drawn from the game of bowls, in which context *bias* means the
'one-sided form of the bowl which gives an oblique motion to it' (Onions).
     187. *several*] separate, distinctive (*O.E.D.*, adj., 1).
     192. *ingrateful*] 'displeasing, disagreeable' (*O.E.D.*, 1). Gifford's emend-
ation imposes a modern rule of usage, violating seventeenth-century practice
along the way; see Abbott (§ 442).

Of your sweet disposition, madam; make me
Your servant, lady, by her fair example [*Kisses Isabella.*]
To favour me – [*Aside*] I never knew one turn   195
Her cheek to a gentleman that came to kiss her
But sh' had a stinking breath. [*To Sentlove and Haircut*]
                    Your servant, gentlemen;
Will Sentlove, how is't?
Celestina. [*To Isabella*]   I am sorry, coz,
To accuse you; we in nothing more betray
Ourselves to censure of ridiculous pride   200
Than answering a fair salute too rudely.
O, it shows ill upon a gentlewoman
Not to return the modest lip if she
Would have the world believe her breath is not
Offensive.
Bornwell.   Madam, I have business   205
With you.
Sentlove. [*To Haircut*] His looks are pleasant.
Celestina.   With me, sir?
Bornwell. I hear you have an ex'lent wit, madam,
I see you're fair.
Celestina.   The first is but report,
And do not trust your eyesight for the last,
'Cause I presume y'are mortal and may err.   210
Haircut. [*To Sentlove*] He's very gamesome.
Bornwell.   Y'ave an ex'lent voice:
They say you catched it from a dying swan,
Which, joined to the sweet harmony of your lute,
You ravish all mankind.
Celestina.   Ravish mankind?

213. Which] *Q;* With which *conj. Gifford.*   the sweet harmony] *Q subst.;* the
harmony *Gifford.*

---

197. *stinking breath*] a more common complaint than persons accustomed to
twentieth-century standards in hygiene and dentistry might suppose; as
Stone observes (p. 487), 'both sexes must very often have had bad breath from
the rotting teeth and constant stomach disorders which can be documented
from many sources'.

212. *catched*] a permissible substitute for 'caught'. Onions observes that
Shakespeare uses 'caught' 31 times, 'catched' 4 times (see 'catch', vb.).
Abbott (§ 344) cites *L.L.L.*, V.ii.69–70: 'None are so surely caught, when they
are catched, / As wit turned fool.'

213–14. *Which . . . mankind*] Gifford's conjecture, though it makes perfect

Bornwell. With their consent.

Celestina.   It were the stranger rape.   215
    But there's the less indictment lies against it,
    And there is hope your little honesties
    Cannot be much the worse; for men do rather
    Believe they had a maidenhead than put
    Themselves to th'rack of memory how long   220
    'Tis since they left the burden of their innocence.

Bornwell. Why, you are bitter, madam.

Celestina.   So is physic:
    I do not know your constitution. [*Draws Bornwell aside.*]

Bornwell. You shall if please you, madam.

Celestina.   Y'are too hasty;
    I must examine what certificate   225
    You have, first, to prefer you.

Bornwell.   Fine! Certificate?

Celetstina. Under your lady's hand and seal.

Bornwell.   Go to,
    I see you are a wag.

---

224. if] *Q;* if't *Gifford.*

---

sense, is based on a punctilious desire to improve the playwright's grammar.
As it stands, the clause can be paraphrased thus: 'that voice of yours, when
heard in conjunction with your already ravishing lute, allows you to enrapture
everyone'.

217–21.] Throughout this passage, Celestina is mocking the sexual assumptions of her patriarchal society. Even though she may indeed 'ravish all
mankind' (l. 214), men need not really fear an attack on their chastity (*little
honesties*). The distinctively female connotations of *maidenhead* and the mock-
heroic tone of *burden of . . . innocence* are further ironic judgements on sexual
attitudes among men.

222. *physic*] medicine.

223. *constitution*] possibly a pun, conflating the two senses implied in the
following: 'I did think, by the excellent constitution of thy leg, it was formed
under the star of a galliard' (*Tw.N.*, I.iii.118–20); 'else nothing in the world /
Could turn so much the constitution / Of any constant man' (*Mer.V.*,
III.ii.245–7). Cf. Onions, who cites both examples. The physical sense alone
governs Bornwell's interpretation of the remark.

227. *Under . . . seal*] This remark turns the 'certificate' of the previous lines
into a marriage licence; hence Bornwell's embarrassment and admission of
'wedlock' (l. 229).

Go to] An expression of protest or incredulity (Onions). The illogical
beauty of idiomatic expressions is nicely illustrated by observing that the
precise equivalent for *go to* in contemporary speech is 'come on'.

Celestina.   But take heed how
   You trust to't.
Bornwell.   I can love you in my wedlock
   As well as that young gallant o'th' first hair,   230
   Or the knight bachelor, and can return
   As amorous delight to thy soft bosom.
Celestina. Your person and your language are both strangers.
Bornwell. But may be more familiar: I have those
   That dare make affidavit for my body.   235
Celestina. D'ee mean your surgeon?
Bornwell.   My surgeon, madam?
   I know not how you value my abilities
   But I dare undertake, as much, to express
   My service to your ladyship; and, with
   As fierce ambition fly to your commands   240
   As the most valiant of these lay siege to you.
Celestina. You dare not, sir.
Bornwell.   How, madam?
Celestina.   I will justify't.
   You dare not marry me, and I imagine
   Some here, should I consent, would fetch a priest
   Out of the fire.

---

232. thy] *Q;* your *Gifford.*   241. these lay] *Gifford;* these, 'lay *Q.*

---

229. *I . . . wedlock*] In appealing to the double standard, Bornwell aligns himself with conservative and patriarchal opinion. Stone observes, p. 505, that 'the only period in which the double standard was seriously questioned was the 1630s and 1640s. Courtiers like Sir Kenelm Digby, who led a chequered sex life, claimed that breach of chastity "is no greater fault in them [women] than in men", while the Puritan John Milton adopted a similar position.' Still, Bornwell's attitude was the dominant one; cf. Keith Thomas, 'The Double Standard', *Journal of the History of Ideas*, XX (1959), 195–216.

230. *o'th' first hair*] 'just beginning to grow a beard' (Papousek).

231. *knight bachelor*] Referring to Sentlove, Bornwell gives him 'the full title of a gentleman who has been knighted' (*O.E.D.*), with a pun, no doubt, on his status as an unmarried male adult.

236. *D'ee*] obsolete contraction for 'do ye' or 'do you' (*O.E.D.*).

surgeon] the authority required to 'certify that he is free from venereal disease' (Spencer).

244–5. *fetch . . . fire*] produce a clergyman (to perform the marriage ceremony) from his hiding-place in the hearth. This paraphrase is based on Papousek, who explains at length: 'The mention of a priest in the fireplace refers to the fact that recusant (Catholic) families frequently hid a priest who

Bornwell.   I have a wife, indeed.   245
Celestina. And there's a statute not repealed, I take it.
Bornwell. Y'are in the right: I must confess y'ave hit,
    And bled me in a master vein.
Celestina.   You think
    I took you on the advantage; use your best
    Skill at defence, I'll come up to your valour   250
    And show another work you dare not do:
    You dare not, sir, be virtuous.
Bornwell.   I dare,
    By this fair hand I dare, and ask a pardon
    If my rude words offend thy innocence
    Which, in a form so beautiful, would shine   255
    To force a blush in them suspected it
    And from the rest draw wonder.
Haircut.   I like not
    Their secret parley; shall I interrupt 'em?
Isabella. By no means, sir.
Sentlove.   Sir Thomas was not wont
    To show so much a courtier.
Mariana.   He cannot   260
    Be prejudicial to you. Suspect not
    Your own deserts so much; he's married.
Bornwell. I have other business, madam. You keep
    Music; I came to try how you can dance.
Celestina. You did? [*Aside*] I'll try his humour out of breath.   265
    Although I boast no cunning, sir, in revels,
    If you desire to show your art that way
    I can wait on you.
Bornwell. [*Taking her hand*] You much honour me.
    Nay, all must join to make a harmony.   *They dance.*

263–4. keep / Music; I] *lineation of this ed.; keepe musicke, I Q.*

---

was being sought by the government as an outlaw, in a secret hiding place
built into the fireplace in many large houses.'

248. *bled . . . vein*] Bornwell figuratively compares the psychological purification which Celestina has induced in him to the much-practised physical
cure of blood-letting. Burton (*Anatomy*, II.iv.3, p. 582) observes that 'particular kinds of blood-letting in use are three', the first of which, and that
referred to here, consists of 'opening a Vein in the arm with a sharp knife, or in
the head, knees, or any other part, as shall be thought fit'.

265. *try . . . breath*] test his inclination to the point of exhaustion.

Bornwell. I have nothing now, madam, but to beseech   270
 (After a pardon for my boldness) you
 Would give occasion to pay my gratitude.
 I have a house will be much honoured
 If you vouchsafe your presence, and a wife
 Desires to present herself your servant.   275
 I came with the ambition to invite you;
 Deny me not, your person you shall trust
 On fair security.
Celestina.   Sir, although I use not
 This freedom with a stranger, you shall have
 No cause to hold me obstinate.
Bornwell.   You grace me.   280
 Sir William Sentlove –
Haircut. [*To Celestina*] I must take my leave;
 You will excuse me madam, court attendances –
Celestina. By any means.
Bornwell.   Ladies, you will vouchsafe
 Your company?
Isabella and Mariana. We wait upon you, sir.   *Exeunt.*

 272.] would give me the opportunity to return the favour of hospitality.
 275. *present . . . servant*] be formally introduced to you.
 276. *ambition*] The context requires the obsolete meaning: 'a strong desire
. . . to . . . do anything creditable, etc.' (*O.E.D.*).
 278. *use not*] am not accustomed to practising.
 280. *grace*] confer honour upon (Onions).

The Third Act.

ACT III, SCENE i

Enter Lord *unready;* HAIRCUT *preparing his periwig, table, and looking-glass.*

Lord. What hour is't?
Haircut.   'Bout three o'clock, my lord.
Lord. 'Tis time to rise.
Haircut.   Your lordship went but late
    To bed last night.
Lord.   'Twas early in the morning.

Enter Secre[tary].

Secretary. [*To Decoy, offstage*] Expect a while. [*To Lord*] My lord is
    busy?
Lord. What's the matter?

---

2. Lord.] *Gifford; Bor. Q.*   8. What's] *conj. Gifford;* What *Q.*

0.1 unready] 'not fully clothed' (Onions). Since the nobleman who first appears in this scene has been given no proper name, I refer to him throughout by the sobriquet 'Lord Unready'; this procedure has the advantage of avoiding verbal confusion with any other personages, terrestrial or celestial.

0.1–2.] The precise attention given to Lord Unready's toilet in the S.D. here and elsewhere (see IV.iii.11.1–2) implies a mode of theatrical action specifically suited to the staging conditions of the private theatres, and presumably tailored to the tastes of their audiences. In *The Humorous Courtier*, V.ii (*Wks*, IV, 593), also a Cockpit play, Shirley calls for Depazzi to enter with 'CRISPINO *curling his hair*'. At Blackfriars an even more elaborate ritual of adornment was staged in *The Fatal Dowry*, IV.i.0.1–3 (Massinger, *Plays*, I, 63): '*Enter* NOVALL JUNIOR, *as newly dressed, a* TAYLOR, BARBER, PERFUMER. . . . NOVALL *sits in a chaire, Barber orders his haire, Perfumer gives powder, Taylor sets his clothes*'.

4. *Expect*] See II.ii.65n.

Secretary.   Here is a lady   5
    Desires access to you upon some affairs
    She says may specially concern your lordship.
Lord. A lady? What's her name?
Secretary.   Madam Decoy.
Lord. Decoy? prithee admit her.

                         Enter DECOY.

                              Have you business, madam,
    With me?
Decoy.   And such, I hope, as will not be   10
    Offensive to your lordship.
Lord.   I pray speak it.
Decoy. I would desire your lordship's ear more private.
Lord. [*To Haircut and Secretary*] Wait i'th' next chamber till I
    call.   [*To Decoy*] Now, madam.
                         Exeunt [HAIRCUT *and* Secretary].
Decoy. Although I am a stranger to your lordship,
    I would not lose a fair occasion offered   15
    To show how much I honour and would serve you.
Lord. Please you to give me the particular,
    That I may know the extent of my engagement;
    I am ignorant by what desert you should
    Be encouraged to have care of me.
Decoy.   My lord,   20
    I will take boldness to be plain: beside
    Your other excellent parts, you have much fame
    For your sweet inclination to our sex.
Lord. How d'ee mean, madam?
Decoy.   I' that way your lordship
    Hath honourably practised upon some   25
    Not to be named; your noble constancy
    To a mistress hath deserved our general vote,

17–18.] Lord Unready interprets Decoy's offer of service as a form of
toadying. Thus, his reply can be paraphrased, 'Let me know the precise
nature (*particular*) of your offer, so that I can deduce what you will regard as
my reciprocal obligation (*engagement*).'

19. *desert*] suitably ambiguous: his own or her deserving.

22. *parts*] See II.ii.185n.

25. *practised upon*] pursued, but with innuendo of 'imposed upon by artifice', 'deluded'.

27. *mistress*] identified as Bella Maria at l. 70.

    And I (a part of womankind) have thought
    How to express my duty.
Lord.   In what, madam?
Decoy. Be not so strange, my lord; I know the beauty   30
    And pleasures of your eyes: that handsome creature
    With whose fair life all your delight took leave,
    And to whose memory you have paid too much
    Sad tribute.
Lord.   What's all this?
Decoy.   This: if your lordship
    Accept my service, in pure zeal to cure   35
    Your melancholy, I could point where you might
    Repair your loss.
Lord.   Your ladyship, I conceive,
    Doth traffic in flesh merchandise.
Decoy.   To men
    Of honour, like yourself; I am well known
    To some in court, and come not with ambition,   40
    Now, to supplant your officer.
Lord.   What is
    The lady of pleasure you prefer?
Decoy.   A lady
    Of birth and fortune, one upon whose virtue

30. know] *Q;* knew *Gifford.*   34. This: if] *Gifford;* This, if *Q.*

---

    30. *strange*] reserved; not affable or encouraging (*O.E.D.*).

    30–1. *I . . . eyes*] i.e., I am aware of the kind of beauty and the sorts of pleasures which appeal to your eyesight.

    36. *melancholy*] Both medical and literary tradition in the Renaissance supported the view that extreme grief caused by the death of a loved one could produce a dominance of the melancholy humour and thereby a dangerous physical and mental condition. See Burton's *Anatomy*, I.ii.3.4 (pp. 225–6) and I.ii.4.7 (p. 305).

    41. *officer*] 'an agent, in this case a procurer' (Papousek); doubtless Decoy suspects Haircut of performing this function.

    What] who (Abbott, § 254).

    42. *The . . . pleasure*] Bentley asserts, V, 1126, giving full documentation, that 'there is evidence that the phrase was normally used in the time to mean "prostitute"'. The present context implies that the expression is a euphemism for 'high-class prostitute', a synonym for 'courtesan'; see ll. 53–5n. As Forsythe observes, p. 93, Shirley is unusually fond of incorporating the title of a play into its text; see, among many instances, *The Maid's Revenge*, V.iii (*Wks*, I, 184): 'Oh, see / A MAID'S REVENGE with her own Tragedy'.

    prefer] recommend (Onions).

I may presume – the Lady Aretina.

Lord. Wife to Sir Thomas Bornwell?

Decoy.   The same, sir.   45

Lord. Have you prepared her?

Decoy. Not for your lordship, till I have found your pulse;
    I am acquainted with her disposition:
    She has a very appliable nature.

Lord. And, madam, when expect you to be whipped   50
    For doing these fine favours?

Decoy.   How, my lord?
    Your lordship does but jest; I hope you make
    A difference between a lady that
    Does honourable offices and one
    They call a bawd. Your lordship was not wont   55
    To have such coarse opinion of our practice.

52. jest; I hope you make] *This ed.;* jeast I hope, you make *Q;* jest, I hope; you
make *Gifford.*

---

47. *pulse*] i.e., amorous inclinations. The pulse was reputed to be an accurate index of erotic interest; cf. Burton, *Anatomy,* III.ii.3, p. 723: 'Josephus Struthius, that Polonian, in the fifth Book of his Doctrine of Pulses, holds that this, and all other passions of the mind, may be discovered by the Pulse. And if you will know, saith he, whether the men suspected be such or such, touch their arteries, &c. And in his fourth Book, he speaks of this particular Pulse, Love makes an unequal pulse, &c.; he gives instance of a Gentlewoman, a Patient of his, whom by this means he found to be much enamoured, and with whom: he named many persons, but at the last when his name came whom he suspected, her pulse began to vary, and to beat swifter, and so by often feeling her pulse, he perceived what the matter was.' Decoy, of course, has no intention of adopting these medical procedures, but she is clearly interested in making a diagnosis.

49. *appliable*] 'docile, compliant, well disposed' (*O.E.D.*, citing this example).

50. *whipped*] a common punishment for bawdry; see l. 59n.

53–5. *difference . . . bawd*] Decoy is invoking a distinction amusingly illustrated in a letter by James Howell to Sir James Crofts, dated at Orleans, 5 March 1622; see *Familiar Letters,* ed. Jacobs (1890), pp. 141–2, where Howell describes an incident in which the Duke of Epernon, during a visit to Paris, 'treated with a Pander to procure him a Courtesan, and if she was a *Damoisel* (a Gentlewoman) he would give so much, and if a *Citizen,* he would give so much: The Pander did his office, but brought him a Citizen clad in *Damoisel's* apparel, so she and her Maquerel were paid accordingly. The next day after, some of his Familiars having understood hereof, began to be pleasant with the Duke, and to jeer him, that he . . . should suffer himself to be so cozen'd, as to pay for a Citizen after the rate of a Gentlewoman: The little Duke grew half wild hereupon, and commenced an action of Fraud against the Pander'.

Lord. The Lady Aretina is my kinswoman.

Decoy. What if she be, my lord? The nearer blood
   The dearer sympathy.

Lord.   I'll have thee carted.

Decoy. Your lordship wo' not so much stain your honour   60
   And education, to use a woman
   Of my quality –

Lord.   'Tis possible you may
   Be sent off with an honourable convoy
   Of halberdiers.

Decoy.   O, my good lord!

Lord. Your ladyship shall be no protection,   65
   If thou but stay'st three minutes.

Decoy.   I am gone.
   When next you find rebellion in your blood,
   May all within ten mile o'th' court turn honest.   *Exit.*

Lord. I do not find that proneness since the fair
   Bella Maria died; my blood is cold,   70
   Nor is there beauty enough surviving
   To heighten me to wantonness. [*To Haircut, offstage*]
   Who waits?

---

66. thou but stay'st] *Q subst.;* you but stay *Gifford.*

58–9. *The nearer . . . sympathy*] a variation of the proverb, 'The nearer the kin the further in' (Tilley, K 39). Cf. Hobbes, *Leviathan* (1651), ii.19 (ed. Oakeshott, 1960, pp. 128–9): 'it is always presumed that the nearer of kin, is the nearer in affection'.

59. *carted*] characteristically linked with whipping (see l. 50 above) as an appropriate punishment for bawdry; cf. Chapman *et al., Eastward Ho*, ed. Van Fossen (1979), V.iii.69–71: 'Say he should be condemned to be carted or whipped for a bawd, or so'. The public exposure entailed by carting could be perceived by offenders not only as humiliation but also as free advertising. Maquerelle, the bawd in Marston's *The Malcontent*, ed. Hunter (1975), has devised a scheme whereby she is 'better known . . . than if she had been five times carted' (V.i.33–4).

60. *wo' not*] See II.i.135n.

64. *halberdiers*] civic guards who carry halberds as official badges (*O.E.D.*); in this context, a whimsical name for police officers (Papousek). In *The Wedding*, IV.iii (Shirley, *Wks*, I, 425), Rawbone imagines himself led to execution 'riding up Holborn in a two-wheeled chariot, with a guard of halbardiers'.

68. *honest*] chaste (Neilson).

69. *proneness*] susceptibility (to sexual passion). Cf. Middleton, *Women Beware Women*, ed. Mulryne (1975), III.ii.55–6: 'I would not have a husband of that proneness / To kiss me before company, for a world.'

Enter HAIRCUT [*with* Secretary].

And what said my lady?

Haircut. The silent language of her face, my lord,
 Was not so pleasant as it showed upon   75
 Her entrance.

Lord.   Would any man that meets
 This lady take her for a bawd?

Haircut.   She does
 The trade an honour, credit to the profession:
 We may in time see baldness, quarter noses
 And rotten legs to take the wall of foot-cloths. 80

Lord. I ha' thought better; [*To Secretary*] call the lady back,
 I wo' not lose this opportunity.
 Bid her not fear; the favour is not common,
 And I'll reward it. I do wonder much [*Exit* Secretary.]
 Will Sentlove was not here today.   85

Haircut. I heard him say this morning he would wait
 Upon your lordship.

Enter Secre[tary] *and* DECOY.

      She is returned, sir.

Secretary. Madam, be confident my lord's not angry.

---

87. lordship. She] *lineation as in Neilson;* Lordship. | She *Q.*

79–80. *baldness . . . legs*] symptoms of venereal disease, according to I. T.,
The Hunting of the Pox (1619), sig. B3–3v. Baldness as a symptom is frequently alluded to, as in *M.N.D.*, I.ii.87: 'Some of your French crowns have no
hair at all', and *The Atheist's Tragedy*, ed. Ribner (1964), IV.iv.31: 'Those
falling diseases cause baldness'. In *The Knight of the Burning Pestle*, ed.
Doebler (1967), III.i.396–401, Sir Pockhole suffers the other symptoms: 'riding hard this way / Upon a trotting horse, my bones did ache; / And I, faint
knight, to ease my weary limbs, / Light at this cave, when straight this furious
fiend, / With sharpest instrument of purest steel, / Did cut the gristle of my
nose away'.

80. *take . . . wall*] assume a position of precedence; literally, to assume 'the
right or privilege of walking next the wall as the cleaner and safer side of a
pavement, sidewalk, etc.' (*O.E.D.*).

foot-cloths] emblems 'of dignity and state'; literally, a foot-cloth is 'a large
richly-ornamented cloth laid over the back of a horse and hanging down to the
ground on each side' (*O.E.D.*). For a comparable specimen of the metaphor,
see Middleton's *The Phoenix*, V.i.26–7 (*Works*, ed. Bullen, 1885, I, 196):
'Think all thy seed young lords, and by this act / Make a foot-cloth'd
posterity.'

Lord. You return welcome, madam; you are better
    Read in your art, I hope, than to be frighted   90
    With any shape of anger when you bring
    Such news to gentlemen. Madam, you shall
    Soon understand how I accept the office.
Decoy. You are the first lord, since I studied carriage, that
    showed such infidelity and fury upon so kind a message.   95
    Every gentleman will show some breeding, but if one
    (right honourable) should not have noble blood.
Lord. You shall return my compliment in a letter to my Lady
    Aretina; favour me with a little patience. [*To Haircut*]
    Show her that chamber.   100
Decoy. Ill attend your lordship. *Ex*[*eunt* Decoy *and* HAIRCUT].
Lord. [*To Secretary*] Write. 'Madam, where your honour is in
    danger, my love must not be silent'.

       Enter SENTLOVE *and* [ALEXANDER] KICKSHAW.

    Sentlove and Kickshaw!
Alexander. Your lordship's busy.   105
Lord. Writing a letter; nay, it sha' not bar any discourse.
Secretary. – 'Silent'.
Lord. [*Continues dictation.*] 'Though I be no physician, I may
    prevent a fever in your blood'. [*To Sentlove and Alex-*
    ander] And where have you spent the morning's   110
    conversation?

---

89. *Lord.*] Con. MS subst., Gifford; Bor. Q.   94–107.] *verse in Q, divided*
carriage, / That . . . fury / Upon . . . gentleman / Will . . . honourable /
Should . . . returne / My . . . Lady / *Aretina* . . . patience, / Shew . . .
Lordship. / Write . . . danger, / My . . . silent. / *Sentlove* . . . busie. / Writing
. . . barre / Any.

---

91. *shape*] mere appearance, pretence.

94. *carriage*] 'conveyance of merchandise; in this case bawdry' (Papousek).
To study *carriage* is undoubtedly to become skilful in questions of sexual
behaviour; cf. *Rom.*, I.iv.92–4: 'This is the hag, when maids lie on their backs,
/ That presses them and learns them first to bear, / Making them women of
good carriage.'

96–7. *but . . . blood*] except in the case of someone who, though otherwise
quite noble, should turn out not to have an adequately passionate sexual
nature.

109. *fever*] 'a state of intense nervous excitement, agitation, heat' (*O.E.D.*).
Since blood was thought to be the spring of the sexual passions, the fever in
Aretina's blood is clearly a state of sexual agitation.

Sentlove. Where you would have given the best Barbary in
   your stable to have met on honourable terms.
Lord. What new beauty? You acquaint yourselves with none
   but wonders.   115
Sentlove. 'Tis too low a miracle.
Lord. 'Twill require a strong faith.
Secretary. – 'Your blood'.
Lord. [*Dictates.*] 'If you be innocent, preserve your fame lest
   this Decoy madam betray it to your repentance'. By what   120
   name is she known?
Sentlove. Ask Alexander, he knows her!
Alexander. Whom?
Sentlove. The Lady Celestina.
Lord. He has a vast knowledge of ladies; 'las poor Alexander!   125
   When dost thou mean thy body shall lie fallow?
Alexander. When there is mercy in a petticoat, I must turn
   pilgrim for some breath.

112–22.] *verse in Q, divided* Barbary / In ... termes. / What ... selves / With
... miracle. / Twill ... bloud. / If ... *Decoy* / Madam ... repentance. / By
... knowne? / Aske.   116. low a miracle] *Q;* low, – a miracle
Gifford.   125–30.] *verse in Q, divided Alexander!* / When ... fallow? / When
... petticote, / I ... thinke / Twere ... it / Upon.

---

112. *Barbary*] a strain of horses bred in Morocco, and reputed to be second
only to Arabian horses in swiftness and grace, according to *The Horse-mans
Honour: Or, the Beautie of Horsemanship* (1620), sig. C3: 'these are in beauty,
shape, and quality like unto the *Arabian,* only somewhat lesse of stature, and
of a much gentler disposition; their color for the most is gray, or lyard and
fraynd with red fraynes in many parts of their bodies, especially about their
heads, and the setting of their necks'. Cf. *Ham.,* V.ii.143–4: 'The king, sir,
hath wagered with him six Barbary horses.'
   115–16. *wonders . . . miracle*] a rough theological distinction used here for
purposes of gentlemanly *badinage.* Browne, in *Religio Medici,* i.15, 27 (*Prose,*
ed. Endicott, 1967, pp. 21, 35) includes the processes of nature among 'those
generall pieces of wonder' which incite 'admiration'; miracles, on the other
hand, are 'the extraordinary effects of the hand of God'. The currency of both
terms in the Petrarchan tradition can be demonstrated by appealing to a
somewhat confusing line from Sidney's 'First Song' in *Astrophil and Stella*
(*Poems,* ed. Ringler, 1962, p. 197): 'Only with you not miracles are wonders'.
In general, a *wonder* is any event or object that causes admiration; a *miracle* is a
phenomenon which amazes because it violates natural laws. In his response to
Sentlove (l. 117), Lord Unready implies that, although it is easy to accept the
notion of the lady's beauty as a (natural) wonder, it would be difficult to
believe that she is a genuine (supernatural) miracle.
   127–8.] The metaphors, especially *mercy* and *pilgrim,* parody the language

Lord. I think 'twere cooler travel if you examine it upon the
    hoof through Spain.   130
Sentlove. Through Ethiopia.
Lord. Nay, less laborious to serve a prenticeship in Peru, and
    dig gold out of the mine, though all the year were dogdays.
Secretary. – 'To repentance'.
Lord. [*Dictates.*] 'In brief, this lady, could you fall from virtue,   135
    within my knowledge will not blush to be a bawd'.
Sentlove. But hang't, 'tis honourable journey work; thou art

132–42.] *verse in Q, divided* prentiship / In . . . mine, / Though . . . repentance, / In . . . vertue, / Within . . . Bawde. / But . . . worke, / Thou . . . sir, /
Let . . . knight, / Which . . . Pheasant, / And . . . uncontrould / And . . .
more, / Th'art.   133. though all the year were] *Qb subst.;* Where all the yeare
is *Qa.*

---

of Petrarchan love-making; see the sonnet which Shakespeare divides between the lovers in *Rom.*, I.v.93–106. The sense of Alexander's remark is as
follows: when at last I meet a woman merciful enough not to require the
services of my body, then and only then will my body 'lie fallow' while I
practise abstinence in order to catch my breath.

    130. *Spain*] an intemperately hot land, according to such travellers as James
Howell, in a letter from Valencia to Dr Fr. Mansel, dated 1 March 1620; see
Familiar Letters, ed. Jacobs (1890), pp. 58–9: 'Tho' it be the same glorious
Sun that shines upon you in *England* which illuminates also this Part of the
Hemisphere . . . yet he dispenseth his Heat in different Degrees of Strength:
those Rays that do but warm you in *England*, do half roast us here; those
Beams that irradiate only, and gild your Honeysuckle Fields, do scorch and
parch this chinky gaping Soil, and so put too many Wrinkles upon the Face of
our common Mother the Earth.'

    131. *Ethiopia*] 'used vaguely for the whole of Africa S. of Egypt and the
Sahara desert' (Sugden).

    132. *Peru*] 'The name was used for the whole W. coast [of South America]'
(Sugden).

    133. *though . . . were*] The uncorrected reading is textually inadmissible. E
(inner) contains not only this variant, but also the obvious errors (in B and N1
exclusively) at II.ii.277 ('yon' for 'you'), III.i.101.1 (omisson of '*Ex.*'),
III.i.143 ('bawds' for 'bawd'), III.i.164 (comma for query), and III.i.169
('your' for 'her'). The evidence is tabulated in Appendix B, p. 200. Although
most edd. print the corrected reading, Baskervill and Papousek adopt the
uncorrected reading: the former giving no reasons for his choice, the latter
advancing a confused justification with no textual support.

    dogdays] the hottest season of the year, corresponding to the zodiacal month
of Cancer, and calculated with reference to the greater and lesser dog stars
(*O.E.D.*). Cf. Webster, *The White Devil*, ed. Brown (1960), III.ii.202: 'Frost
i'th' dog-days! strange!'

famous by't, and thy name's up.

Alexander. So, sir. Let me ask you a question, my dear knight:
    which is less servile, to bring up the pheasant and wait, or   140
    sit at table uncontrolled and carve to my own appetite?

Sentlove. No more, th'art witty, as I am –

Secretary. – 'A bawd'.

Sentlove. How's that?

Alexander. O, you are famous by't, and your name's up, sir.   145

Lord. [*Dictates.*] 'Be wise, and reward my caution with timely
    care of yourself; so I shall not repent to be known, your
    loving kinsman and servant'. [*To Sentlove and Kickshaw*]
    Gentlemen, the Lady Celestina, is she so rare a thing?

Alexander. If you'll have my opinion, my lord, I never saw so   150
    sweet, so fair, so rich a piece of nature.

Lord. I'll show thee a fairer presently, to shame thy eyes and
    judgement; [*Showing him a miniature*] look o' that.
    [*Taking the letter from Secretary*] So, I'll subscribe. [*Signs
    the letter.*] Seal it; I'll excuse your pen for the direction.   155

---

143. bawd] *Qb;* bawds *Qa.*   146–55.] *verse in Q, divided* with / Timely . . .
repent / To . . . servant. / Gentlemen . . . *Celestina.* / Is . . . my / Opinion . . .
saw / So . . . nature. / Ile . . . shame / Thy . . . subscribe / Seale.

---

138. *thy name's up*] you have a good reputation; cf. the proverb, 'If one's
name be up he may lie in bed' (Tilley, N 28).

140–1. *which . . . appetite?*] The question implies an extended analogy in
which Sentlove in his role as pander (cf. II.ii.88–91) is compared to the waiter
who serves a delicacy in the hope of getting his share of it later, while Alexander in his role as lady-killer is compared to the man who consumes the meal
without compunction.

141. *carve*] indulge (Onions, 2).

145. *your name's up*] See l. 138n.

151. *piece*] specimen; often used as a synonym for girl or young woman
(Onions). See *Tit.,* I.i.312–13: 'go, give that changing piece / To him that
flourished for her with his sword'; and *The Changeling,* ed. Bawcutt (1958),
IV.i.54–5: ''tis a nice piece / Gold cannot purchase'.

152–3. *eyes . . . judgement*] The relationship between visual perception
(*eyes*) and intellectual penetration (*judgement*) here emerges as a theme to be
played in many variations during the remainder of the scene. See l. 196n.

155. *I'll . . . direction*] This is not, as Papousek believes, a request that the
Secretary address the letter to Aretina, but a casual dismissal of this usual
procedure. The address is unnecessary because the letter will be delivered in
person by Madam Decoy, who is waiting 'i'the' next chamber' (l. 160). It is
unwanted, because Lord Unready wishes to keep his communication with
Aretina hidden by a veil of absolute discretion.

Alexander. Bella Maria's picture; she was handsome.
Sentlove. But not to be compared.
Lord. Your patience, gentlemen; I'll return instantly.   *Exit*.
Alexander. Whither is my lord gone?
Secretary. To a lady i'th' next chamber.   160
Sentlove. What is she?
Secretary. You shall pardon me, I am his secretary.
Sentlove. I was wont to be of his counsel. [*Aside*] A new officer,
          and I not know't? I am resolved to batter all other with the
          praise of Celestina; I must retain him.   165

                    Enter Lord.

Lord. Has not that object convinced your erring judgements?
Alexander. What, this picture?
Lord. Were but your thoughts as capable as mine
          Of her idea, you would wish no thought
          That were not active in her praise, above   170
          All worth and memory of her sex.
Sentlove   She was fair,
          I must confess, but had your lordship looked
          With eyes more narrow and some less affection
          Upon her face –
Alexander.   I do not love the copies
          Of any dead; they make me dream of goblins.   175
          Give me a living mistress, with but half
          The beauty of Celestina. Come, my lord,
          'Tis pity that a lord of so much flesh
          Should waste upon a ghost, when they are living
          Can give you a more honourable consumption.   180

161–6.] *verse in Q, divided* she? / You . . . Secretary. / I . . . officer / And . . .
batter / All . . . *Celestina* / I . . . object / Convinc't.   164. batter] *Gifford;*
'batter *Q*.   169. her] *Qb;* your *Qa*.

___

161. *What*] who; cf. l. 41n.
163. *officer*] See l. 41n.
169. *her idea*] the Platonic idea (or form) of her excellence; cf. V.iii.54n.
173. *narrow*] capable of close observation; cf. *Shr*., III.ii.142: 'The narrow-
prying father, Minola'.
174. *copies*] images or pictures (*O.E.D.*).
180. *consumption*] general term for any disease characterised by wasting
away; here probably a synonym for love-melancholy. Cf. Rodamont's assertion in *St Patrick for Ireland*, II.i (Shirley, *Wks*, IV, 380): 'I am not sick, but I
am troubled with a desperate consumption.'

Sentlove. Why, do you mean, my lord, to live an infidel?
    Do, and see what will come on't. Observe still,
    And dote upon your vigils; build a chamber
    Within a rock: a tomb among the worms,
    Not far off, where you may (in proof apocryphal)   185
    Court 'em not devour the pretty pile
    Of flesh your mistress carried to the grave.
    There are no women in the world; all eyes
    And tongues and lips are buried in her coffin.
Lord. Why, do you think yourselves competent judges   190
    Of beauty, gentlemen?
Both.   What should hinder us?
Alexander. I have seen and tried as many as another
    With a mortal back.
Lord.   Your eyes are bribed,
    And your hearts chained to low desires; you cannot
    Enjoy the freedom of a sense.

---

186. not devour] *Q subst.;* not to devour *conj. Gifford.*   189. tongues]
Gifford; tongue *Q.*   194. low] *This ed.;* some *Q.*

---

181. *an infidel*] i.e., to Venus or love.
182. *Observe still*] continue your (false) devotion; i.e., 'worship ever'
(Schelling).
185. *in proof apocryphal*] by way of conducting a sham experiment.
186. *not devour*] not to devour (see Abbott, § 349). The rule invoked here is
that 'to' is often omitted from the infinitive phrase when used with certain
kinds of auxiliary verbs, especially those expressing wishes or preferences; cf.
Lear, IV.v.35: 'desire her [to] call her wisdom to her'. In view of the permis-
siveness of seventeenth-century grammar on this point, Gifford's conjecture
should not be allowed to grow into a full-fledged emendation, as it has in some
edd. (Gosse, Neilson, Schelling).
pile] possibly a pun, embracing both the usual meaning of 'heap' or
'mound', and the secondary sense almost equivalent to 'nap': i.e., the smooth,
downy surface of a textile fabric, especially velvet. For oblique confirmation
of the secondary meaning, cf. *The Revenger's Tragedy,* ed. Foakes (1966),
I.i.46-7: 'To have their costly three-pil'd flesh worn off / As bare as this'.
193. *mortal back*] A strong back was taken as evidence of virility; see *The
Alchemist,* ed. Mares (1967), II.ii.37-9: 'I will make me a back / With the
elixir, that shall be as tough / As Hercules, to encounter fifty a night.'
bribed] subject to corrupting influences; i.e., unable to see beyond the level
of the senses. Cf. Lord Unready's use of the phrase 'corrupted optics' at
l. 199.
194. *low*] The emendation of this ed. is based on the assumption that the
copy contained the word 'lowe' which the compositor misread as 'some'. In

Alexander.   Your lordship   195
    Has a clear eyesight, and can judge and penetrate.
Lord. I can, and give a perfect censure of
    Each line and point, distinguish beauty from
    A thousand forms which your corrupted optics
    Would pass for natural.
Sentlove.   I desire no other   200
    Judge should determine us; and if your lordship
    Dare venture but your eyes upon this lady,
    I'll stand their justice and be confident
    You shall give Celestina victory
    And triumph o'er all beauties past and living.   205
Alexander. I dare, my lord, venture a suit of clothes you will be
    o'ercome.
Lord. You do not know my fortitude.
Sentlove. Nor frailty: you dare not trust yourself to see her.
Lord. Think you so, gentlemen? I dare see this creature, to   210
    make you know your errors and the difference of her
    whose memory is my saint. Not trust my senses? I dare see
    and speak with her. Which holds the best acquaintance to
    prepare my visit to her?
Sentlove. I will do't, my lord.   215

---

205. o'er] *Gifford;* ors *Q.*   206–14.] *verse in Q, divided* clothes, / You . . .
fortitude / Nor . . . her. /Thinke . . . creature / To . . . difference / Of . . .
trust / My . . . her, / Which . . . prepare / My.   210. gentlemen?] *Gifford;*
gentlemen, *Q.*

---

working from secretary hand, this would be an easy mistake. And on literary
grounds, *low* is preferable because it continues the thought of the previous
line, suggesting that the hearts of the two libertines in question (like their
eyes) are restricted by their inability to experience more than material
pleasure.

   195. *freedom . . . sense*] the ability to see clearly and hence exercise good
judgement.

   196. *clear . . . penetrate*] Unabashed by Lord Unready's claim that libertines cannot properly see or discern, Alexander compliments him on the clar-
ity of his physical and moral vision. Cf. Beatrice-Joanna in *The Changeling*,
ed. Bawcutt (1958), I.i.72–6: 'Our eyes are sentinels unto our judgments, /
And should give certain judgment what they see; / But they are rash sometimes, and tell us wonders / Of common things, which when our judgments
find, / They can then check the eyes, and call them blind.'

   199. *corrupted optics*] See note to 'bribed' at l. 193.

   201. *determine*] decide between (Onions).

Alexander. She is a lady free in entertainments.
Lord. I would give this advantage to your cause:
    Bid her appear in all the ornaments
    Did ever wait on beauty, all the riches
    Pride can put on, and teach her face more charm   220
    Than ever poet dressed up Venus in;
    Bid her be all the graces and the queen
    Of love in one – I'll see her, Sentlove, and
    Bring off my heart (armed but with single thought
    Of one that's dead) without a wound, and when   225
    I have made your folly prisoner, I'll laugh at you.
Sentlove. She shall expect you; trust to me for knowledge.
Lord. I'm for the present somewhere else engaged;
    Let me hear from you.   [*Exit*.]
Sentlove.   So, I am glad he's yet
    So near conversion.
Alexander.   I am for Aretina.   230
Sentlove. No mention of my lord.
Alexander.   Prepare his lady:
    'Tis time he were reduced to the old sport;
    One lord like him more would undo the court.   *Exeunt*.

218. her] *conj. Gifford;* him *Q.*   224. but with] *F. D. Hoeniger;* but *Q;* with
Con. MS; but with a *conj. Gifford;* but in *conj. Harrier.*   225. that's]
Gifford; that is *Q.*   233. *Exeunt*] *Gifford; Exit Q.*

218. *her*] Gifford's emendation is justified both by the meaning and by the
parallel construction at l. 222.

222–3. *all . . . one*] For a detailed discussion of the three graces in
Renaissance iconography and their relationship to Venus, see E. Wind, *Pagan
Mysteries in the Renaissance*, revised ed. (1968), pp. 36–52. As a Neoplatonic
triad labelled 'Pulchritudo-Amor-Voluptas' (p. 43), the graces may be inter-
preted as three aspects of the goddess of love.

224. *Bring off*] 'deliver, rescue' (Onions).

but with] That the reading of Q requires emendation was first recognised by
the annotator who produced Con. MS. His solution was to mark *but* for
deletion and to write *with* above the line. I owe my solution to F. D. Hoeniger,
who points out that the annotator's only mistake was to substitute the word
with rather than merely adding it.

225–6. *when . . . prisoner*] i.e., after your foolish presumption has been
defeated and captured by my single-minded resolution. The word *prisoner*
completes the jousting metaphor set up in the previous lines.

Act III, Scene ii

Enter ARETINA *with a letter*, DECOY.

Decoy. He is the ornament of your blood, madam;
    I am much bound to his lordship.
Aretina.   He gives you
    A noble character.
Decoy.   'Tis his goodness, madam.
Aretina. [*Aside*] I wanted such an engine: my lord has
    Done me a courtesy to disclose her nature;   5
    I now know one to trust, and will employ her.
    [*To Decoy*] Touching my lord, for reasons which I shall
    Offer to your ladyship hereafter, I
    Desire you would be silent; but to show
    How much I dare be confident in your   10
    Secrecy, I pour my bosom forth: I
    Love a gentleman on whom there wo' not
    Need much conjuration to meet – your ear – [*Whispers.*]
Decoy. I apprehend you, and I shall be happy
    To be serviceable. I am sorry   15
    Your ladyship did not know me before now;
    I have done offices, and not a few
    Of the nobility but have done feats
    Within my house, which is convenient
    For situation, and artful chambers,   20
    And pretty pictures to provoke the fancy.

Enter LITTLEWORTH.

Littleworth. Madam, all pleasures languish in your absence.
Aretina. Your pardon a few minutes, sir. [*Aside to Decoy*] You
    must
    Contrive it thus.

10–15.] *lineation of this ed;* your secrecie, / I . . . gentleman / On . . . conjur-
ation / To . . . eare – / I . . . shall / Be *Q*.   12. on] *Q subst.;* One *Gosse.*   13.
Need] *Gifford subst.;* meet *Q*.   19. is convenient] *Qb;* is so convenient
Qa.   21. And] *Qb;* Such *Qa*.

---

    4. *engine*] contrivance, device (Onions), but here a person who helps to
'engineer' a scheme or plot.
    12. *wo' not*] See II.i.135n.

Littleworth. [*Withdrawing*] I attend, and shall account it
    Honour to wait on your return.
Aretina.   [*Aside to Decoy*] He must not   25
    Have the least knowledge of my name or person.
Decoy. I have practised that already for some great ones,
    And dare again to satisfy you, madam;
    I have a thousand ways to do sweet offices.
Littleworth. [*Aside*] If this Lady Aretina should be honest   30
    I ha' lost time. She's free as air: I must
    Have closer conference, and if I have art,
    Make her affect me in revenge.
Decoy.   [*Aside to Aretina*] This evening?
    Leave me to manage things.
Aretina.   You will oblige me.
Decoy. You shall commend my art and thank me after. *Ex[it].*   35
Aretina. [*To Littleworth*] I hope the revels are maintained
    within.
Littleworth. By Sir Thomas and his mistress.
Aretina.   How! his mistress?
Littleworth. The Lady Celestina: I ne'er saw
    Eyes shoot more amorous interchange.
Aretina.   Is't so?
Littleworth. He wears her favour with more pride.
Aretina.   Her favour?   40

25. must] *Qb;* may *Qa.*   33. evening?] *Qb;* evening *Qa.*   40. more]
Gifford; ore *Qb;* meere *Qa.*

---

27. *practised*] performed (Onions).

30. *honest*] chaste.

31. *free . . . air*] proverbial (Tilley, A 88). The significance of the phrase can
be inferred from its use in Marston and Barkstead's *The Insatiate Countess,*
I.i.54 (*The Works of John Marston,* ed. Bullen, 1887, III, 133), where Isabella,
the character referred to in the title, rejoices in the death of her husband
because it has removed the restrictions of marriage and left her 'free as air'.

33. *affect*] be fond of, love.

in revenge] i.e., Aretina may even the score in her game with Bornwell by
embarking on her own flirtation.

37. *mistress*]understood here 'in the wanton sense'; see V.iii.158.

40. *more*] Gifford's emendation can be supported on bibliographical and
palaeographical grounds. The compositor read *e* for *o* (a common misreading), and, in accordince with his spelling preferences, he doubled the *e* to
produce 'meere' in Qa. The proofreader crossed out *eere* and wrote in *ore*
above the line, hoping to arrive again at *more.* But then the press corrector
substituted *ore* for the entire word, producing the reading of Qb. If this is
correct, Gifford simply restored the lost *m.*

Littleworth. A feather that he ravished from her fan.
     And is so full of courtship, which she smiles on.
Aretina. [*Aside*] 'Tis well.
Littleworth. And praises her beyond all poetry.
Aretina. I'm glad he has so much wit.
Littleworth.   [*Aside*] Not jealous?   45
Aretina. [*Aside*] This secures me: what would make other
          ladies pale
     With jealousy, gives but a licence to my wand'rings.
     Let him now tax me if he dare – and yet,
     Her beauty's worth my envy, and I wish
     Revenge upon it, not because he loves,   50
     But that it shines above my own.

                    Enter ALEX[ANDER].

Alexander.   Dear madam –
Aretina. I have it! You two gentlemen profess
     Much service to me; if I have a way
     To employ your wit and secrecy –
Both.   You'll honour us.
Aretina. You gave a high and worthy character   55
     Of Celestina.
Alexander.   I remember, madam.
Aretina. Do either of you love her?
Alexander.   Not I, madam.
Littleworth. I would not, if I might.
Aretina.   She's now my guest,
     And by a trick invited by my husband
     To disgrace me. You gentlemen are held   60
     Wits of the town: the consuls that do govern
     The senate here, whose jeers are all authentic;
     The taverns and the ordinaries are

43–4. well. / And] *lineation as in Gifford;* well. And *Q.*   52. it! You] *Gifford*
subst.; it, you *Q.*   57. her?] *Qb;* her. *Qa.*   58. not, if] *Qb;* not if *Qa.*

61–2. *consuls . . . senate*] 'a hyperbolical comparison of Alexander and
Littleworth to the two annually elected magistrates who held supreme authority in the Roman Republic' (Papousek).

63. *ordinaries*] establishments serving the multiple functions of restaurant,
bar and gaming-house. According to Cotton (sig. B2v), 'an *Ordinary* is a
handsom house, where every day, about the hour of twelve, a good Dinner is

Made academies where you come, and all
Your sins and surfeits made the time's example;   65
Your very nods can quell a theatre,
No speech or poem good without your seal;
You can protect scurrility and publish;
By your authority, believed, no rapture
Ought to have honest meaning.

Alexander.   Leave our characters.   70
Littleworth. And name the employment.
Aretina.   You must exercise
The strength of both your wits upon this lady,
And talk her into humbleness or anger,
Both which are equal to my thought. If you
Dare undertake this slight thing for my sake,   75
My favour shall reward it; but be faithful,
And seem to let all spring from your own freedom.

Alexander. This all? We can defame her, if you please,
My friend shall call her whore, or anything,
And never be endangered to a duel.   80
Aretina. How's that?

65. made the time's] *Qb subst.;* made times *Qa.*   68–9. scurrility and publish; / By] *Neilson;* scurrility, and publish / By *Q;* scurrility, and publish, / By *Gifford.*   81–5.] *verse in Q, divided* that? / He . . . . man / Will . . . satisfaction, / But . . . us. / They.

_____

prepared by way of *Ordinary*, composed of variety of dishes, in season, well-drest, with all other accommodations fit for that purpose, whereby many Gentlemen of great Estates and good repute, make this place their resort, who after Dinner play a while for recreation, both moderately and commonly, without deserving reproof'.

66.] Significant facial expressions from you are enough to dominate the mood of an audience at a theatrical performance. Cf. the Prologue to *The Example* (Shirley, *Wks*, III, 282): 'he that can / Talk loud, and high, is held the witty man, / And censures finely, rules the box, and strikes / With his court nod consent to what he likes'.

67. *seal*] imprimatur; stamp of approval.

68–9. *You . . . By*] I follow Neilson's punctuation here because it achieves the desirable result of making sense of a difficult passage. The semi-colon at the end of the line places *protect* and *publish* into grammatical parallelism: both are alternatives which the gallants may adopt. Hence, the line may be paraphrased, 'when you discover indecency, you have the power to choose whether to expose (*publish*) or hide (*protect*) it'.

69. *rapture*] i.e., expression of enthusiasm.

74. *equal . . . thought*] a variation of the phrase, 'equal to me', meaning 'it makes no difference' (*O.E.D.*).

Alexander. He can endure a cudgelling, and no man will fight
after so fair a satisfaction. But leave us to our art, and do
not limit us.

Aretina. They are here. Begin not, till I whisper you.   85

    Enter SIR THOMAS, CELESTINA, MARIANA, ISABELLA.

[To Celestina] *Je vous prie, madame, d'excuser
l'importunité de mes affaires, qui m'ont fait offenser, par mon
absence, une dame de laquelle j'ai reçu tant d'obligation.*

*Celestina. Pardonnez-moi, madame; vous me faites trop
d'honneur.*   90

*Aretina. C'est bien de la douceur de votre naturel que vous tenez
cette langage; mais, j'espère que mon mari n'a pas manqué de
vous entretenir en mon absence.*

Celestina. En verité, monsieur nous a fort obligé.

Aretina. Il eût trop failli, s'il n'eût tâché de tout son pouvoir à   95
vous rendre toutes sortes de services.

Celestina. C'est de sa bonté qu'il nous a tant favorisé.

85.1 MARIANA] *Con. MS subst., Gifford; Marcana Q.*   88. *obligation*] *Q;*
obligations Gifford.   92. *cette*] *Gifford; Ceste Q; ce Knowland.*

85.]See l. 201 below.

86–120.] For the socially ambitious in 1635, French was more than 'one of
the finest tongues for ladies to show their teeth in' (ll. 124–5). The marriage of
Charles I to Henrietta Maria of France in 1625 was in part responsible for the
growing popularity of French as the language of *politesse*, especially among
cultivated women. The translations which follow are indebted to (sometimes
identical with) those given by Baskervill and Papousek. I have consulted
Cotgrave on every problematic word or phrase, and have based my solutions
on his advice.

86–8.] I prithee, madam, to pardon the urgency of my affairs which have
caused me to offend, by my absence, a lady to whom I am so much obliged.

89–90.] Pardon me, madam; you do me too much honour.

91–3.] It is doubtless by virtue of the sweetness of your natural disposition
that you maintain such discourse; but I hope that my husband has not failed to
entertain you in my absence.

92. cette langage] Although Cotgrave, like modern grammarians, gives
the gender of *langage* as masculine, I have thought it unwise to attribute to
Shirley greater fluency in French than he evidently possessed.

94.] In truth, the gentleman has greatly obliged us.

95–6.] He would have done exceedingly amiss, had he not endeavoured
with all his ability to render you all manner of service.

97.] It is owing to his liberality that we have been so highly favoured.

Aretina. De la vôtre plutôt, madame, que vous fait donner
    d'interprétation si bénigne à ses efforts.

Celestina. Je vois bien que la victoire sera toujours à madame, et   100
    de langage et de la courtoisie.

Aretina. Vraiment, madame, que jamais personne a plus désiré
    l'honneur de votre compagnie, que moi.

Celestina. Laissons en, je vous supplie, des compliments; et per-
    mettez à votre servante de vous baiser les mains.   105

Aretina. Vous m'obligez trop.

Bornwell. [*To Celestina*] I have no more patience; let's be
    merry again in our own language, madam. Our mirth
    cools.

        Enter FREDERICK [*with* Steward].

Our nephew!   110

Aretina. [*Aside*] Passion of my brain!

Frederick. Save you gentlemen, save you ladies.

Aretina. [*Aside*] I am undone.

Frederick. I must salute, no matter at which end I begin.

Aretina. There's a compliment.   115

Celestina. Is this your nephew, madam?

Aretina. Je vous prie, madame, d'excuser les habits et le rude
    comportement de mon cousin. Il est tout fraîchement venu de
    l'université, où on l'a tout gâté.

---

101. *courtoisie*] Knowland subst.; *courtesie* Q.   107–8.] verse in Q, divided
agen / In.   108. language, madam. Our] *This ed.;* language, Madam our *Q;*
language: madam our *Gifford.*

  98–9.] Rather to yours, madam, which has caused you to place so gracious
an interpretation upon his endeavours.

  100–1.] Now I perceive that the victory will always be yours, madam, both
in discourse and in courtesy.

  101. courtoisie] Since Cotgrave gives only this French spelling (and lists
'courtesie' among the English synonyms), it is reasonable to suppose that the
spelling in Q is the compositor's misreading of the correct French word in the
copy.

  102–3.] In truth, madam, no one has ever desired the honour of your company more than I.

  104–5.] Let us, I entreat you, leave these compliments; and please allow
your servant to kiss your hands.

  106.] You are too kind.

  117–19.] Prithee, madam, excuse the apparel and the unmannerly
behaviour of my cousin. He has but newly arrived from the university, where
they have ruined him utterly.

Celestina. Excusez-moi, madame, il est bien accompli.   120

Frederick. This language should be French, by the motions of
  your heads and the mirth of your faces.

Aretina. [*Aside*] I am dishonoured.

Frederick. 'Tis one of the finest tongues for ladies to show their
  teeth in. If you'll Latin, I am for you – or Greek it; my   125
  tailor has not put me into French yet. [*To Celestina*] *Mille
  basia, basia mille.*

Celestina. Je ne vous entends pas, monsieur; I understand you
  not, sir.

Frederick. Why so! You and I then shall be in charity, for   130
  though we should be abusive, we ha' the benefit not to
  understand one another. Where's my aunt? I did hear
  music somewhere, and my brains (tuned with a bottle of
  your capering claret) made haste to show their dancing.

Littleworth. [*To Aretina*] Please you, madam, they are very   135
  comfortable.

Steward. Alas, madam, how would you have me help it? I did
  use all means I could, after he heard the music, to make
  him drunk in hope so to contain him; but the wine made
  him lighter, and his head flew hither ere I missed his heels.   140

Alexander. Nay, he spoke Latin to the lady.

121–6.] *verse in* Q, *divided* motions / Of . . . dishonor'd. / Tis . . . their / Teeth
. . . it, / My . . . yet, / *Mille.*   125. Latin, I] *Spencer;* Latin I *Q;* Latin it, I
Gifford.   128–40.] *verse in* Q, *divided monsieur,* / I . . . so? / You . . . charity,
/ For . . . benefit / Not . . . Aunt? / I . . . braines / Tun'd . . . claret / Made . . .
Madam, / They . . . Madam / How . . . use / All . . . musicke, / To . . . him /
But . . . head / Flew.

120.] Excuse me, madam, he is thoroughly accomplished.

124–5. *show . . . teeth*] Cf. *The Revenger's Tragedy,* ed. Foakes (1966),
II.i.14–16, where Dondolo, after advising Castiza that a man wishes to 'Show
his teeth in your company', glosses the phrase as follows: 'Why, speak with
you, Madonna.'

126–7. Mille basia] a fragment of the following lines from Catullus (v.7–8):
'da mi basia mille, deinde centum, / dein mille altera, dein secunda centum.'
See *Catullus, Tibullus, and Pervigilium Veneris,* Loeb Classical Library
(1913), pp. 6–9, where F. W. Cornish translates as follows: 'Give me a
thousand kisses, then a hundred, then another thousand, then a second
hundred.' Frederick's inverted repetition of the phrase is evidently an attempt at elegant variation.

135. *they*] i.e., the comfits which Littleworth is fond of dispersing; see
I.i.194–5, 236.

Aretina. O, most unpardonable! Get him off quickly and discreetly, or if I live –

Steward. 'Tis not in my power. He swears I am an absurd
sober fellow; and if you keep a servant in his house to cross   145
his humour, when the rich sword and belt comes home,
he'll kill him.

Aretina. What shall I do? Try your skill, Master Littleworth.

Littleworth. He has ne'er a sword. [*To Frederick*] Sweet Mr
Frederick –   150

Bornwell. [*To Celestina*] 'Tis pity, madam, such a scion should
be lost; but you are clouded.

Celestina. Not I, sir; I never found myself more clear at heart.

Bornwell. I could play with a feather. Your fan, lady. [*Takes
her fan.*] Gentlemen! Aretina! [*Sings.*] Ta ra ra ra. [*To*   155
Celestina] Come, madam.

Frederick. [*To Littleworth*] Why, my good tutor in election,
you might have been a scholar!

Littleworth. But I thank my friends they brought me up a little
better. Give me the town wits, that deliver jests clean from   160
the bow, that whistle in the air and cleave the pin at
twelvescore. Ladies do but laugh at a gentleman that has

142–7.] *verse in Q, divided* off / Quickly . . . live – / Tis . . . am / An . . . keepe /
A . . . humour, / When.   146. comes] *Q;* come *Gifford.*   151–65.] *verse in
Q, divided* should / Be . . . sir, / I . . . heart. / I . . . Lady, / Gentlemen . . .
Madam. / Why . . . election? / You . . . thanke / My . . . better, / Give . . .
jeasts / Cleane . . . aire, / And . . . doe / But . . . learning. / Tis . . . suspected, /
Leave . . . you; / come.   157–8. election, you . . . scholar!] *Gifford subst.;*
election? / You , . . scholler. *Q.*

---

146. *when . . . home*] 'i.e., when he receives his inheritance upon reaching
his majority' (Papousek). A literal reading of the clause is also permissible, in
view of the fact that Frederick soon expects to be dressed in gentleman's
attire; see l. 178n.

160–1. *clean . . . bow*] i.e., adroitly and with precision, as the metaphor
based on archery implies.

161. *cleave the pin*] In archery, to cleave the pin is to aim the arrow so deftly
that it hits the pin which holds in place the cloth (or clout) at the centre of the
target; see Marlowe, *1 Tamb.*, II.iv.8–9 (*Plays*, p. 69): 'For kings are clouts
that every man shoots at, / Our crown the pin that thousands seek to cleave'.
Cf. Shakespeare, *L.L.L.*, IV.i.135.

162. *twelvescore*] The normal distance in archery was 240 paces (or yards).
Ascham, in *Toxophilus* (1571), sig. H3, refers familiarly to 'the down wynd
twelve score marke'. See also *2H4*, III.ii.43–6, where Shallow praises the

any learning; 'tis sin enough to have your clothes suspected. Leave us, and I will find a time to instruct you. Come,
here are sugar-plums. 'Tis a good Frederick.   165
Frederick. Why, is not this my aunt's house in the Strand? the
noble rendezvous? [*Celestina laughs.*] Who laughs at me?
Go, I will root here if I list, and talk of rhetoric, logic,
Latin, Greek, or anything – and understand 'em, too.
Who says the contrary? Yet, in a fair way, I contemn all   170
learning and will be as ignorant as he, or he, or any taffeta,
satin, scarlet, plush, tissue, or cloth o'bodkin gentleman
whose manners are most gloriously infected. [*To
Celestina*] Did you laugh at me lady?
Celestina. Not I, sir! But if I did show mirth upon your ques-   175
tion, I hope you would not beat me, little gentleman.
Frederick. How, little gentleman! You dare not say these words

166–78.] *verse in Q, divided* strand? / The . . . me? / Go . . . talke / Of . . .
thing, / And . . . contrary? / Yet . . . learning, / And . . . he, / Or . . . plush, /
Tissue . . . gentleman, / Whose . . . infected; / Did . . . sir? / But . . . question, /
I . . . gentleman. / How . . . say / These.   171. be as ignorant] *Qb;* be
ignorant *Qa.*   172. cloth o' bodkin] *Gifford;* cloath, a bodkin *Q;* cloth-a-
bodkin *Baskervill.*

bowmanship of an acquaintance by claiming that he 'would have clapped i'
the clout at twelve score, and carried you a forehand shaft a fourteen and
fourteen and a half, that it would have done a man's heart good to see'.

165. *sugar-plums*] See I.i.195n.

166. *Strand*] See I.ii.79n.

171. *he . . . he*] Clearly Frederick is pointing to Littleworth and Alexander
as he speaks.

taffeta] a fairly expensive glossy silk fabric, 'used for every kind of garment
in the wardrobe of both men and women'. It was often associated with a sense
of false finery, because 'deceit in finishing taffeta was practised by unscrupu-
lous persons. Inferior and deceptively woven material was gummed and
glossed to give an attractive appearance' (Linthicum, p. 124).

172. *satin . . . tissue*] All of these materials are said by Linthicum, pp. 88,
117–22, to belong to the highly desirable and hence very expensive class of
seventeenth-century fabrics.

cloth o' bodkin] a variety of cloth of gold or silver (see I.i.91n.). 'It was
characterized by raised designs of animals, plants, branches, and geometric
figures, and made in many colours.' Originally produced in Baghdad, its
manufacture spread to France and England after the fourteenth century (Linthicum, p. 115).

173. *gloriously*] ostentatiously; see II.i.34n.

infected] a malapropism, doubtless inspired by sack. Frederick means to say
'affected'.

to my new clothes and fighting sword.

Aretina. Nephew Frederick!

Frederick. Little gentleman. 'Tis an affront both to my   180
blood and person. I am a gentleman of as tall a birth as any
boast nobility. Though my clothes smell o' the lamp, my
coat is honourable – right honourable – full of or and argent. A little gentleman!

Bornwell. Coz, you must be patient; my lady meant you no   185
dishonour, and you must remember she's a woman.

Frederick. Is she a woman? That's another matter. [*To
Celestina*] D'ee hear, my uncle tells me what you are.

Celestina. So, sir.

Frederick. You called me little gentleman.   190

Celestina. I did, sir.

Frederick. A little pink has made a lusty ship strike her topsail,

180–90.] *verse in Q, divided* gentleman, / This . . . person, / I . . . birth / As
. . . clothes / Smell . . . honourable, / Right . . . argent, / A . . . patient, / My
. . . and / You . . . woman. / Is . . . matter, / Dee . . . are. / So.   180. 'Tis]
Gifford; This *Q.*   182. boast] *Qb;* least *Qa.*   192–9.] *verse in Q, divided*
ship / Strike . . . Elephant, / A . . . all / False . . . gentleman / Be . . . Ladiship
/ Top . . . uncle? / Tother . . . I /Will . . . phylosophy. / Come Nephew, / You
. . . Madam. / Waite.

---

178. *new . . . sword*] i.e., the emblems of gentlemanly culture which Frederick intends to purchase with the money he received from Aretina (see
II.i.139–40). Cf. l. 146n.

181. *tall*] 'goodly, fine, "proper"' (Onions, 1).

181–2. *any boast*] any who boast (Abbott, § 244).

182. *smell . . . lamp*] proverbial (Tilley, C 43). To smell of the candle or the
lamp is to betray laborious scholarly activity.

182–3. *my . . . honourable*] 'My coat of arms indicates a family of honor.
The surface meaning of the phrase is that his clothes are good enough, and
honestly worn, in contrast to the rich clothing of the "gentlemen"'
(Papousek).

183. *or*] the heraldic term for gold, one of the two metals (along with argent)
of heraldry. Having the sun as its planet and topaz as its stone, *or* is indeed,
according to G. Legh's *The Accidents of Armory* (1563), sig. B1–2v, a mark of
honour: 'For looke how much this metall excelleth all others in the kind
thereof, as in finenesse and puritie: So much shoulde the bearer thereof, excell
all other, in prowes and vertue.' In moral terms, *or* signifies 'wisedom, riches,
magnanimitie, joyfulnes and elation of mynde'.

183–4. *argent*] the heraldic term for silver, the second of the two metals of
heraldry. According to G. Legh's *The Accidens of Armory* (1563), sig. B3v–4,
argent is associated with the moon and with pearls; it signifies 'chastitie, vir-
ginitie, cleare conscience, & Charitie'.

192. *pink*] a small sailing vessel 'used for coasting and fishing' (*O.E.D.*,
sb., 1).

the Crow may beard the Elephant, a whelp may tame the
Tiger (spite of all false decks and murderers), and a little
gentleman be hard enough to grapple with your ladyship,   195
top and top-gallant. Will you go drink, uncle, t'other enchanted bottle? You and I will tipple and talk philosophy.

Bornwell. Come, nephew. [*To Celestina*] You will excuse a
minute's absence, madam. [*To Steward*] Wait you on us.

Steward. My duty, sir.   200

Aretina. [*To Alexander and Littleworth*] Now, gentlemen.

Ex[eunt] all but Cel[estina], Alex[ander], and Little[worth].

Alexander. Madam, I rather you accuse my language
        For speaking truth, than virtue suffer in
        My further silence; and it is my wonder
        That you, whose noble carriage hath deserved   205
        All honour and opinion, should now
        Be guilty of ill manners.

Celestina.   What was that
        You told me, sir?

Littleworth.   Do you not blush, madam,
        To ask that question?

Celestina.   You amaze, rather,

196–7. uncle, t'other . . . bottle?] *Gifford subst.;* uncle? / Tother . . . bottle,*Q.*

---

strike] 'to lower (sails, masts)' as a token of surrender (*O.E.D.*, vb., 17).

193–4. *the Crow . . . Tiger*] Since *Crow, Elephant* and *Tiger* are capitalised
in Q, the likelihood is that they should be taken as proper names for actual or
imaginary ships. A *whelp* is 'one of a fleet of auxiliary war vessels established
in Charles I's reign' for the purpose of attending upon *H.M.S. Lion* (*O.E.D.*,
sb., 5). To *beard* an opponent is to offer open defiance (*O.E.D.*, vb., 3).

194. *false decks*] 'The *false deck* was a slight one raised over the other, as a
defence against boarders' (Gifford).

murderers] small cannon (*O.E.D.*, 2), as implied in *The Changeling*, ed.
Bawcutt (1958), I.i.222–3: 'How shall I dare to venture in his castle, / When
he discharges murderers at the gate?'

196. *top . . . top-gallant*] The phrase is 'short for *topsail* and *topgallant sail*'
according to *O.E.D.* ('top', sb.1, 9c); figuratively, as in this instance, it means
'with all sail set, in full array or career'.

201.] This is the signal which Aretina promised at l. 85; Alexander and
Littleworth are now free to subject Celestina to the verbal insolence which
ensues.

201.1.] The staging of the remainder of this scene is difficult to visualise,
partly because of an inconsistency in the stage directions. If only the three
specified characters remain on the platform, and only Bornwell returns (l.
224.1), then there would appear to be no motivation for Celestina's question,

My cheek to paleness; what mean you by this?   210
I am not troubled with the hiccup, gentlemen,
You should bestow this fright upon me.
Littleworth.   Then
Pride and ill memory go together.
Celestina.   How, sir?
Alexander. The gentleman on whom you exercised
Your thin wit was a nephew to the lady   215
Whose guest you are; and though her modesty
Look calm on the abuse of one so near
Her blood, the affront was impious.
Littleworth.   I am ashamed on't.
You, an ingenious lady, and well mannered?
I'll teach a bear as much civility.   220
Celestina. You may be master of the college, sir,
For aught I know.
Littleworth.   What college? of the bears?

210. mean you] *Gifford;* you meane *Q.*   214. exercised] *conj. Gifford;*
exercise *Q.*   222. of the bears] *spoken by Littleworth in Q; assigned to
Celestina by Gifford (conj.).*

'How shall I / Acquit your lady's silence?' (ll. 321–2). I argue in the Introduction, pp. 32–3, that the solution to this problem lies in the use of the above.
Shortly after her exit, perhaps at l. 214, Aretina should reappear, silently, at
an observation post above. This would allow her to overhear the battle of
insults, to be the legitimate object of Celestina's question, and to return by a
backstage route to the platform level in time for her next speech (l. 326).
    211–12.] As Baskervill points out, the two clauses are connected with an
implied 'so that' (cf. Abbott, § 244), and are based on 'the belief that fright
cured the hiccups'.
    219. *ingenious*] interchangeable with 'ingenuous' in the sense of 'befitting a
well-born person' (Onions, 5).
    220.] Bears were thought to be sluggishly resistant to training; see E.
Topsell, *The Historie of Foure-Footed Beastes* (1607), sig. E2v: 'Concerning
the industrie or naturall disposition of a beare, it is certaine that they are very
hardlie tamed, and not to bee trusted though they seeme never so tame.'
    221. *master . . . college*] The role assigned to Littleworth here is a parody of
that played by Gasparo in Shirley's *Love Tricks: Or the School of Complement*;
cf. I.i.196n.
    222. *of the bears*] Subsequent edd. follow Gifford in assigning this phrase to
Celestina rather than Littleworth. Since either procedure makes perfect
sense, I have not rearranged the dialogue in Q.
    223. *a plot*] Celestina becomes aware, at this point, that she is the victim of a
conspiracy; perhaps she has noticed that Aretina is watching the scene from
her observaton observation post above (see l. 201.1n.).

Celestina. Have you a plot upon me? D'ee possess
　　Your wits, or know me, gentlemen?

　　　　　　　Enter BORNWELL.

Bornwell. [*Aside*]　　　　　　　　　How's this?
Alexander. Know you? Yes, we do know you to an atom.　　225
Littleworth. Madam, we know what stuff your soul is made on.
Celestina. But do not bark so like a mastiff, pray,
　　[*Aside*] Sure they are mad. [*To them*] Let your brains
　　　　stand a while
　　And settle, gentlemen; you know not me.
　　What am I?
Littleworth.　　　Th'art a puppet, a thing made　　230
　　Of clothes and painting, and not half so handsome
　　As that which played Susanna in the fair.
Celestina. I heard you visited those canvas tragedies –
　　One of their constant audience, and so taken
　　With Susan, that you wished yourself a rival　　235

224.1.] Gifford specifies that Bornwell should enter '*behind*', a virtually
unavoidable procedure on the Cockpit stage (see Appendix A). He should
take a position on the platform at some distance from the three characters
whom he is observing, but sufficiently downstage to allow for asides to the
audience. The three verbal combatants should be unaware of (or at least not
concerned with) Bornwell's presence until he addresses them in ll. 283–4.

230. *puppet*] The best piece of evidence about seventeenth-century pup-
petry is the puppet-play written by Littlewit and staged by Leatherhead in
Bartholomew Fair, ed. Horsman (1960), V.iv.113–351. G. Speaight, who
discusses Jonson's play and many other contemporary references in *The
History of the English Puppet Theatre* (1955), pp. 54–69, believes that 'glove
puppets were the usual form of puppet show during the first half of the
seventeenth century' (p. 65).

232. *Susanna*] 'The History of Susanna' is one of the books of the Apocry-
pha. Susanna, wife of Joakim, has her outdoor bath rudely interrupted by the
two wicked elders (see l. 236) who proposition her, attempt to blackmail her,
and when all else fails, accuse her of adultery and condemn her to death. Only
the intervention of Daniel, who rigorously cross-questions the elders, rescues
Susanna and restores her reputation. A dramatic version of the story, attributed to Thomas Garter and entitled *The Most Virtuous & Godly Susanna*,
M.S.R. (1937), places the beleaguered heroine at the centre of a moral inter-
lude in which her assailants are called Volputas and Sensuality. It would be a
relatively small step from these allegorical characters to the dramatic short-
hand of the puppet-master.

233. *canvas tragedies*] so named because of the 'canvas booths' in which
puppet-plays were performed (Papousek).

       With the two wicked elders.
Alexander.   You think this
       Is wit, now? Come, you are –
Celestina.   What, I beseech you?
       Your character will be full of salt and satire,
       No doubt. What am I?
Alexander.   Why, you are a woman.
Celestina. And that's at least a bow wide of your knowledge.   240
Alexander. Would be thought handsome (and might pass i'th'
              country
       Upon a market day) but miserably
       Forfeit to pride and fashions, that if heaven
       Were a new gown, you'd not stay in't a fortnight.
Celestina. It must be miserably out of fashion, then;   245
       Have I no sin but pride?
Alexander.   Hast any virtue?
       Or but a good face to excuse that want?
Celestina. You praised it yesterday.
Alexander.   That made you proud.
Celestina. More pride?
Alexander.   You need not so close up the praise:
       I have seen a better countenance in a   250
       Sibyl.
Celestina.   When you wore spectacles of sack,
       Mistook the painted cloth, and kissed it for
       Your mistress.
Alexander.   Let me ask you a question:
       How much have you consumed in expectation

---

240. your] *Gifford;* you *Q.*   242. but miserably] *Q;* but so miserably
Gifford.   249. not so] *This ed.;* not to *Q;* not. To *Spencer.*   250-4. a / Sibyl
. . . sack, / Mistook . . . for / Your . . . question: / How] *lineation of this ed.;*
Sibill. / When . . . mistooke / The . . . mistresse. / Let . . . much / Have *Q.*

   238.] Your description of my character will be bitter and satiric.

   240. *bow*] 'bowshot' (Baskervill); i.e., about 240 paces. Cf. l. 162n.

   249. *You . . . praise*] i.e., pride isn't the only way of reacting to praise (with
an undercurrent of 'Don't interrupt me just when I'm about to tell you what I
really think of you'). My emendation corrects a common misreading (*t* for *s*)
and allows *so* to mean 'in this manner'.

   251. *Sibyl*] here used informally in the sense of 'a prophetess; a fortune-
teller, a witch' (*O.E.D.*, 2). The legendary ugliness of the Cumaean Sibyl (to
whom Apollo granted an abnormally long life) is also implied.

   252. *painted cloth*] i.e., decorated wall hangings; cf. I.ii.11n.

    That I would love you?

Celestina.   Why, I think as much   255
    As you have paid away in honest debts
    This seven year! [*Aside*] 'Tis a pretty impudence,
    But cannot make me angry.

Littleworth. [*To Alexander*]   Is there any
    Man that will cast away his limbs upon her?

Alexander. [*To Celestina*] You do not sing so well as I
        imagined,   260
    Nor dance; you reel in your coranto, and pinch
    Your petticoat too hard; y'ave no good ear
    To th' music, and incline too much one shoulder,
    As you were dancing on the rope – and falling;
    You speak abominable French, and make   265
    A curtsy like a dairymaid. [*Aside*] Not mad?

Littleworth. [*To Alexander*] Do we not sting her handsomely?

Bornwell. [*Aside*] A conspiracy!

Alexander. [*To Celestina*] Your state is not so much as 'tis
        reported
    When you confer notes – all your husband's debts   270
    And your own reconciled – but that's not it
    Will so much spoil your marriage.

Celestina.   As what, sir?
    Let me know all my faults.

Alexander.   Some men do whisper
    You are not over honest.

Celestina.   All this shall not
    Move me to more than laughter, and some pity.   275
    Because you have the shapes of gentlemen,

255-7. Why, . . . year!] *Gifford subst.;* Why? . . . yeare, *Q;* Why . . . year.
Gosse.

---

    261. *coranto*] the usual English name for the 'courante', a dance in quick
triple time characterised by steps which are 'delightfully simple and light,
producing the effect of a sprightly skipping motion' (Dolmetsch, p. 133).

    262. *petticoat*] See I.i.296n.

    264. *dancing . . . rope*] i.e., tightrope walking. For comment on the popular-
ity of rope-dancing shows, see Strutt, pp. 196–201.

    268.] If Bornwell has noticed that Aretina is watching the scene from her
observation post above (see l. 201.1n.), it would be entirely natural for him to
draw this inference.

    270. *confer*] 'to bring together, gather, collect; to add together' (*O.E.D.*, 1).
notes] bills or accounts (*O.E.D.*, sb.2, 15).

And though you have been insolent upon me,
I will engage no friend to kick or cudgel you,
To spoil your living and your limbs together;
I leave that to diseases that offend you   280
And spare my curse – poor silken vermin – and
Hereafter shall distinguish men from monkeys.

Bornwell. Brave soul! [*To Alexander and Littleworth*] You
brace of horse-leeches. [*To Celestina*] I have heard their
barbarous language, madam; y'are too merciful. They   285
shall be silent to your tongue; pray punish 'em.

Celestina. They are things not worth my character, nor mention of any clean breath: so lost in honesty, they cannot
satisfy for wrongs enough, though they should steal out of
the world at Tyburn.   290

Littleworth. We are hanged already.

Celestina. Yet will I talk a little to the pilchards.
You two, that have not 'twixt you both the hundredth
Part of a soul, coarse woollen-witted fellows
Without a nap, with bodies made for burdens;   295
You that are only stuffings for apparel
(As you were made but engines for your tailors
To frame their clothes upon and get them custom)
Until men see you move, yet then you dare not,

284–9.] *verse in Q, divided* heard / Their . . . mercifull, / They . . . e'm. / They
. . . mention / Of . . . honesty / They . . . enough / Though.

---

280. *diseases . . . you*] doubtless a reference to venereal disease; cf.
III.i.79–80n.

284. *horse-leeches*] literally, 'blood-suckers', but often used as a general
term of contempt; cf. Webster, *The Duchess of Malfi*, ed. Brown (1964),
I.i.52–4: 'could I be one of their flattering panders, I would hang on their ears
like a horse-leech till I were full, and then drop off'.

287. *character*] characterising (Neilson).

288. *in honesty*] i.e., where the question of honesty is concerned, in matters
of honesty; see Abbott, § 162.

290. *Tyburn*] 'the place of execution for Middlesex criminals', i.e. gallows,
located 'in the angle between Edgware Rd and Bayswater Rd' (Sugden).

292. *pilchards*] a variety of small fish, used here as a term of contempt, and
further defined indirectly by Feste in *Tw.N.*, III.i.32–4: 'fools are as like
husbands as pilchers are to herrings, the husband's the bigger'.

295. *nap*] the smooth outer surface of a textile fabric. Thus to be 'without a
nap' is to be rough and abrasive; cf. *Cor.*, II.i.223: 'The napless vesture of
humility'.

297. *engines*] mannequins (Schelling).

Out of your guilt of being the ignobler beast,   300
But give a horse the wall (whom you excel
Only in dancing of the brawl, because
The horse was not taught the French way); your two faces –
One fat like Christmas, t'other lean like Candlemas,
And prologue to a Lent – both bound together   305
Would figure Janus, and do many cures
On agues and the green disease by frighting;
But neither can, with all the characters
And conjuring circles, charm a woman (though
Sh' had fourscore years upon her and but one   310
Tooth in her head) to love or think well of you;
And I were miserable to be at cost
To court such a complexion as your malice
Did impudently insinuate. But I waste time
And stain my breath in talking to such tadpoles.   315
Go home and wash your tongues in barley-water,

---

302. brawl] *This ed.;* brawles *Q.*

---

301. *give . . . wall*] accede (to a horse) a position of precedence; i.e., the opposite of 'taking' the wall (cf. III.i.80n).

302. *brawl*] Also known as the 'branle', 'this dance derives its name from the French word "branler", to swing from side to side, since the steps of the branle go alternately from left to right. The English converted the name into "brawl", and drew false analogies therefrom' (Dolmetsch, p. 55). The reading of this ed. is based on the assumption that the plural form (*brawles*) is unidiomatic for the name of a dance when it follows the definite article, and on the observation that the compositor had plenty of trouble with terminal *s* elsewhere: see the errors in connection with 'Straddles' (I.i.203), 'come' (I.ii.18), 'bawd' (III.i.143), 'tongues' (III.i.189), and 'riches' (V.i.54).

304. *Candlemas*] Celebrated on 2 February, this feast commemorates the purification of the Virgin Mary.

307. *green disease*] a variant of 'green sickness', defined by Partridge as follows: '*Chlorosis* – an anaemic sickness of young women (with consequent greenish complexion). The Elizabethan dramatists emblemized it as a sign of a girl's love-sickness, or of vague desire, for a man.' Burton is entirely conventional in claiming that 'the Green-sickness . . . often happeneth to young women' (*Anatomy*, III.ii.3, pp. 721–2).

313. *complexion*] disposition, temperament (Onions, 2).

316. *barley-water*] 'a drink, made by the decoction of pearl barley, used as a demulcent' (*O.E.D.*). For Shirley, this drink seems to have implied restraint bordering on the ascetic; cf. *The Gamester*, III.i (*Wks*, III, 227): 'you gentlemen / Are such strange creatures, so unnatural, / So infinitely chaste, so mortified / With beef and barley-water'.

Drink clean tobacco, be not hot i'th' mouth,
And you may 'scape the beadle; so I leave you
To shame and your own garters. [*To Bornwell*] Sir, I must
Entreat you, for my honour, do not penance 'em: 320
They are not worth your anger. How shall I
Acquit your lady's silence?
Bornwell.   Madam, I
Am sorry to suspect, and dare revenge.
Celestina. No cause of mine.
Bornwell.   It must become me to
Attend you home.

321–2. How shall I . . . silence?] *Gifford;* how I shall . . . silence. *Q.*   324–5.
to / Attend you home. You] *lineation as in Harrier;* to attend you home. / You
Q.

---

317. *Drink . . . tobacco*] S. Rowlands uses the same idiom in *Humors
Ordinarie* (1603), sig. C2v: 'I here bequeath, if I doe chance to die, / To you
kinde friends, & boone companions all, / A pound of good *Tobacco*, sweet and
drie, / To drinke amongst you at my Funerall.' To *drink* tobacco is standard
seventeenth-century usage, and implies nothing more esoteric than inhaling
smoke through a pipe; see J. E. Brooks, ed., *Tobacco: Its History Illustrated by
the Books, Manuscripts and Engravings in the Library of George Arents, Jr*
(1937–52), I, 46, n. 8. The virtues of *clean* (i.e., unadulterated) tobacco are
extolled by Bobadill in *Every Man in his Humour*, III.v.82–95 (Jonson, *Wks*,
III, 355): 'Further, take it in the nature, in the true kind so, it makes an
antidote, that (had you taken the most deadly, poysonous plant in all *Italy*) it
should expell it, and clarifie you, with as much ease, as I speake. . . . I doe hold
it, and will affirme it (before any Prince in *Europe*) to be the most soveraigne,
and precious weede, that ever the earth tendred to the use of man.'
    be . . . mouth] i.e., avoid the unpleasant side-effects which Cob attributes to
'this roguish *tabacco*' in *Every Man in his Humour*, III.v.106–8 (Jonson, *Wks*,
III, 356): 'it's good for nothing, but to choke a man, and fill him full of smoke,
and embers'. Figuratively, Celestina is warning her assailants to abstain from
offensive or libellous conversation.
    318. *beadle*] an 'inferior parish officer who might punish petty offences'
(Onions).
    319. *your . . . garters*] an allusion to the surprisingly popular proverb, 'he
may go hang himself in his own garters' (Tilley, G 42). Shirley exploits this
notion in *The Ball*, III.iv (*Wks*, III, 52), and again in *The Bird in a Cage*, III.ii
(*Wks*, II, 414): 'I leave your wise signiorships to the mercy of your garters,
which is a speedy way, after a little time, to make yourselves invisible indeed.'
But none of these examples can rival Falstaff's recommendation to Prince Hal
in *1H4*, II.ii.40–1: 'Go hang thyself in thine own heir-apparent garters!'
Worn by both men and women, garters 'were bands tied usually just below
the knee' (Linthicum, p. 263).
    321–2. *How . . . silence?*] clearly a reference to Aretina; see l. 201.1n.

Celestina.   You are noble. Farewell, mushrooms.   325
                               [*Exeunt* CELESTINA *and* BORNWELL.]

                               [*Enter* ARETINA.]

Aretina. Is she gone?

Littleworth. I think we peppered her.

Alexander. I am glad 'tis over, but I repent no service for you,
          madam.

                    Enter Servant *with a letter.*

          To me? [*Examines the letter.*] From whence – a jewel. A   330
          good preface, be happy the conclusion.

Aretina. Some love letter –   *He smiles upon't.*

Littleworth. [*To Aretina*] He has a hundred mistresses. You
          may be charitable, madam; I ha' none. He surfeits, and I
          fall away i'th' kidneys.   335

Alexander. [*To Servant*] I'll meet.   [*Exit* Servant.]
          [*Aside*] 'Tis some great lady, questionless, that has taken
          notice and would satisfy her appetite.

Aretina. Now, Mr Alexander, you look bright o' the sudden;
          another spirit's in your eye.   340

Alexander. Not mine, madam; only a summons to meet a
          friend.

Aretina. What friend?

Littleworth. By this jewel, I know her not!

Aretina. 'Tis a she friend. I'll follow, gentlemen; we may have   345

327–31.] *verse in Q, divided* her. / I . . . over, / But . . . Madam. / To . ¦ .
preface, / Be.   333–5.] *verse in Q, divided* may / Be . . . none, /
He.   337–47.] *verse in Q, divided* has / Taken . . . appetite. / Now . . . sud-
daine, / Another . . . eye. / Not . . . Madam, / Onely . . . friend. / What . . .
not! / Tis . . . gentlemen, / We . . . goe. / I.   344.] *spoken by Littleworth in Q;
assigned to Alexander by Baskervill.*

---

325. *mushrooms*] contemptible upstarts; see Ford's comparable use of the
word in *The Broken Heart*, ed. Spencer (1980), IV.i.98, 'Sirrah, low mushrooms never rival cedars', and Peacham's in *The Compleat Gentleman* (1634),
sig. X*2–4: 'how may we . . . discerne and know an intruding upstart, shot up
with last nights Mushroome, from an ancient & deserved Gentleman'.

335. *fall away*] The obsolete meaning, 'to lose flesh or substance; to shrink'
(*O.E.D.*, 'fall', vb., 79e), is primary, but 'to decay, pine away, perish' (79f) is
also implied.

kidneys] here used figuratively for physical condition or constitution (see
O.E.D., 2, 2b), with sexual innuendo understood (cf.IV.ii.17n.).

a game at cent before you go.

Alexander. I shall attend you, madam.

Littleworth. 'Tis our duty.

                    [*Exeunt* ALEXANDER *and* LITTLEWORTH.]

Aretina. I blush while I converse with my own thoughts:

    Some strange fate governs me, but I must on;   350

    The ways are cast already, and we thrive

    When our sin fears no eye nor perspective.   *Exit.*

---

346. *cent*] 'a game at cards, supposed to have resembled piquet; a score of a hundred was the game' (Gosse). Often spelled 'sant' (as it is in Q), 'saunt', or even 'saint', the game was played in taverns as well as private chambers, to judge by S. Rowlands's *Humors Ordinarie* (1603), sig. E1v: 'Tut, he hath Cards for any kind of game, / *Primero, Saunt*, or what soever name.' Shirley refers to it also in *The Example*, III.i. (*Wks*, III, 319): 'If it please you, lady, / We'll pass that time at cent.'

352. *perspective*] The obsolete meaning of 'optical instrument' (*O.E.D.*, sb., 2) is doubtless intended, as it is in Webster, *The Duchess of Malfi*, ed. Brown (1964), IV.ii.356–9: 'a guilty conscience / Is . . . a perspective / That shows us hell!'

The Fourth Act.

Enter two men leading ALEXANDER,
blind[fold]ed, and go off suddenly.

Alexander. I am not hurt. My patience to obey 'em
    (Not without fear to ha' my throat cut else)
    Did me a courtesy. [*Removes blindfold.*] Whither ha' they
        brought me?
    'Tis devilish dark: the bottom of a well
    At midnight, with but two stars on the top,   5
    Were broad day to this darkness. I but think
    How like a whirlwind these rogues caught me up
    And smotherèd my eyesight; let me see,
    These may be spirits, and for aught I know
    Have brought me hither over twenty steeples.   10
    Pray heaven they were not bailiffs (that's more worth
    My fear) and this a prison; all my debts
    Reek in my nostril, and my bones begin
    To ache with fear to be made dice. And yet

0.1–2.] The action here described is reminiscent of that in Middleton's *The Witch*, M.S.R. (1950), III.i.945–6: '*Enter Duchesse, leading Almachildes (blindfold)*'. The purpose of the blindfold in Middleton is to allow the Duchess to proposition and (apparently) seduce Almachildes without revealing the truth until the final scene: 'the Woman that his blinded folly knew / was onely a hirde-Strumpet' (V.iv.2165–6). Cf. *The Alchemist*, ed. Mares (1967), III.v.15.1, where Face and Subtle prepare Dapper for his encounter with the Fairy Queen, and Jonson specifies that '*They blind him with a rag.*'

11. *bailiffs*] arresting officers; technically a bailiff is an 'officer of justice under a sheriff, who executes writs, distrains, and arrests' (Onions).

13–14. *bones . . . dice*] Since 'dice are usually made of bone or ivory' (Strutt, p. 272), Alexander's irrational fear is based on a conceivable (though unlikely) prospect.

This is too calm and quiet for a prison;   15
What if the riddle prove I am robbed? And yet
I did not feel 'em search me. [*Music sounds*] How now?
   Music!

   Enter DECOY, *like an old woman, with a light.*

And a light! What beldam's this? (I cannot pray.)
   What art?
Decoy.   A friend. Fear not, young man, I am
   No spirit.
Alexander.   Off!
Decoy.   Despise me not for age,   20
   Or this coarse outside, which I wear not out
   Of poverty; thy eyes be witness, 'tis
   No cave or beggar's cell th'art brought to. [*Gives him
      gold.*] Let
   That gold speak here's no want, which thou may'st spend
   And find a spring to tire even prodigality,   25
   If thou beest wise.
Alexander. [*Aside*]   The devil was a coiner
   From the beginning; yet the gold looks current.
Decoy. Th'art still in wonder. Know, I am mistress of
   This house, and of a fortune that shall serve
   And feed thee with delights. 'Twas I sent for thee,   30
   The jewel and the letter came from me;
   It was my art, thus to contrive our meeting,
   Because I would not trust thee with my fame
   Until I found thee worth a woman's honour.
Alexander. [*Aside*] Honour and fame? The devil means to have   35
   A care on's credit. Though she sent for me,
   I hope she has another customer

18. *beldam's*] The informal meaning of *beldam* was 'loathsome old woman,
hag' (Onions, 2).

25. *spring . . . prodigality*] a source (of money) not to be exhausted even by
lavish expenditure.

26. *coiner*] 'a maker of counterfeit coin' (*O.E.D.*, 2), but also 'a man regarded as a coin-stamper in the mint of sexual intercourse' (Partridge).

27. *current*] 'genuine, authentic' (*O.E.D.*, adj., 5) as opposed to counterfeit.
Cf. *R3*, IV.ii.8–9: 'Ah, Buckingham, now do I play the touch, / To try if thou
be current gold indeed.'

35–6. *have . . . credit*] be wary of his reputation.

37. *customer*] 'a male frequenter of brothels' (Partridge).

To do the trick withal. I would not turn
Familiar to a witch.
Decoy.   What say'st? Canst thou
Dwell in my arms tonight? shall we change kisses   40
And entertain the silent hours with pleasure,
Such as old Time shall be delighted with
And blame the too swift motion of his wings
While we embrace?
Alexander. [*Aside*]   Embrace! She has had no teeth
This twenty years, and the next violent cough   45
Brings up her tongue – it cannot possibly
Be sound at root. I do not think but one
Strong sneeze upon her, and well meant, would make
Her quarters fall away; one kick would blow
Her up like gunpowder and loose all her limbs.   50
She is so cold, an incubus would not heat her;
Her phlegm would quench a furnace, and her breath
Would damp a musket bullet.

42. Time] *Gifford;* time *Q.*

38. *To . . . withal*] with whom to perform the deed of darkness (see Abbott,
§ 196).
39. *Familiar*] attendant spirit. 'The familiar . . . is an almost exclusively
English (and Scottish) contribution to the theory of Witchcraft. . . . The
Devil, so it was held, having made a compact with the witch, gave her a low-
ranking demon in the shape of a small domestic animal to advise her and
perform small malicious errands, including murder' (Robbins).
42–3.] The allusion to the allegorical figure of Father Time is entirely conventional. As E. Panofsky observes (*Studies in Iconology*, 1939, p. 71), 'in
Renaissance and Baroque art, Father Time is generally winged and mostly
nude. To his most frequent attribute of a scythe or sickle are added, or sometimes substituted, an hourglass, a snake or dragon biting its tail, or the zodiac;
and in many cases he walks with crutches.' The wings which Time acquired in
the middle ages became a proverbial symbol for the fleeting quality of the
moment (see Tilley, T 327). In *The Grateful Servant*, II.i (Shirley, *Wks*, II,
28), Cleona expresses impatience to see her lover through a variation of the
iconographic pattern: 'Time has no feathers; he walks now on crutches.'
49. *quarters*] hindquarters (*O.E.D.*, sb., 2c).
fall away] disintegrate (see *O.E.D.*, 'fall', vb., 79f). Cf. III.ii.335n.
51. *cold*] 'sexually frigid' (Partridge).
incubus] 'a lewd demon or goblin which seeks sexual intercourse with
women' (Robbins).
52. *phlegm*] One of the four bodily fluids (or humours) believed to be responsible for governing human temperaments. According to Burton
(*Anatomy*, I.i.2.3, p. 129), '*Pituita*, or phlegm, is a cold and moist humour,

Decoy.   Have you, sir,
    Considered?
Alexander.   What?
Decoy.   My proposition:
    Canst love?
Alexander. [*Aside*] I could have done. [*To her*] Whom do
    you mean?   55
    I know you are pleased but to make sport.
Decoy.   Thou art not
    So dull of soul as thou appear'st.
Alexander. [*Aside*]   This is
    But some device; my grannam has some trick in't.
    [*To her*] Yes, I can love.
Decoy.   But canst thou affect me?
Alexander. Although to reverence so grave a matron   60
    Were an ambitious word in me, yet since
    You give me boldness, I do love you.
Decoy.   Then
    Thou art my own.
Alexander.   [*Aside*] Has she no cloven foot?
Decoy. And I am thine, and all that I command
    Thy servants; from this minute thou art happy,   65
    And fate in thee will crown all my desires.
    I grieved a proper man should be compelled
    To bring his body to the common market;
    My wealth shall make thee glorious. And the more
    To encourage thee, howe'er this form may fright   70
    Thy youthful eyes, yet thou wilt find, by light
    Of thy own sense (for other light is banished

71. wilt] *Gifford;* wo't *Q.*

---

begotten of the colder parts of the *chylus* (or white juice coming out of the
meat digested in the stomack) in the liver; his office is to nourish and moisten
the members of the body.' An abundance of this humour was believed to
produce a phlegmatic temperament, and women were said to have a greater
supply of phlegm than men.
   58. *grannam*] specifically 'grandmother', but used as a general term for 'old
woman' as well (*O.E.D.*).
   59. *affect*] 'fancy, like, or love' (*O.E.D.*, vb., 2a).
   68. *common market*] i.e., flesh-market.
   69. *glorious*] splendid; see I.i.273n.
   72. *sense*] '(one's) sensual nature, sexual desire' (Onions, 2).

My chamber) when our arms tie lovers' knots
And kisses seal the welcome of our lips,
I shall not there affright thee, nor seem old,   75
With rivelled veins – my skin is smooth and soft
As ermine's, with a spirit to meet thine,
Active and equal to the queen of love's
When she did court Adonis.

Alexander.   [*Aside*] This doth more
Confirm she is a devil, and I am   80
Within his own dominions. I must on,
Or else be torn a-pieces; I have heard
These succubi must not be crossed.

Decoy.   We trifle
Too precious time away. I'll show you a prospect
Of the next chamber, and then out the candle.   85

Alexander. Have you no sack i'th' house? I would go armed
Upon this breach.

Decoy.   It sha' not need.

Alexander.   One word,
Mother: have not you been a cat in your days?

Decoy. I am glad you are so merry, sir. You observe
That bed?

---

77. ermine's] *This ed.; Ermines Q;* ermines *Gifford.*

---

76. *rivelled*] 'shrunken, shrivelled' (*O.E.D.*, 2).

77. *ermine's*] i.e., 'the fur of the ermine, often having the black tails (formerly pieces of black lamb's-wool) arranged upon it, at regular intervals, for the sake of effect. The whiteness of ermine is often referred to in poetry as an emblem of purity' (*O.E.D.*, sb., 2).

78–9. *queen . . . Adonis*] an allusion to the legend most popularly known through Shakespeare's *Venus and Adonis*, in which the goddess of love comes indelicately near to seducing the beautiful young fertility god.

83. *succubi*] 'A devil in female form, the succubus specializes in seducing men. Although feminine in meaning, in form this medieval Latin word, *succubus*, is masculine' (Robbins); hence the pl., *succubi*.

88. *cat*] Witches were believed to be capable of transforming themselves into cats (or other animals) and back again. R. Scot, in *The Discoverie of Witchcraft* (1584), sig. H6–6v, refutes J. Bodin's formulation of this belief: 'Item, he saith, that diverse witches at *Vernon*, turned themselves into cats, and both committed and received much hurt. . . . Whie witches are turned into cats, he alledgeth no reason, and therefore (to helpe him foorth with that paraphrase) I saie, that witches are curst queanes, and manie times scratch one another, or their neighbours by the faces; and therefore perchance are turned into cats.'

Alexander.   A very brave one.
Decoy.   When you are   90
    Disrobed, you can come thither in the dark.
    You sha' not stay for me; come as you wish
    For happiness.   *Exit.*
Alexander.   I am preferred. If I
    Be modest and obey, she cannot have
    The heart to do me harm, and she were Hecate   95
    Herself. I will have a strong faith, and think
    I march upon a mistress the less evil.
    If I 'scape fire now, I defy the devil.   *Exit.*

ACT IV, SCENE ii

Enter FRED[ERICK], LITTLEW[ORTH], Steward.

Frederick. And how d'ee like me now?
Steward.   Most excellent.
Frederick. Your opinion, Mr Littleworth?
Littleworth.   Your French tailor
    Has made you a perfect gentleman; I may
    Converse now with you, and preserve my credit.
    D'ee find no alteration in your body   5
    With these new clothes?
Frederick.   My body altered? No.
Littleworth. You are not yet in fashion, then: that must

93. preferred. If] *Knowland subst.;* preferd, if *Q.*   97. mistress the] *Know-land.;* Mistris, the *Q.*

90. *brave*] splendid; cf. IV.ii.143n.
95. *and*] if (Abbott, § 101).
Hecate] Jonson glosses this traditional name, in a marginal note to *The Masque of Queens* (*Wks*, VII, 295), as follows: 'Shee was beleev'd to governe, in witchcraft; and is remembered in all theyr invocations.' Similarly, in the *dramatis personae* prefixed to *The Witch*, M.S.R. (1950), Middleton describes '*Heccat*' as the '*cheif Witch*'.
2. *French tailor*] During the reign of Charles I, French sartorial tastes were much admired by the English gentry. In *The Witty Fair One*, II.i (Shirley, *Wks*, I, 295), Sir Nicholas Treedle's Tutor observes that travelling to France is unnecessary because 'all the French fashions are here already, or rather your French cuts'. He then praises the cut of the periwig, the doublet and the leg, which English gentlemen have borrowed from France.

Have a new motion, garb, and posture too,
Or all your pride is cast away; it is not
The cut of your apparel makes a gallant,   10
But the geometrical wearing of your clothes.
Steward. Mr Littleworth tells you right; you wear your hat
    Too like a citizen.
Littleworth.   'Tis like a midwife.
    [*Rearranges Frederick's costume.*] Place it with best
        advantage of your hair;
    Is half your feather moulted? This does make   15
    No show: it should spread over like a canopy;
    Your hot-reined monsieur wears it for a shade
    And cooler to his back. Your doublet must
    Be more unbuttoned hereabouts; you'll not

---

8. *motion*] 'movement of the body acquired by drill and training' (Onions, sb., 3). The word implies formal movement, as in fencing; cf. *Ham.*, IV.vii.99–101: 'The scrimers of their nation / He swore had neither motion, guard, nor eye, / If you opposed them.'

    garb] 'style, manner, fashion' (Onions). *Garb* does not mean simply 'apparel', as is evident from the present context and from Massinger's *The Guardian*, II.v.14–21 (*Plays*, IV, 146): 'Why sir, do Gallants travel? . . . to discourse of / The garb and difference in foreign Females, / As the lusty Girle of *France*, the sober *German*, / The plump *Dutch* Fro . . . The merry *Greek*, *Venetian* Courtesan.'

11. *geometrical*] stylishly precise; in this sense, not in *O.E.D.*

12–13. *you . . . citizen*] Frederick has doubtless been supplied with a large, broad-brimmed velvet hat in the Cavalier style, suitably trimmed with an ostrich feather. The Steward points out that he wears the brim unfashionably flat, as a Puritan would wear his sugarloaf hat. A gentleman of fashion in 1635 would wear the brim cocked. See C. and P. Cunnington, *Handbook of English Costume in the Seventeenth Century*, 2nd ed. (1966), pp. 65–9.

13. *'Tis . . . midwife*] i.e., laughably unfasionable.

15. *feather*] See ll. 12–13n.

17. *hot-reined*] lustful; cf. Marston, *The Malcontent*, ed. Hunter (1975), I.v.7: 'Ah, you whoreson, hot-reined he-marmoset!' Though in a strict medical sense the 'reins' were kidneys, the term was used informally as a synonym for 'loins' (*O.E.D.*, 1–2).

18. *Your doublet*] Frederick's black satin doublet (see II.i.44n.) has been discarded in favour of a more colourful garment. As Linthicum observes, p. 199, there was 'great . . . variety in shape, trimming, and sleeve design' of doublets; indeed, the 'material for the outside, the lining, the lace, the pattern of embroidery or pinking, and the elaborately wrought buttons, all required planning; and the cost of six pounds for a single doublet was not unusual'.

19. *unbuttoned hereabouts*] Normally, 'the doublet was fastened up the front to the top of the collar, sometimes with buttons, sometimes with hooks and

Be a sloven else. A foul shirt is no blemish;   20
You must be confident and outface clean linen!
Your doublet and your breeches must be allowed
No private meeting here. Your cloak's too long;
It reaches to your buttock, and doth smell
Too much of Spanish gravity. The fashion   25
Is to wear nothing but a cape; a coat
May be allowed a covering for one elbow,
And some (to avoid the trouble) choose to walk
In cuerpo, thus.
Steward.   Your coat and cloak's a-brushing
In Long-lane Lombard.

29. cuerpo] *Spencer;* quirpo *Q.*

---

eyes' (Linthicum, p. 198). But, as C. and P. Cunnington point out (*Handbook of English Costume in the Seventeenth Century*, 2nd ed., 1966, p. 20), it became fashionable around 1635 to wear the doublet 'left open from chest level' downward, for the purpose of 'exposing an elegant shirt'. The affected care-lessness recommended by Littleworth is the masculine equivalent of 'sweet disorder'. The image of the melancholy lover (cf. 'Lord Hamlet, with his doublet all unbraced', *Ham.*, II.i.78) has been tamed and incorporated into the world of Cavalier fashion.

   20. *foul*] soiled.

   shirt] a garment made of linen and silk, often trimmed with embroidery (Linthicum, p. 213), and worn underneath the doublet.

   22-3. *Your . . . here*] Littleworth is an expert at following the fashion; 1635 is a very early date for the appearance of what C. and P. Cunnington (*Handbook of English Costume in the Seventeenth Century*, 2nd ed., 1966, p. 22) designate as the '*skimpy doublet*', which 'was usually so short that between doublet and breeches a gap was seen bridged by the protruding shirt. In such case the breeches hung from the hips.'

   23-5. *Your . . . gravity*] Apparently Frederick's cloak resembles the out-moded Spanish style, which called for 'a hooded cloak of hip-length whose circular edge was ornamented by lace, or guards of taffeta, velvet, and other silk' (Linthicum, p. 193). Littleworth, finding this garment out of keeping with the rest of Frederick's costume, discards it, perhaps by giving it to the Steward at l. 29.

   25-9. *The fashion . . . thus*] After 1620, according to Linthicum, p. 195, 'men altered the fashion slightly, wearing the cloak in a variety of ways: hang-ing from the shoulder, wrapped across the chest or back with the right-hand corner flung over the left shoulder – never on straight, with the arms in the sleeves!' During his speech, Littleworth is busily demonstrating these and similar alternatives, after which he apparently gives Frederick's coat and cloak to the Steward.

   28-9. *walk . . . cuerpo*] 'stripped of the upper garment' (Gosse). In J. Minsheu's *The Guide into Tongues* (1617), sig. 3B6v, the phrase *andar en cuerpo* is Englished as 'to goe in hose and doublet without a cloake'.

Frederick.   But what if it rain?   30
Littleworth. Your belt about your shoulder is sufficient
    To keep off any storm; beside, a reed
    But waved discreetly has so many pores
    It sucks up all the rain that falls about one.
    With this defence, when other men have been   35
    Wet to the skin through all their cloaks, I have
    Defied a tempest and walked by the taverns
    Dry as a bone.
Steward.   [*Aside*] Because he had no money
    To call for wine.
Frederick.   Why, you do walk enchanted.
    Have you such pretty charms in town? But stay,   40
    Who must I have to attend me?
Littleworth.   Is not that
    Yet thought upon?
Steward.   I have laid out for servants.
Littleworth. They are everywhere.
Steward.   I cannot yet be furnished
    With such as I would put into his hands.
Frederick. Of what condition must they be, and how   45
    Many in number, sir?
Littleworth.   Beside your fencing,
    Your singing, dancing, riding, and French master,
    Two may serve domestic to be constant waiters
    Upon a gentleman: a fool, a pimp.
Steward. For these two officers I have enquired,   50

39. you do] *Q subst.;* do you *Gifford.*

---

30. *Long-lane Lombard*] Long Lane, a street north of the city wall connecting West Smithfield (the scene of Bartholomew Fair) and Aldersgate Street, 'was chiefly occupied by pawnbrokers and old-clothes dealers'. Sugden, citing this example, points out that 'Lombard means pawnship' in the present context; *O.E.D.* offers confirmation.

31. *belt . . . shoulder*] According to C. and P. Cunnington (*Handbook of English Costume in the Seventeenth Century*, 2nd ed., 1966, p. 22), 'a shoulder belt or baldrick for the sword' became a popular costume accessory after 1630.

32. *reed*] i.e., a cane or walking stick (*O.E.D.*). Gifford may well be right in describing the lines which follow as 'a pleasant description of what our old dramatists call a Plymouth *cloak*', a term defined in *O.E.D.* as obsolete slang for 'a cudgel or staff, carried by one who walked *in cuerpo*, and thus facetiously assumed to take the place of a cloak'.

42. *laid out*] 'been on the lookout' (Baskervill).

50. *officers*] household servants (Onions, 2); cf. III.i.41n.

And I am promised a convenient whiskin.
I could save charges and employ the pie-wench
That carries her intelligence in whitepots;
Or, 'tis but taking order with the woman
That holds the ballads: she could fit him with   55
A concubine to any tune. But I
Have a design to place a fellow with him
That has read all Sir Pandarus' works: a Trojan
That lies concealed and is acquainted with
Both city and suburban fripperies;   60
Can fetch 'em with a spell at midnight to him,
And warrant which are for his turn; can for
A need supply the surgeon, too.

Frederick.   I like
Thy providence: such a one deserves
A livery twice a year.

Steward.   It sha' not   65
Need: a cast suit of your worship's will serve;
He'll find a cloak to cover it out of
His share with those he brings to bed to you.

Frederick. But must I call this fellow pimp?

---

55. holds] *Q;* trolls *conj. Gifford.*   64–8. deserves / A . . . sha'not / Need . . .
serve; / He'll . . . of / His] *lineation of this ed.;* yeare. / It . . . worships / Will
. . . it / Out *Q.*

---

51. *whiskin*] obsolete slang for pander (*O.E.D.*).

52–3. *pie-wench . . . whitepots*] 'the girl who sells pies, who, when acting as a
go-between, would conceal messages in the custard' (Papousek).

54–5. *woman . . . ballads*] presumably a female counterpart of Autolycus,
who offers ballads for sale in *Wint.*, IV.iv.257–85, on such subjects as the
plight of the usurer's wife and the miraculous appearance of a fish.

58. *Sir Pandarus' works*] Pandarus owes his reputation as the archetypal go-
between to Chaucer's depiction of him in *Troilus and Criseyde*. Since he is not
an author, his *works* are his deeds and pandering. Cf. Shakespeare, *Troil.*,
III.ii.191–4: 'since I have taken such pains to bring you together, let all pitiful
goers-between be called to the world's end after my name; call them all
Pandars'.

Trojan] 'cant term for "boon companion, dissolute fellow"' (Onions).

60. *fripperies*] showily dressed persons (*O.E.D.*, 2b), in this case
prostitutes.

63. *A need*] The need in question is doubtless treatment for venereal disease. Cf. II.ii.236n.

64. *providence*] foresight (Neilson).

Littleworth.   It is

   Not necessary: or Jack, or Harry,   70
   Or what he's known abroad by will sound better,
   That men may think he is a Christian.

Frederick. But, hear you Mr Littleworth, is there not
   A method, and degrees of title, in
   Men of this art?

Littleworth.   According to the honour   75
   Of men that do employ 'em. An emperor
   May give this office to a duke, a king
   May have his viceroy to negotiate for him,
   A duke may use a lord, the lord a knight,
   A knight may trust a gentleman; and, when   80
   They are abroad and merry, gentlemen
   May pimp to one another.

Frederick.   Good, good fellowship!
   But for the fool now, that should wait on me
   And break me jests.

Littleworth.   A fool is necessary.

Steward. By any means.

Frederick.   But which of these two servants   85
   Must now take place?

Littleworth.   That question, Mr Frederick,
   The school of heraldry should conclude upon.
   But if my judgement may be heard, the fool
   Is your first man, and it is known a point
   Of state to have a fool.

Steward.   But sir, the other   90
   Is held the finer servant: his employments
   Are full of trust, his person clean and nimble,
   And none so soon can leap into preferment,
   Where fools are poor.

Littleworth.   Not all. There's story for't:
   Princes have been no wiser than they should be;   95

---

70. *or . . . or*] either . . . or.
84. *break . . . jests*] crack jokes for my amusement; see Onions, 'break', 2.
85. *any*] all.
86. *take place*] take precedence over, or go before (*O.E.D.*, 'place', sb., 27c).
87. *school . . . heralrdy*] i.e., the College of Arms (Heralds' College).
94. *Where*] whereas.
story] example, precedent.

Would any nobleman that were no fool
Spend all in hope of the philosopher's stone,
To buy new lordships in another country?
Would knights build colleges? or gentlemen
Of good estates challenge the field and fight   100
Because a whore wo' not be honest? Come,
Fools are a family over all the world.
We do affect one naturally; indeed,
The fool is leiger with us.
Steward.   Then the pimp.
Is extraordinary.
Frederick.   Do not you fall out   105
About their places.

Enter ARETINA.

Here's my noble aunt.
Littleworth. How do you like your nephew, madam, now?
Aretina. Well. Turn about, Frederick. Very well.
Frederick. Am I not now a proper gentleman?
The virtue of rich clothes! Now could I take   110
The wall of Julius Caesar, affront

109. S.H. *Frederick.*] *Con. MS subst., Gifford; Are. Q.*

---

97. *philosopher's stone*] the cherished goal of alchemical experiment, aptly
characterised by Face in *The Alchemist*, ed. Mares (1967), II.v.40–44: "'Tis a
stone, and not / A stone; a spirit, a soul, and a body: / Which if you do dissolve,
it is dissolv'd, / If you coagulate, it is coagulated, / If you make it fly, it flieth.'

102.] A delightful variation of the proverb, 'The world is full of fools'
(Tilley, W 897). The Latin original, 'Stultorum plena sunt omnia', is from
Cicero's *Epistulae ad Familiares*, ix.22 (Cicero, *The Letters to his Friends*,
Loeb Classical Library, 1927–9, II, 270); it is quoted by Marston in *The
Scourge of Villanie* (*The Poems of John Marston*, ed. Davenport, 1961, p. 163)
and again in *The Malcontent*, ed. Hunter (1975), V.iii.44–5.

103. *affect*] 'assume the character of, imitate' (Onions, vb.1, 4).

104. *leiger*] one of many permissible spellings of an obsolete term meaning
'permanently resident' or 'constantly in use'; see *O.E.D.*, 'ledger', adj., 2.
Shirley uses the word also as a synonym for 'resident ambassador' in *The
Humorous Courtier*, II.ii. (*Wks*, IV, 557): 'She did you public grace this morning too / Before the French leiger.' Cf. Webster, *The White Devil*, ed. Brown
(1960), III.i.1–2: 'You have dealt discreetly to obtain the presence / Of all the
grave lieger ambassadors.'

110–11. *take . . . wall*] See III.i.8on.

111–12. *affront . . . lip*] i.e., insult Pompey the Great to his face. This
metaphor may be a gentler variations of the idiom in which one hurls a chal-

Great Pompey's upper lip, and defy the senate;
Nay, I can be as proud as your own heart, madam:
You may take that for your comfort. I put on
That virtue with my clothes, and I doubt not   115
But in a little time I shall be impudent
As any page or player's boy. I am
Beholding to this gentleman's good discipline,
But I shall do him credit in my practice.
Your steward has some pretty notions, too,   120
In moral mischief.

Aretina.   Your desert in this
Exceeds all other service, and shall bind me
Both to acknowledge and reward.

Littleworth.   Sweet madam!
Think me but worth your favour, I would creep
Upon my knees to honour you, and for every   125
Minute you lend to my reward, I'll pay
A year of serviceable tribute.

Aretina.   You
Can compliment.

Littleworth.   [*Aside*] Thus still she puts me off.
Unless I speak the downright word, she'll never
Understand me; a man would think that creeping   130
Upon one's knees were English to a lady.

Enter ALEXANDER.

Alexander. How is't, Jack? Pleasures attend you, madam; how
does my plant of honour?

Aretina. Who is this?

132–43.] *verse in Q, divided* Madam, / How . . . this? / Tis . . . glorious! / Tis
. . . Bucephalus / Waites . . . sir. / I . . . it, / Tis . . . plough / That.

---

lenge in an enemy's teeth; cf. Shakespeare, *1H4*, V.ii.41–2: 'I have thrown / A
brave defiance in King Henry's teeth.' The reckless nature of Frederick's
boast is based in part on Pompey's reputation as a man 'who could not abide to
be ill spoken of'; see Plutarch's *Lives of the Noble Grecians and Romains*, tr.
North, 5th ed. (1631), sig. 3L2.

117. *player's boy*] i.e., apprentice actor.
124. *Think me*] if you think me.
131. *English*] i.e., nothing in excess of normal usage.
133. *plant*] 'scion, offshoot, nurseling; a young person; a novice' (*O.E.D.*,
sb.1, 1c). Alexander is referring to Frederick, for whose social education he
accepted responsibility in II.i.88–94.

Alexander. 'Tis Alexander.   135

Aretina. Rich and glorious!

Littleworth. 'Tis Alexander the Great.

Alexander. And my Bucephalus waits at the door.

Aretina. Your case is altered, sir.

Alexander. I cannot help these things; the fates will have it.   140
    'Tis not my land does this.

Littleworth. [*Aside*] But thou hast a plough that brings it in.

Aretina. [*Aside*] Now he looks brave and lovely.

Frederick. Welcome, my gallant Macedonian.

Alexander. Madam, you gave your nephew for my pupil. I read   145
    but in a tavern: if you'll honour us, the Bear at the Bridge-
    foot shall entertain you. A drawer is my Ganymede: he

145–73.] *verse in Q, divided* pupill, / I . . . us, / The . . . you, / A . . . skinke /
Briske . . . have / A . . . Phesants, / Quailes . . . up / Like . . . Sturgeon / Shall
. . . army, / And . . . will / But . . . mine / Must . . . may / Be . . . Ladies, /
When . . . you; / Come . . . noise, / We . . . boy. / Madam . . . thinke / Of . . .
fraile, / And . . . helpe. / A . . . or / You . . . I / Have . . . coole. / But . . .
charitie / Can . . . cold / Of . . . dare / Be . . . confident / He . . . mad / To.

---

136. *glorious*] splendid; see I.i.270n.

138. *Bucephalus*] the favourite horse of Alexander the Great.

139.] See II.i.121n.

142. *a plough*] The sexual meaning is inescapable, especially if this passage
is compared with its counterparts in Shakespeare; cf. *Ant.*, II.ii.228–9: 'She
made great Caesar lay his sword to bed; / He ploughed her, and she cropped.'

143. *brave*] 'finely arrayed', excellent, attractive (Onions). Cf. Herrick,
'Upon Julia's Clothes', *Poems*, ed. Martin (1965), p. 261: 'Next, when I cast
mine eyes and see / That brave Vibration each way free; / O how that glittering
taketh me!'

144. *Macedonian*] native of Macedonia, the birthplace of Alexander the
Great. Frederick is picking up the mock-heroic tone initiated by Littleworth
at l. 137.

145. *read*] elliptical for 'read lessons (or lectures)', i.e., 'give instruction'
(Onions).

146–7. *Bear . . . Bridge-foot*] The Bear was 'a very well-known tavern'
located at 'the Southwark end' of London Bridge (Sugden). Cf. *Epicoene*,
II.v.112–15 (Jonson, *Wks*, V, 195): 'and when one of the foure-score hath
brought it knighthood ten shillings, it knighthood shall go to the Cranes, or
the Beare at the *Bridge*-foot, and be drunk in feare'.

147. *A . . . Ganymede*] i.e., one of the tapsters is my personal cup-bearer. In
Greek mythology, Ganymede is a beautiful youth who is abducted by the
gods and pressed into service as cup-bearer to Zeus. His name was often used
as a synonym for 'homosexual minion'; cf. *Edward II*, I.iv.180–1 (Marlowe,
Plays, p. 296): 'For never doted Jove on Ganymede / So much as he on cursed
Gaveston'.

shall skink brisk nectar to us; we will only have a dozen
partridge in a dish; as many pheasants, quails, cocks, and
godwits shall come marching up like the trained band; a   150
fort of sturgeon shall give most bold defiance to an army,
and triumph o'er the table.

Aretina. Sir, it will but dull the appetite to hear more, and mine
must be excused; another time I may be your guest.

Alexander. 'Tis grown in fashion now with ladies; when you   155
please, I'll attend you.   [*Exit.*]

Littleworth. Come, Frederick.

Frederick. We'll have music; I love noise! We will outroar the
Thames and shake the bridge, boy.

                              Ex[*eunt* FREDERICK *and* Steward].

Littleworth. Madam, I kiss your hand. Would you would   160
think of your poor servant; flesh and blood is frail, and
troublesome to carry without help.

Aretina. A coach will easily convey it, or you may take water at
Strand bridge.

Littleworth. But I have taken fire.   165

Aretina. The Thames will cool –

Littleworth. But never quench my heart; your charity can only
do that!

Aretina. I will keep it cold, of purpose.

---

157. *Littleworth.*] *This ed.; name and l. 157 spoken by Alexander in previous
edd.; Littleworth | Come Fredericke. Q.*   166. cool –] *Baskervill;* coole. *Q.*

---

148. *skink*] 'to pour out or draw (liquor)' (*O.E.D.*, citing this example).

brisk] 'agreeably acid' (Onions, 3). Cf. *2H4*, V.iii.44: 'A cup of wine that's
brisk and fine'.

nectar] the drink of the gods; i.e., wine.

150. *godwits*] 'marsh birds hunted as game, and prized for their delicate
flavor' (Papousek).

trained band] city militia (Neilson).

151. *fort . . . sturgeon*] 'a sturgeon-pasty' (Schelling).

157.S.H.] Q is clearly wrong in printing *Littleworth* at the end of the previous line. Indeed, the casual confusion of S.H. and dialogue here is the best
single example of the kinds of liberties the compositor took with the manuscript in setting up Q. For further discussion, see Introduction, pp. 38–9.

163. *take water*] embark on a journey by boat.

164. *Strand bridge*] landing-place on the bank of the Thames at the foot of
Strand Lane, between Somerset House and Arundel House (Sugden, citing
only this example).

Littleworth. Now you bless me, and I dare be drunk in   170
  expectation.   [*Exit.*]
Aretina. I am confident he knows me not, and I were worse
  than mad to be my own betrayer.

                    Enter BORN[WELL].

  Here's my husband.
Bornwell. Why, how now Aretina? What, alone?   175
  The mystery of this solitude? my house
  Turn desert o' the sudden? all the gamesters
  Blown up? Why is the music put to silence?
  Or ha' their instruments caught a cold, since we
  Gave 'em the last heat? I must know thy ground   180
  Of melancholy.
Aretina.   You are merry, as
  You came from kissing Celestina.
Bornwell.   I
  Feel her yet warm upon my lip. She is
  Most excellent company: I did not think
  There was that sweetness in her sex. I must   185
  Acknowledge 'twas thy cure to disenchant me
  From a dull husband to an active lover.
  With such a lady, I could spend more years
  Than since my birth my glass hath run soft minutes,
  And yet be young; her presence has a spell   190
  To keep off age, she has an eye would strike
  Fire through an adamant.

---

178. *Blown up*] apparently gambling parlance for 'ruined, devastated', though this sense is not in *O.E.D.* Jonson uses the same phrase in *The Magnetic Lady*, III.vi.133–5 (*Wks*, VI, 560), where 'Narrownesse of mind' is attributed to 'Gamesters, quite blown up'. See also *The Alchemist*, ed. Mares (1967), I.ii.77–9: 'He'll win up all the money i' the town . . . And blow up gamester after gamester, / As they do crackers in a puppet-play.' The comment by Mares is instructive: 'The sense is clear, though the image may seem odd to a modern reader. As an image of the violent reversal of expectations it is thematic to the play, and is physically presented in the explosion of the furnace at IV.v.55.'

192. *adamant*] 'an alleged rock or mineral, as to which vague, contradictory, and fabulous notions long prevailed. The properties ascribed to it show a confusion of ideas between the diamond (or other hard gems) and the loadstone or magnet' (*O.E.D.*). Cf. Chapman, *Bussy D'Ambois*, ed. Brooke (1964), III.ii.213–14: 'if my heart were not hooped with adamant, the conceit of this would have burst it'.

Aretina.   I have heard as much
    Bestowed upon a dull-faced chambermaid
    Whom love and wit would thus commend. True beauty
    Is mocked when we compare thus, itself being   195
    Above what can be fetched to make it lovely.
    Or, could our thoughts reach something to declare
    The glories of a face or body's elegance –
    That touches but our sense; when beauty spreads
    Over the soul, it calls up understanding   200
    To look what thence is offered, and admire.
    In both I must acknowledge Celestina
    Most excellently fair – fair above all
    The beauties I ha' seen, and one most worthy
    Man's love and wonder.
Bornwell.   Do you speak, Aretina,   205
    This with a pure sense to commend, or is't
    The mockery of my praise?
Aretina.   Although it shame
    Myself, I must be just and give her all
    The excellency of women; and were I
    A man –
Bornwell.   What then?
Aretina.   I know not with what loss   210
    I should attempt her love. She is a piece
    So angelically moving, I should think
    Frailty excused to dote upon her form,
    And almost virtue to be wicked with her.   *Exit.*
Bornwell. What should this mean? This is no jealousy,   215
    Or she believes I counterfeit. I feel
    Something within me (like a heat) to give

200. it] *This ed.;* and *Q.*   201. what] *Con. MS, conj. Gifford;* when *Q.*

---

    195. *compare thus*] i.e., make such comparisons.
    196. *what . . . fetched*] the imagery which can be invented (i.e., far-fetched
metaphors). Cf. *H5*, II.ii.114–17: 'All other devils that suggest by treasons /
Do botch and bungle up damnation / . . . with forms being fetched / From
glist'ring semblances of piety.'
    211. *piece*] See III.i.151n.
    212–14. *I . . . her*] The rhetorical strategy of this passage is similar to that in
Ford's *'Tis Pity*, ed. Roper (1975), I.ii.202–3: 'Such lips would tempt a saint;
such hands as those / Would make an anchorite lascivious.'

Her cause, would Celestina but consent.
What a frail thing is man: it is not worth
Our glory to be chaste. While we deny   220
Mirth and converse with women, he is good
That dares the tempter, yet corrects his blood.   *Exit.*

ACT IV, SCENE iii

[Enter] CELESTINA, MARIANA, ISABELLA.

Celestina. I have told you all my knowledge. Since he is pleased
to invite himself, he shall be entertained, and you shall be
my witnesses.
Mariana. Who comes with him?
Celestina. Sir William Sentlove, that prepared me for the   5
honourable encounter. I expect his lordship every
minute.

Enter SENTLOVE.

Sentlove. My lord is come.
Celestina. He has honoured me.

Enter Lord, HAIRCUT.

Sentlove. My lord, your periwig is awry.   10
Lord. [*To Haircut*] You, sir.   *While Haircut is busy about his
                                    hair, Sentlove goes to Celestina.*
Sentlove. You may guess at the gentleman that's with him: it is

220. chaste. While] *This ed.;* chaste, while *Q.*   221. women, he] *Q;* women.
He *Gifford.*   *1–6.*] *verse in Q, divided* pleasd / To . . . entertaind, / And . . .
him. / Sir . . . for / The . . . expect / His.   *9–10.*] *one line of verse in
Q.*   12–18.] *verse in Q, divided* him. / It . . . observe / And . . . sir, / I . . .
may / Have . . . reveng'd / She . . . confesse, / But.

220–21.] The punctuation of Q probably represents the compositor's attempt to make sense of inadequately (or very sparsely) punctuated manuscript copy. For further discussion, see Introduction, p. 39.
221. *converse*] here used as a noun, meaning 'intercourse, (hence) conversation' (Onions).
222. *corrects . . . blood*] restrains his desire.
11.1–2.] Haircut's obsequious attention to his patron's appearance prevents him from noticing that Celestina is present.
13. *and*] if.

his barber, madam; d'ee observe and your ladyship want a
shaver.

Haircut. [*To Lord*] She is here, sir. [*Aside*] I am betrayed.   15
  Sentlove, your plot! I may have opportunity to be revenged.

                                                   Exit.

Sentlove. [*To Lord*] She in the midst.

Lord. She's fair, I must confess; but does she keep this distance
  out of state?

Celestina. [*To Lord*] Though I am poor in language to express   20
  How much your lordship honours me, my heart
  Is rich and proud in such a guest. I shall
  Be out of love with every air abroad,
  And for this grace done my unworthy house,
  Be a fond prisoner, become anchorite,   25
  And spend my hours in prayer to reward
  The blessing and the bounty of this presence.

Lord. Though you could turn each place you move in to
  A temple, rather than a wall should hide
  So rich a beauty from the world, it were   30
  Less want to lose our piety and your prayer;
  A throne were fitter to present you to
  Our wonder, whence your eyes (more worth than all
  They look on) should chain every heart a prisoner.

Sentlove. [*Aside*] 'Twas pretty well come off.

Lord.   By your example   35
  I shall know how to compliment; [*Kisses her.*] in this
  You more confirm my welcome.

Celestina.   I shall love
  My lips the better if their silent language
  Persuade your lordship but to think so truly.

Lord. You make me smile, madam.

Celestina.   I hope you came not   40
  With fear that any sadness here should shake
  One blossom from your eye; I should be miserable
  To present any object should displease you.

Lord. You do not, madam.

24. this] *Con. Ms, Gifford;* his *Q.*

---

  14. *shaver*] a pun which doubles the insult by combining the literal meaning
(barber) and the secondary sense of 'a humorous fellow, joker, wag' (*O.E.D.*,
1–3).

  19. *state*] 'social protocol' (Harrier).

Celestina.   As I should account
　　It no less sorrow if your lordship should   45
　　Lay too severe a censure on my freedom.
　　I wo' not court a prince against his justice,
　　Nor bribe him with a smile to think me honest.
　　Pardon, my lord, this boldness and the mirth
　　That may flow from me; I believe my father   50
　　Thought of no winding sheet when he begot me.
Lord. [*Aside*] She has a merry soul. It will become
　　Me ask your pardon, madam, for my rude
　　Approach – so much a stranger to your knowledge.
Celestina. Not, my lord, so much stranger to my knowledge;   55
　　Though I have but seen your person a far off,
　　I am acquainted with your character,
　　Which I have heard so often I can speak it.
Lord. You shall do me an honour.
Celestina.   If your lordship
　　Will be patient.
Lord.   And glad to hear my faults.   60
Celestina. That's as your conscience can agree upon 'em;
　　However, if your lordship give me privilege,
　　I'll tell you what's the opinion of the world.
Lord. You cannot please me better.
Celestina.   Y'are a lord
　　Born with as much nobility as would,   65
　　Divided, serve to make ten noblemen
　　Without a herald; but with so much spirit
　　And height of soul as well might furnish twenty.
　　You are learned (a thing not compatible now
　　With native honour) and are master of   70
　　A language that doth chain all ears and charm

59–60. lordship / Will be] *lineation of this ed.;* Lordship will / Be *Q.*   61.
That's] *This ed.;* That *Q.*   71. ears] *Gifford;* yeares *Q.*

---

67. *herald*] i.e., a member of the Heralds' College with authority to grant
arms.
69–70. *You . . . honour*] Ideally, learning and honour go hand in hand; see
Peacham, *The Compleat Gentleman* (1634), sig. C1v: 'Since Learning then is
an essential part of Nobilitie, as unto which wee are beholden, for whatsoever
dependeth on the culture of the minde; it followeth, that who is nobly borne,
and a Scholler withall, deserveth double Honour.' Cf. II.i.31–4.

All hearts where you persuade; a wit so flowing,
And prudence to correct it, that all men
Believe they only meet in you; which, with
A spacious memory, make up the full wonders.   75
To these, you have known valour, and upon
A noble cause know how to use a sword
To honour's best advantage, though you wear none;
You are as bountiful as the showers that fall
Into the spring's green bosom (as you were   80
Created lord of fortune, not her steward);
So constant to the cause in which you make
Yourself an advocate, you dare all dangers,
And men had rather you should be their friend
Than justice or the bench bound up together.   85

Lord. But did you hear all this?

Celestina.   And more, my lord.

Lord. Pray, let me have it, madam.

Celestina. To all these virtues, there is added one
    (Your lordship will remember when I name it,
    I speak but what I gather from the voice   90
    Of others); it is grown to a full fame
    That you have loved a woman.

Lord.   But one, madam?

Celestina. Yes, many. Give me leave to smile, my lord;
    I shall not need to interpret in what sense.
    But you have showed yourself right honourable,   95
    And for your love to ladies have deserved
    (If their vote might prevail) a marble statue.
    I make no comment on the people's text.
    My lord, I should be sorry to offend.

Lord. You cannot, madam; these are things we owe   100
    To nature for.

Celestina.   And honest men will pay
    Their debts.

76. known] *Q subst.;* join'd *conj. Gifford;* showne *conj. Harrier.*   78. wear]
Gifford; were *Q.*

72. *wit*] A word of much broader significance in the seventeenth century
than today, *wit* is used here in the sense of 'imagination' (Onions, 2).
    98.] I will not be so tactless as to divulge the inscription which popular
opinion would affix to the statue in your honour.

Lord.   If they be able, or compound.

Celestina. She had a hard heart, would be unmerciful,
         And not give day to men so promising;
         But you owed women nothing.

Lord.   Yes, I am   105
         Still in their debt, and I must owe them love:
         It was part of my character.

Celestina.   With your lordship's
         Pardon, I only said you had a fame
         For loving women, but of late men say
         You have against the imperial laws of love   110
         Restrained the active flowings of your blood,
         And with a mistress buried all that is
         Hoped for in love's succession – as all beauty
         Had died with her and left the world benighted!
         In this you more dishonour all our sex   115
         Than you did grace a part, when everywhere
         Love tempts your eye to admire a glorious harvest,
         And everywhere, as full blown ears submit
         Their golden heads, the laden trees bow down
         Their willing fruit and court your amorous tasting.   120

Lord. I see men would dissect me to a fibre;
         But do you believe this?

Celestina.   It is my wonder,
         I must confess, a man of nobler earth
         Than goes to vulgar composition,
         Born and bred high, so unconfined, so rich   125
         In fortunes and so read in all that sum
         Up human knowledge, to feed gloriously
         And live at court (the only sphere wherein
         True beauty moves, nature's most wealthy garden,
         Where every blossom is more worth than all   130

105. owed] *Q subst.;* owe *Knowland.*

---

102. *compound*] 'make a settlement' (Harrier).
104. *give day to*] pay attention to, take notice of (Baskervill).
111. *active . . . blood*] i.e., desire.
122. *my wonder*] something I marvel at.
124. *vulgar composition*] the making of ordinary mortals.
127. *gloriously*] splendidly; see I.i.273n.
130. *blossom*] a person considered to be 'lovely and full of promise' (Onions, 1), i.e., a beautiful young woman.

The Hesperian fruit by jealous dragon watched,
Where all delights do circle appetite
And pleasures multiply by being tasted)
Should be so lost with thought of one turned ashes.
There's nothing left, my lord, that can excuse you,   135
Unless you plead what I am ashamed to prompt
Your wisdom to –
Lord.   What's that?
Celestina.   That you have played
The surgeon with yourself –
Lord.   And am made eunuch.
Celestina. It were much pity.
Lord.   Trouble not yourself:
I could convince your fears with demonstration   140
That I am man enough, but knew not where
(Until this meeting) beauty dwelt. The court
You talked of must be where the queen of love is,
Which moves but with your person: in your eye
Her glory shines, and only at that flame   145
Her wanton boy doth light his quick'ning torch.
Celestina. Nay, now you compliment. I would it did,
My lord, for your own sake.
Lord.   You would be kind
And love me, then?
Celestina.   My lord, I should be loving
Where I found worth to invite it, and should cherish   150
A constant man.

134. turned] *Gifford subst.;* turne *Q.*   137. What's] *Gifford;* What *Q.*

131.] One of the labours of Hercules consisted of stealing the golden apples from a tree, jointly guarded by a dragon and the nymphs known as Hesperides, in a garden at the western edge of the world.

140–1. *I . . . enough*] Lord Unready's eagerness to vouch for his virility recalls Bornwell's appeal, in II.ii.234–5, to 'those / That dare make affidavit for my body'.

143. *queen of love*] i.e., Venus.

146. *wanton boy*] i.e., Cupid.

quick'ning] life-giving, revitalising (Onions, 'quicken').

torch] E. Panofsky points out, in *Studies in Iconology* (1939), p. 128, that a torch-bearing Cupid stands for Platonic love, as opposed to the sensual desire which blind Cupid represents. Cf. V.iii.54n.

147. *I . . . did*] The meaning of this clause is clear enough, namely: 'I wish what you have been saying were true.' Thus the antecedent of *it* must be 'the court' (l. 142) which dances in time with an idealised Celestina.

Lord.   Then you should me, madam.

Celestina. But is the ice about your heart fallen off?
    Can you return to do what love commands?
    Cupid, thou shalt have instant sacrifice,
    And I dare be the priest.

Lord.   Your hand, your lip. [*Kisses her.*]   155
    Now I am proof 'gainst all temptation.

Celestina. Your meaning, my good lord?

Lord.   I, that have strength
    Against thy voice and beauty, after this
    May dare the charms of womankind; thou art,
    Bella Maria, unprofanèd yet;   160
    This magic has no power upon my blood.
    Farewell, madam; if you durst be the example
    Of chaste as well as fair, thou wert a brave one.

Celestina. I hope your lordship means not this for earnest.
    Be pleased to grace a banquet.

Lord.   Pardon, madam.   165
    [*Preparing to go*] Will Sentlove, follow; I must laugh at
      you.

Celestina. My lord, I must beseech you stay, for honour
    For her whose memory you love best.

Lord.   Your pleasure.

Celestina. And by that virtue you have now professed,
    I charge you to believe me, too. I can   170
    Now glory that you have been worth my trial,
    Which I beseech you pardon; had not you
    So valiantly recovered in this conflict,
    You had been my triumph without hope of more
    Than my just scorn upon your wanton flame.   175
    Nor will I think these noble thoughts grew first
    From melancholy (for some female loss,
    As the fantastic world believes), but from
    Truth and your love of innocence, which shine
    So bright in the two royal luminaries   180

---

   165. *banquet*] not used here in the sense of a complete formal meal, but rather as a term for refreshments consisting of 'sweetmeats, fruit, and wine' (Onions, 2).

   178. *fantastic*] given to fantasy and false belief; i.e., credulous.

   180–1. *two . . . court*] 'This tribute to the nuptial virtues of Charles and Henrietta was not unmerited. The compliment, though frequent enough on

At court, you cannot lose your way to chastity.
Proceed, and speak of me as honour guides you.

                    Exit Lord [*with* SENTLOVE].

I am almost tired; come, ladies, we'll beguile
Dull time, and take the air another while.   *Exeunt*.

---

the stage, was not always paid at so small an expense of truth' (Gifford). A
similar tribute is paid in *The Triumph of Peace*, Shirley's masque 'presented in
the Banquetting-house at Whitehall, before the King and Queens Majesties,
and a great assembly of lords and ladies' (*Wks*, VI, 261), in which the musicians bowed to the royal pair before performing an ode which begins as follows: 'To you, great king and queen, whose smile / Doth scatter blessings
through this isle, / To make it best / And wonder of the rest, / We pay the duty
of our birth; / Proud to wait upon that earth / Whereon you move, / Which
shall be nam'd / And by your chaste embraces fam'd, / The paradise of love'
(*Wks*, VI, 277).

182. *Proceed*] Celestina's gesture will make it obvious that she is inviting
Lord Unready to enter another chamber, in which the banquet is about to be
served.

The Fifth Act.

Enter ARETINA *and* Servant.

Aretina. But hath Sir Thomas lost five hundred pounds
    Already?
Servant.   And five hundred more he borrowed.
    The dice are notable devourers, madam,
    They make no more of pieces than of pebbles,
    But thrust their heaps together to engender.   5
    'Two hundred more,' the caster cries; this gentleman:
    'I am w'ee. I ha' that to nothing, sir.' The caster
    Again: ''Tis covered.' And the table too,
    With sums that frighted me. Here one sneaks out,
    And with a martyr's patience, smiles upon   10
    His money's executioner, the dice,

6. more,' the caster cries; this] *This ed.;* more the Caster cries this *Q; more the
caster!* cries this *Gifford;* more!" the caster cries this *Baskervill.*   7. w'ee. I]
Q; *with you. – I Gifford;* wi' ye. – I *Neilson;* w'ee." – "I *Spencer.*   7–8.
nothing, sir.' The caster / Again:' 'Tis covered'. And] *Baskervill subst.;* no-
thing sir, the Caster / Agen, tis covered, and *Q; nothing, sir.* | Again; '*Tis
covered!* and *Gifford;* nothing, sir. The caster / Again." 'Tis covered, and
Neilson; nothing, sir,' the caster / Again. 'Tis covered, and *Knowland.*

    4. *pieces*] gold coins worth twenty-two shillings each; cf. I.i.223.
    6. *caster*] in a game such as hazard, the person whose turn it is to roll the
dice. Cotton points out, in his description of the rules of hazard, sig. M4v, that
'the *Chance* is the *Casters*, and the *Main* theirs who are concerned in play with
him'.
    6–8.] The punctuation of this passage is confusing, both in Q and in most
modern edd. It would appear that the caster is declaring the stake for his next
roll ('Two hundred more'), that his opponent produces a matching sum with a
careless flourish ('I ha' that to nothing'), and that the caster confirms the
wager with ''Tis covered'.
    7. *w'ee*] with you. See II.ii.181n.

Commands a pipe of good tobacco, and
I'th' smoke on't vanishes; another makes
The bones vault o'er his head, swears that ill throwing
Has put his shoulder out of joint, calls for   15
A bone-setter; that looks to th' box, to bid
His master send him some more hundred pounds,
Which lost, he takes tobacco and is quiet;
Here a strong arm throws in-and-in, with which
He brusheth all the table, pays the rooks   20

16. bone-setter; that] *Gifford subst.;* bone setter that *Q.*

---

14. *bones*] archaic slang for dice; cf. W. Rowley, *A New Wonder, A Woman Never Vext* (1632), sig. C2v: 'Now the dice are mine; set now a faire / Boord; a faire passage sweet bones.' The term was obviously derived from the common practice of making dice out of bone (Strutt, p. 272). Cf. IV.i.13–14.

16. *bone-setter*] probably a pimp. See the gloss provided by Vindice and Lussurioso in *The Revenger's Tragedy*, ed. Foakes (1966), I.iii.42–5: '*Luss.* What hast been, of what profession? / *Vind.* A bone-setter. / *Luss.* A bone-setter? / *Vind.* A bawd, my lord; one that sets bones together.' Thus, the gambler described in this passage (ll. 13–16), demoralised by bad luck, seeks consolation from a prostitute.

that] 'that one' (Schelling); i.e., the former, the gambler who is said to have left the table for the solace of tobacco (ll. 9–13).

box] The 'bank' in a gaming establishment, where reckonings are kept and loans are made; see I.i.105n.

17. *His master*] probably the proprietor of the establishment, who would be in charge of any loans made from the 'box'. This interpretation gains support from the following conversation between Wilding and Hazard in *The Gamester*, III.iv (Shirley, *Wks*, III, 242): '*Haz.* If thou wilt have any money, speak before I launch out, and command it. / *Wild.* A hundred pieces. / *Haz.* Call to the master o' the house, by this token—thou wilt venture again, then?'

19. *in-and-in*] the best possible roll in a game of the same name. See Cotton, sig. M2–2v: '*Inn and Inn* is a Game very much used in an *Ordinary*, and may be play'd by two or three, each having a *Box* in his hand. It is play'd with four Dice. You may drop what you will, Six-pences, Shillings, or Guinneys; every Inn you drop, and every *Inn and Inn* you sweep all; but if you throw out . . . your Adversary wins all. . . . Here you are to observe that *Out* is when you have thrown no Dubblets on the four Dice; *Inn* is when you have thrown two Dubblets of any sort. . . . *Inn and Inn* is, when you throw all Dubblets, whether all of a sort or otherwise, *viz.* four Aces, four Deuces, or four Cinques, or two Aces, two Deuces, two Treys, two Qu[a]ters, or two Cinques, two Sixes, and so forth.' Cf. *The Gamester*, III.iv (Shirley, *Wks*, III, 240): 'A curse upon these reeling dice! that last in-and-in was out my way ten pieces.'

20. *brusheth . . . table*] wins the entire stake (Baskervill).

rooks] Professional hustlers in a gambling establishment, according to Cotton, sig. B3v, 'may all pass under the general and common appellation of *Rooks*'.

That went their smelts apiece upon his hand,
Yet swears he has not drawn a stake this seven year.
But I was bid make haste; my master may
Lose this five hundred pounds ere I come thither.   *Exit.*

Aretina. If we both waste so fast, we shall soon find   25
Our state is not immortal; something in
His other ways appears not well already.

Enters SIR THOMAS [*with* Servants].

Bornwell. Ye tortoises, why make you no more haste?
Go, pay to th' master of the house that money,
And tell the noble gamesters I have another   30
Superfluous thousand pound; at night, I'll visit 'em.
D'ee hear?

Servant.   Yes, and please you.

Bornwell.   Do't, ye drudges.
                    [*Exeunt* Servants.]

[*Sings.*] Ta ra ra –
Aretina!

Aretina.   You have a pleasant humour, sir.

Bornwell. What, should a gentleman be sad?

Aretina.   You have lost.   35

Bornwell. A transitory sum. As good that way
As another.

Aretina.   Do you not vex within for't?

Bornwell. I had rather lose a thousand more than one
Sad thought come near my heart for't. Vex for trash?
Although it go from other men like drops   40
Of their life blood, we lose with the alacrity
We drink a cup of sack or kiss a mistress.
No money is considerable with a gamester:
They have souls more spacious than kings. Did two
Gamesters divide the empire of the world,   45
They'd make one throw for't all, and he that lost

27. appears] *conj. Knowland;* appeare *Q.*

---

21. went . . . smelts] placed their half-guinea bets. For the slang meaning of
smelt, see *O.E.D.,* sb.2.
    22. drawn . . . stake] won any money (Onions, 'draw', 8). Cf. Shakespeare,
Wint., I.ii.244–8: 'thou must be counted . . . a fool / That seest a game played
home, the rich stake drawn, / And tak'st it all for jest'.

> Be no more melancholy than to have played for
> A morning's draught. Vex a rich soul for dirt,
> The quiet of whose every thought is worth
> A province?

Aretina.   But when dice have consumed all,   50
> Your patience will not pawn for as much more.

Bornwell. Hang pawning! Sell outright, and the fear's over.

Aretina. Say you so? I'll have another coach tomorrow
> If there be riches above ground.

Bornwell.   I forgot
> To bid the fellow ask my jeweller   55
> Whether the chain of diamonds be made up;
> I will present it to my Lady Bellamour,
> Fair Celestina.

Aretina.   This gown I have worn
> Six days already; it looks dull. I'll give it
> My waiting woman, and have one of cloth   60
> Of gold embroidered; shoes and pantables
> Will show well of the same.

Bornwell.   I have invited
> A covey of ladies and as many gentlemen
> Tomorrow to the Italian ordinary:
> I shall have rarities and regalias   65

54. riches] *Con. MS;* rich *Q.*   61. embroidered] *Gifford subst.;* enbrodered
Q.   65. regalias] *Gifford;* regalli as *Q.*

51.] You will not be able to pawn your patience for a sum equal to what you
have lost.

60–1. *cloth . . . embroidered*] *Cloth of gold* was a fabric made by one of a
variety of methods of interweaving gold with silk or wool (Linthicum, p. 114).
When the design of this fabric included embroidery, it was often referred to as
'cloth o' bodkin'. (See III.ii.172n.).

61. *pantables*] More commonly called 'pantofles', these were thick-soled
outer shoes, worn by both men and women over their regular shoes, construc-
ted out of cork and often elaborately decorated. Though notoriously difficult
to walk in, pantables 'were in universal favour at Court and among gallants' in
the late sixteenth century. Understandably, they were taken as emblems of
vanity and pride. See Linthicum, pp. 250–3.

64. *ordinary*] an establishment serving the multiple functions of restaurant,
bar and gaming-house; see III.ii.63n.

65. *regalias*] As used here, 'regalia' is an obsolete variant of 'regalo', meaning 'a choice or elegant repast or entertainment' (*O.E.D.*). Cf. the letter by
James Howell to Ben Jonson, dated 3 May 1635 (*Familiar Letters,* ed. Jacobs,
1890, p. 324): 'I thank you for the last *regalo* you gave me at your *Musæum*,
and for the good company.'

To pay for, madam; music, wanton songs,
And tunes for silken petticoats to dance to.
Aretina. And tomorrow have I invited half the court
    To dine here; what misfortune 'tis your company
    And ours should be divided! After dinner   70
    I entertain 'em with a play.
Bornwell.   By that time
    Your play inclines to the epilogue, shall we
    Quit our Italian host and whirl in coaches
    To the Dutch magazine of sauce – The Stillyard –
    Where deal and backrag (and what strange wine else   75
    They dare but give a name to in the reckoning)
    Shall flow into our room and drown Westphalias,
    Tongues, and anchovies, like some little town
    Endangered by a sluice, through whose fierce ebb
    We wade and wash ourselves into a boat,   80
    And bid our coachmen drive their leather tenements
    By land while we sail home with a fresh tide
    To some new rendezvous.
Aretina.   If you have not
    'Pointed the place, pray bring your ladies hither;
    I mean to have a ball tomorrow night,   85

---

67. for] *This ed.; of Q.*

---

67. *petticoats*] See I.i.296n. As used here, the word is a textbook case of
synecdoche, in which the part stands for the whole (i.e., the garment for the
wearer).

74. *magazine . . . sauce*] 'storehouse of sauce, tavern' (Baskervill).

The Stillyard] a hall situated on the north bank of the Thames, between
Church Lane and Dowgate, 'where the merchants of the Hanseatic League
had their headquarters. . . . In 1597 they were expelled from the country; and
the Hall then became a favourite resort for the drinking of Rhenish wines.
Neats' tongues and other provocatives of thirst could be obtained there'
(Sugden).

75. *deal*] 'some unidentified kind of wine, supposed to have been of Rhenish
origin' (*O.E.D.*, sb.4).

backrag] '*i.e.* Baccarach, a famous Rhine wine' (Gosse).

77. *Westphalias*] ham or bacon from Westphalia. Moryson, IV, 168, claims
that in England 'the flesh of Hogges and Swine is more savoury, than in any
other parts, excepting the bacon of Westphalia'. Cf. Webster, *The White
Devil*, ed. Brown (1960), V.i.181, and Jonson, *Bartholomew Fair*, ed. Horsman (1960), V.iv.309.

81. *leather tenements*] 'i.e., their coaches' (Papousek).

And a rich banquet for 'em, where we'll dance
Till morning rise and blush to interrupt us.
Bornwell. Have you no ladies i'th' next room, to advance
A present mirth? What a dull house you govern!
Farewell, a wife's no company. – Aretina,   90
I've summed up my estate, and find we may have
A month good yet.
Aretina.   What mean you?
Bornwell.   And I'd rather
Be lord one month of pleasures, to the height
And rapture of our senses, than be years
Consuming what we have in foolish temperance,   95
Live in the dark and no fame wait upon us.
I will live so posterity shall stand
At gaze when I am mentioned.
Aretina.   A month good,
And what shall be done then?
Bornwell.   I'll over sea
And trail a pike; with watching, marching, lying   100
In trenches, with enduring cold and hunger
And taking here and there a musket shot,
I can earn every week four shillings, madam.
And if the bullets favour me to snatch
Any superfluous limb, when I return   105
(With good friends) I despair not to be enrolled
Poor Knight of Windsor. For your course, madam,
No doubt you may do well; your friends are great,

---

98. *At gaze*] 'in the attitude of gazing, especially in wonder, expectancy,
bewilderment, etc.' (*O.E.D.*, 'gaze', sb., 3b).

100. *trail . . . pike*] i.e., enlist as a pikeman in the infantry. '"To trail a pike"
—that is to say, to hold the steel head in the hand and let the butt trail on the
ground—was a common phrase to signify service in the infantry, for in those
days gentlemen voluneteers worked their way up from the ranks, and more
than one peer trailed a pike in the regiments of Maurice of Nassau'
(*Shakespeare's England*, I, 115).

107. *Poor . . . Windsor*] The same phrase occurs in Chapman, *et al., Eastward Ho*, ed. Van Fossen (1979), IV.i.185–6, where the following explanation
is offered: 'properly a pensioner of the Military Knights of Windsor, founded
in 1349 to support retired soldiers; by the seventeenth century a slang term for
"pauper"'. This is also the precise economic and social rank occupied by Sir
John Falstaff in *Wiv.* Cf. *The Constant Maid*, III.i (Shirley, *Wks*, IV, 486):
'you must have clothes / Fitting your state. . . . You'll not look in those / Like
a poor knight of Windsor'.

Or, if your poverty and their pride cannot
Agree, you need not trouble much invention   110
To find a trade to live by: there are customers.
Farewell, be frolic, madam; if I live
I will feast all my senses, and not fall
Less than a Phaeton from my throne of pleasure,
Though my estate flame like the world about me.   *Exit.*   115
Aretina. 'Tis very pretty.

ACT V, SCENE ii

Enter DECOY.

Aretina. Madam Decoy!
Decoy. What, melancholy after so sweet a night's work? Have
    not I showed myself mistress of my art?
Aretina. A lady.
Decoy. That title makes the credit of the act a storey higher.   5
    Y'ave not seen him yet; I wonder what he'll say.
Aretina. He's here.

---

115. *Exit*] set *in righthand margin opposite* melancholy *(V.ii.2) in* Q.   2–6.]
verse in Q, *divided* melancholy / After . . . I / Shew'd . . . Lady. / That . . . act /
A . . . yet, / I.

111.] a belligerent and nasty line, to judge by the glosses given by Partridge
for *trade* ('the trade of whore, bawd', etc.) and *customer* ('a male frequenter of
brothels').

112. *frolic*] merry (Onions).

114. *Phaeton*] The sun of Helios (the sun-god), Phaeton was permitted to
guide the sun's chariot for a day. But he was unable to manage the solar steeds,
and would have set the world on fire, had not Zeus dispatched him with a
thunderbolt. Thus, Phaeton became 'the standard image of glittering failure'
(Harrier).

0.1.] Previous edd. print Act V as a single continuous scene, in keeping with
the convention that a new scene begins only after the stage has been cleared. Q
throughout does not mark scene divisions (only act divisions), Gifford being
responsible for dividing Acts I–IV into scenes. Since Act V is clearly divisible
into three units of dramatic structure, held together by *liaison des scènes* (a
technique borrowed from France and gaining in popularity among Caroline
playwrights), I have indicated new scenes beginning with the entrance of
Madam Decoy here, and with the entrance of Lord Unready at V.iii.

Enter ALEXANDER *and* FREDERICK.

Alexander. Bear up, my little myrmidon. Does not Jack
    Littleworth follow?

Frederick. Follow? He fell into the Thames at landing.   10

Alexander. The devil shall dive for him ere I endanger my silk
    stockings for him. Let the watermen alone: they have
    drags and engines. When he has drunk his julep, I shall
    laugh to see him come in pickled the next tide.

Frederick. He'll never sink, he has such a cork brain.   15

Alexander. Let him be hanged or drowned, all's one to me. Yet
    he deserves to die by water cannot bear his wine credibly.

Frederick. Is not this my aunt?

Alexander. And another handsome lady; I must know her.

Frederick. My blood is rampant, too; I must court somebody.   20
    As good my aunt as any other body.

8–14.] *verse in Q, divided* up | My . . . *Littleworth* | Follow . . . Thames | At
. . . him | Ere . . . him, | Let . . . engins, | When . . . laugh | To.   16–33.]
verse in Q, divided me, | Yet . . . cannot | Beare . . . Aunt? | And . . . her. | My
. . . some body, | As . . . body. | Where . . . bridge, | At . . . began | To . . .
company | Was . . . lay, | a . . . *roba* | For . . . dull; | We . . . vagaries; | When
. . . Ladies | Play . . . mirth | Without . . . fancies, | That . . . read | A . . .
behave | My.

---

8. *myrmidon*] i.e., loyal follower. Technically, the myrmidons were soldiers
from Thessaly, 'famed for loyalty and ruthlessness' (Harrier), whom Achilles
led at the siege of Troy. But the word seems to have acquired new status as
drinking slang, as in Shakespeare, *Tw.N.*, II.iii.26–7: 'My lady has a white
hand, and the Myrmidons are no bottle-ale houses.'

12. *watermen*] Since the Thames was a major transportation artery in
London, 'there were innumerable wherries for hire at all the public stairs,
with their watermen crying, "Eastward Ho!" or "Westward Ho!". . . . John
Taylor, the water-poet, affirmed that 2,000 small boats were to be found about
London, and that "the number of watermen, and those that lived and were
maintained by them, and by the labour of the oar and scull, betwixt the bridge
of Windsor and Gravesend, could not be fewer than 40,000"' (*Shakespeare's
England*, II, 154).

13. *drags*] 'apparatus for recovering objects from the bottom of rivers or
pools; especially for recovering the bodies of drowned persons' (*O.E.D.*, sb.,
2d).

engines] contrivances (Neilson).

julep] 'a sweetened drink containing medicine' (Harrier).

15. *cork brain*] In seventeenth-century usage, a 'cork-brain' was 'a light-
headed or giddy person' (*O.E.D.*, 'cork', sb.1, 11d).

17. *cannot bear*] who (understood) cannot bear (Abbott, § 244).

credibly] creditably (Spencer).

Aretina. Where have you been, cousin?

Frederick. At the bridge, at the Bear's Foot, where our first
    health began to the fair Aretina, whose sweet company
    was wished by all. We could not get a lay, a tumbler, a   25
    device, a *bona roba* for any money. Drawers were grown
    dull; we wanted our true firks and our vagaries. When
    were you in drink, aunt?

Aretina. How?

Frederick. Do not ladies play the good fellows too? There's no   30
    true mirth without 'em. I have now such tickling fancies.
    That doctor of the chair of wit has read a precious lecture,
    how I should behave myself to ladies, as now, for example.

Aretina. Would you practise upon me?

Frederick. I first salute you. [*Kisses her hand.*] You have a soft   35

23. At the bridge, at the Bear's Foot] *Q subst.*; At the Bear / At the Bridge-foot
Gifford.   35–47.] *verse in Q, divided* you, / You . . . so / All . . . smile, / And
. . . draw / Off . . . hand / More . . . owne / Lip . . . thus, / Prepare . . .
Palmistry, / Which . . . Lady / But . . . line / I . . . out / Is . . . semicircle /
Enclosing . . . *Saturne,* / If . . . Lady / Whom . . . careere, / And . . . forward,
/ You.

---

23. *At . . . Foot*] Gifford's emendation springs from a kind but misguided
desire to impose correctness on the speech of a man who is manifestly drunk.
The correct name of the popular tavern (the Bear at the Bridge-foot) is given
by Alexander in IV.ii.146–7.

25. *lay*] The context implies 'a woman who is readily available for sexual
intercourse' (*O.E.D.*, sb.7, 7d), even though no example of this usage is recorded prior to 1932.

    tumbler] another term for a sexually available woman; see I.ii.43n. Cf. *The
Gamester*, III.i (Shirley, *Wks*, III, 228): 'I know not what to make on her; she
may be / A tumbler, for all this; I'll to her again.'

26. *device*] undoubtedly slang for courtesan; in this sense, not in *O.E.D.* In
The Gamester, III.iv (Shirley, *Wks*, III, 242), Wilding refers to Penelope,
with whom he has arranged a midnight meeting, as 'the flesh device at home
that expects' (i.e., waits).

    bona roba] a woman dressed in an overtly enticing and flashy way. J. Florio,
in *A Worlde of Wordes* (1598), defines *buonarobba* with engaging high spirits:
'as we say, good stuffe, a good wholesome plum-cheeked wench'. Shirley
offers a virtual definition in *The Humorous Courtier*, II.ii (*Wks*, IV, 557): 'He
ne'er convers'd with an Italian bona roba, a plump lady, that fills her gown.'

    Drawers] tapsters (Onions).

27. *firks*] pranks, as in Ford's *The Broken Heart*, ed. Spencer (1980),
III.ii.155: 'These are his megrims, firks, and melancholies.'

    vagaries] capricious, uninhibited behaviour (*O.E.D.*).

32. *doctor . . . wit*] i.e., Alexander, who was appointed Frederick's social
tutor in II.i.88–94. Here Frederick is continuing the conceit whereby Alexander claims to 'read but in a tavern' (IV.ii.145–6).

　　hand, madam; are you so all over?

Aretina. Nephew!

Frederick. Nay, you should but smile, and then again I kiss you

　　– and thus draw off your white glove and start to see your

　　hand, more excellently white. I grace my own lip with this		40

　　touch, and turning gently, thus, prepare you for my skill

　　in palmistry, which out of curiosity no lady but easily app-

　　lies to. The first line I look, with most ambition to find

　　out, is Venus' girdle: a fair semicircle enclosing both the

　　mount of Sol and Saturn; if that appear, she's for my turn,		45

　　a lady whom nature has prepared for the career; and,

　　Cupid at my elbow, I put forward. You have this very line,

　　aunt.

Aretina. [*Aside*] The boy's frantic.

Frederick. You have a couch or palate; I can shut the chamber		50

　　door, enrich a stranger when your nephew's coming in to

　　play.

---

43. look] *Gifford*; tooke *Q*.　　50. palate] *Q subst.*; palett *Gifford;* pallet
Gosse.　　50–56.] *verse in Q, divided* shut / The . . . when / Your . . . more. /
Are . . . bloud? / Here . . . sport, / And.　　51. in to] *This ed.;* into *Q*.

---

　　42. *palmistry*] Jonson parodies this dubious art in *The Alchemist*, ed. Mares
(1967), IV.ii.44–50, where Subtle's method of inspecting Dame Pliant's hand
anticipates Frederick's treatment of Aretina's.

　　42–3. *applies*] yields (Neilson).

　　44. *Venus' girdle*] a key term in palmistry, defined as follows by R. Sanders
in *Physiognomie, and Chiromancie* (1653), sig. H1: 'Now to enter into the
Discourse of *Venus* Girdle, We say that it is a Semicircle that begins between
the fore-finger and the middle finger, and ends between the fourth finger and
the little one; which Semicircle includes within its semi-circumference the
two mounts of *Saturn* and the *Sun*. . . . It is to be noted, that this Line or
Girdle is not often found in hands; for among a thousand men or women,
there are hardly four that have it; for it signifies a monstrous uncleanness, and
fornication'.

　　45. *mount . . . Saturn*] According to R. Sanders (see l. 44n.), sig. B4–C2v,
these are the fleshy prominences situated at the base of the ring finger and the
base of the middle finger respectively, the hand being divided into regions
corresponding to the influence of the seven astrological planets.

　　46. *career*] any rapid and energetic burst of activity (Onions); hence, 'sexual
encounter'.

　　50. *palate*] variant form of 'pallet', in the sense of 'a small, poor, or mean
bed or couch' (*O.E.D.*, sb.2, 1). Cf. Chapman, *Bussy D'Ambois*, ed. Brooke
(1964), III.ii.190–2: 'I . . . stole at midnight from my pallet.'

　　50–2. *I . . . play*] The general drift of these lines is clear enough: Frederick
insinuates that he will be a discreet and convenient lover. The grammar,

Aretina. No more.

Frederick. Are you so coy to your own flesh and blood?

Alexander. [*Presenting Decoy to Frederick*) Here, take your   55
playfellow; I talk of sport, and she would have me marry
her.

Enter LITTLEWORTH *wet.*

Frederick. Here's Littleworth. Why, how now, tutor?

Littleworth. I ha' been fishing.

Frederick. And what ha' you caught?   60

Littleworth. My belly full of water.

Alexander. Ha, ha! Where's thy rapier?

Littleworth. My rapier is drowned, and I am little better; I was
up by th'heels, and out came a tun of water, beside wine.

Alexander. 'T has made thee sober.   65

Littleworth. Would you have me drunk with water?

Aretina. I hope your fire is quenched by this time.

Frederick. It is not now as when your worship walked by all the
taverns, Jack, dry as a bone.

Alexander. You had store of fish under water, Jack.   70

Littleworth. It has made a poor John of me.

58–68.] *verse in Q, divided* Heres *Littleworth.* / Why . . . fishing. / And . . .
water. / Ha . . . drown'd, / And . . . heeles, / And . . . wine. / 'T . . . drunk /
With . . . time. / It . . . walkd / By.   63. rapier is drowned] *Gifford subst.;*
rapier's is drown'd *Q;* rapier's drown'd *Knowland.*   64. tun] *Q;* ton *Gifford.*

---

however, is confusing, perhaps on account of Frederick's inebriation, but
more likely as a result of an error in the printing house. I suspect that a line of
copy belonging between 'when' and 'your' has been omitted. Such an omitted
line probably began with 'Your', since this is the catchword on sig. I2, 'when'
being the last word proper. If two consecutive lines of copy began with
'Your', the error would have been easily made.

64. *tun*] 'a measure of capacity for wine and other liquids' equal to 4 hogs-
heads or 252 old wine-gallons (*O.E.D.*, sb., 2).

68–9.] Frederick is mocking the boast made by Littleworth in IV.ii.35–8.

70. *store*] plenty (*O.E.D.*, sb., 4b).

71. *poor John*] salted hake (Onions). The metaphor implies humiliation in a
manner roughly parallel to Falstaff's imaginary deflation in *1H4*, II.iv.120–1:
'if manhood . . . be not forgot upon the face of the earth, then am I a shotten
herring'.

Frederick. I do not think but if we cast an angle into his belly we
    might find some pilchards.

Littleworth. And boiled by this time. Dear madam, a bed.

Alexander. Carry but the water-spaniel to a grass plot where he   75
    may roll himself; let him but shake his ears twice in the
    sun, and you may grind him into a posset.

Frederick. Come, thou shalt to my bed, poor pickerel.

                                           [*They help him
                                                  disrobe.*]

Decoy. Alas, sweet gentleman.

Littleworth. I have ill luck, and I should smell by this time; I   80
    am but new ta'en I am sure, sweet gentlewoman.

Decoy. Your servant.

Littleworth. Pray, do not pluck off my skin; it is so wet, unless
    you have good eyes, you'll hardly know it from a shirt.

Decoy. Fear nothing.   85

Aretina. He has sack enough, and I may find his humour.

                        Exeunt [all but Aretina and Alexander].

Alexander. And how is't with your ladyship? You look without
    a sunshine in your face.

Aretina. You are glorious in mind and habit.

Alexander. Ends of gold and silver.   90

Aretina. Your other clothes were not so rich. Who was your
    tailor, sir?

72–84.] *verse in Q, divided* angle / Into . . . Pilchards. / And . . . bed. / Carry
. . . grasseplot / Where . . . shake / His . . . him / Into . . . bed / Poore . . .
gentleman. / I . . . gentlewoman. / Your . . . skin, / It . . . eyes / You'le.   80.
and] *Q;* an *Gifford.*   87–100.] *verse in Q, divided* looke / Without . . . glorious / In . . . silver. / Your . . . was / Your . . . since, / They . . . backe, / I . . .
by, / They . . . enough / To . . . selfe / A . . . necessary / Dependances . . .
garters, / And . . . conformitie, / Bootes . . . in, / My . . . new, / The.

---

72. *angle*] fishing-hook (Onions).

75. *water-spaniel*] 'a variety of spaniel, much used for retrieving water-fowl'
(*O.E.D.*).

77. *posset*] 'drink composed of hot milk curdled with ale, wine, &c., formerly used as a delicacy and as a remedy' (Onions).

86. *may . . . humour*] a flippant remark, as there can be no difficulty in
discovering the malignant 'humour' that causes Littleworth's indisposition.

89. *glorious*] Both 'vainglorious' (in mind) and 'splendid' (in habit, i.e.,
apparel) are implied; see II.i.34n. and I.i.273n.

90. *Ends*] fragments (Onions, sb., 2).

Alexander. They were made for me long since. They have
    known but two bright days upon my back (I had a
    humour, madam, to lay things by); they will serve two   95
    days more, I think. I ha' gold enough to go to th' mercer:
    I'll now allow myself a suit a week as this, with necessary
    dependances – beaver, silk stockings, garters, and roses in
    their due conformity. Boots are forbid a clean leg, but to
    ride in. My linen every morning comes in new; the old   100
    goes to great bellies.
Aretina. You are charitable.
Alexander. I may dine w'ee sometime, or at the court, to meet
    good company (not for the table). My clerk o'th' kitchen's
    here, a witty epicure, a spirit that to please me with what's   105
    rare can fly a hundred mile a day to market and make me
    lord of fish and fowl. I shall forget there is a butcher, and,
    to make my footman nimble, he shall feed on nothing but
    wings of wild-fowl.
Aretina. These ways are costly.   110
Alexander. Therefore I'll have it so; I ha' sprung a mine.

96. more, I think. I ha'] *This ed.;* more, I thinke I ha *Q;* more: I think I have
Gifford.   103–8.] *verse in Q, divided* Court / To . . . table, / My . . . Epicure,
/ A . . . rare / Can . . . market, / And . . . shall / Forget . . . make / My . . .
nothing / But.   108. footman] *Gifford;* footmen *Q.*

---

    95. *humour*] whim.
    98. *dependances*] accessories (Papousek).
    beaver] beaver hat.
    silk stockings] These, according to Linthicum, p. 261, 'became the "only
weare" among gallants, for they showed off the comeliness of the wearer's leg
much better than did the woolen ones'.
    garters] ornamental bands of silk worn just below the knee (Linthcum, p.
263). Cf. III.ii.319n.
    roses] i.e., rosettes or shoe-roses which, according to C. and P. Cunnington
(*Handbook of English Costume in the Seventeenth Century*, 2nd ed., 1966,
p. 56), 'grew very large and among the very fashionable might at times cover
the whole foot'.
    98–9. *in . . . conformity*] 'arranged in a harmonious pattern' (Papousek).
    99. *clean*] well-shaped (Spencer).
    101. *great bellies*] pregnant women (Harrier).
    103. *w'ee*] with you. See II.ii.181n.
    104. *not . . . table*] i.e., not for the purpose of eating.
    108. *footman*] I accept Gifford's emendation because *he* requires a singular
antecedent.

Aretina. You make me wonder, sir, to see this change of for-
    tune; your revenue was not late so plentiful.

Alexander. Hang dirty land and lordships; I wo' not change
    one lodging I ha' got for the Chamber of London.   115

Aretina. Strange, of such a sudden to rise to this estate. No
    fortunate hand at dice could lift you up so, for 'tis since
    last night; yesterday you were no such monarch.

Alexander. There be more games than dice.

Aretina. It cannot be a mistress, though your person is worth   120
    love; none possibly are rich enough to feed as you have
    cast the method of your riots. A princess, after all her
    jewels, must be forced to sell her provinces.

Alexander. Now you talk of jewels! What do you think of this?
    [*Gives her a jewel.*]

Aretina. A rich one.   125

Alexander. You'll honour me to wear't. [*Shows her trinkets.*]
    This other toy I had from you. This chain I borrowed of
    you; a friend had it in keeping. [*Gives them to her.*] If your
    ladyship want any sum, you know your friend and
    Alexander.   130

Aretina. Dare you trust my security?

Alexander. There's gold. [*Gives her gold.*] I shall have more
    tomorrow.

Aretina. You astonish me. Who can supply these?

Alexander. A dear friend I have; she promised we should meet   135
    again i'th' morning.

Aretina. Not that I wish to know more of your happiness than I

112–18.] *verse in Q, divided* change / Of . . . late / So . . . Lordships, / I . . . got
/ For . . . sudden, / To . . . hand / At . . . since / Last.   120–24.] *verse in Q,
divided* be / A . . . love, / None . . . feed / As . . . riots, / A . . . must / Be . . .
talke / Of.   127–32.] *verse in Q, divided* toy / I . . . you, / A . . . Ladiship /
Want . . . *Alexander*. / Dare . . . gold, / I.   135–42.] *verse in Q, divided* have,
/ She . . . morning. / Not . . . know / More . . . aready / Heart . . . lay / My . . .
die / Ere . . . well, / But.

---

114. *wo' not*] See II.i.135n.

115. *Chamber . . . London*] the treasury of the city; cf. Massinger's poem,
'London's Lamentable Estate' (*Plays*, IV, 400), ll. 34–6: 'the *Chambers
Threasurie* / out of the Surplusage of her cram'd-Store, / could warrant full
Supply from any *Shore*'.

127. *toy*] trifle (Onions, 1).

     have a ready heart to congratulate: be pleased to lay my
     wonder.

Alexander. 'Tis a secret.   140

Aretina. Which I'll die ere I'll betray.

Alexander. You have always wished me well, but you shall
     swear not to reveal the party.

Aretina. I'll lose the benefit of my tongue.

Alexander. Nor be afraid at what I say. What think you first of 145
     an old witch, a strange ill-favoured hag, that for my com-
     pany last night has wrought this cure upon my fortune? I
     do sweat to think upon her name.

Aretina. How sir, a witch?

Alexander. I would not fright your ladyship too much at first, 150
     but witches are akin to spirits. The truth is – nay, if you
     look pale already, I ha' done.

Aretina. Sir, I beseech you.

Alexander. If you have but courage, then, to know the truth,
     I'll tell you: in one word, my chief friend is the devil.   155

Aretina. What? Devil? How I tremble!

Alexander. Have a heart. 'Twas a she-devil, too: a most insa-
     tiate, abominable devil with a tail thus long.

Aretina. Goodness defend me! Did you see her?

Alexander. No, 'twas i'th' dark. But she appeared first to me 160

---

138. a ready] *Baskervill;* aready *Q;* already *Gifford.*   145–48.] *verse in Q,*
divided be / A fraid . . . first / Of . . . hag / That . . . wrought / This . . . sweat /
To.   150–8.] *verse in Q, divided* much / At . . . Spirits, / The . . . already, / I
. . . have / But . . . you / In . . . devill. / What . . . heart, / Twas . . . insatiate /
Abominable . . . taile / Thus.   156. What? Devil?] *This ed.;* What devill?
Q.   160–71.] *verse in Q, divided* me / I'th . . . brought / I . . . Goblins, /
More . . . venter / Upon . . . blacke / An . . . sure / It . . . nothing, / I . . . sure
/ As . . . quake? / I . . . morning, / Where.

---

    138. *lay*] allay (Schelling).

    151. *witches . . . spirits*] The powers of witches were thought to be conferred
on them by evil spirits (demons). Cf. Burton, *Anatomy*, I.ii.1.3, p. 176: 'You
have heard what the Devil can do of himself, now you shall hear what he can
perform by his instruments. . . . Much harm had never been done, as Erastus
thinks, had he not been provoked by witches to it.'

    157. *Have a heart*] i.e., be courageous. As used here, the phrase borders on
both 'to have the heart' (to do something) and 'take heart' (*O.E.D.*, 'heart',
sb., 48–9). The familiar twentieth-century meaning ('show some kindness') is
irrelevant here.

i'th' likeness of a beldam, and was brought (I know not
how nor whither) by two goblins more hooded than a
hawk.

Aretina. But would you venture upon a devil?

Alexander. Ay, for means.   165

Aretina. [*Aside*] How black an impudence is this! [*To him*] But
are you sure it was the devil you enjoyed?

Alexander. Say nothing. I did the best to please her, but as sure
as you live, 'twas a hell-cat.

Aretina. D'ee not quake?   170

Alexander. I found myself the very same in the morning, where
two of her familiars had left me.

Enter Servant.

Servant. [*To Aretina*] My lord is come to visit you.   [*Exit.*]

Alexander. No words, as you respect my safety. I ha' told tales
out of the devil's school; if it be known, I lose a friend. 'Tis   175
now about the time I promised her to meet again. At my
return I'll tell you wonders. Not a word.   *Exit.*

Aretina. 'Tis a false glass; sure, I am more deformed. What
have I done? My soul is miserable.

161. beldam] *Gifford;* Bedlam *Q.*   164. venture] *Gifford;* venter *Q.*   171.
in the] *This ed.;* in i'th *Q;* i' the *Gifford;* i'th' *Neilson.*   174–9.] *verse in Q,
divided* words, / As . . . tales / Out . . . knowne / I . . . time / I . . . my /
Returne . . . word. / Tis . . . deform'd, / What.

161. *beldam*] old woman or hag; cf. IV.i.18n.

162. *hooded*] In falconry, 'a hood was placed on the hawk's head to ensure
her perfect quiescence when not taken on hand' (*Shakespeare's England*, II,
356). Turberville, in *The Book of Faulconrie or Hawking* (1575), sig. I7–8,
gives detailed instructions for teaching a hawk to grow accustomed to the
hood.

169. *hell-cat*] i.e., a witch, see IV.i.88n.

174–5. *told . . . school*] a variant of the proverb, 'to tell tales out of school'
(Tilley, T 54), which implies indiscreet gossiping. Cf. Shirley, *The Grateful
Servant*, III.iv (*Wks*, II, 59): 'You are then a novice in the art of Venus, and
will tell tales out of the school'.

178. *false glass*] i.e., imperfect mirror. Aretina believes that the image of
herself which Alexander has thrown back to her is a distorted one.

ACT V, SCENE iii

Enter Lord.

Lord. I sent you a letter, madam.
Aretina.   You expressed
  Your noble care of me, my lord.

Enter BORNWELL, CELESTINA.

Bornwell.   [*Saluting*] Your lordship
  Does me an honour.
Lord. [*To Celestina*] Madam, I am glad
  To see you here; I meant to have kissed your hand
  Ere my return to court.
Celestina.   Sir Thomas has   5
  Prevailed to bring me, to his trouble, hither.
Lord. You do him grace.
Bornwell.   [*To Aretina*] Why, what's the matter, madam?
  Your eyes are tuning Lachrimae.
Aretina.   As you
  Do hope for heaven, withdraw, and give me but
  The patience of ten minutes.
Bornwell.   Wonderful!   10
  I wo' not hear you above that proportion.
  She talks of heaven. Come, where must we to counsel?
Aretina. You shall conclude me when you please.   [*Exit.*]
Bornwell.   I follow.
Lord. [*Aside*] What alteration is this? I, that so late
  Stood the temptation of her eye and voice,   15
  Boasted a heart 'bove all licentious flame,

0.1.] Neither in Q nor in previous edd. is Act V divided into scenes; see V.ii.0.1n.

8. *tuning Lachrimae*] i.e., preparing to weep. As Gosse points out, *Lachrimae* is the informal title of an extremely popular song from Dowland's *The Second Book of Songs or Ayres* (1600), sig. C1, which begins as follows: 'Flow teares from your springs, / Exild for ever let me mourne: / wher nights black bird hir sad infamy sings, / there let me live forlorne.'

11. *wo' not*] See II.i.135n.

13. *conclude me*] The context implies 'conclude our interview'. I have not found this phrase elsewhere, but I suspect it of being a polite variation of 'have done with me'.

At second view turn renegade and think
I was too superstitious and full
Of phlegm not to reward her amorous courtship
With manly freedom.

Celestina.   [*To Bornwell*]   I obey you, sir.   20
Bornwell. I'll wait upon your lordship presently.   [*Exit.*]
Lord. [*Aside*] She could not want a cunning to seem honest
When I neglected her. I am resolved.
[*To Celestina*] You still look pleasant, madam.
Celestina.   I have cause,
My lord, the rather for your presence, which   25
Hath power to charm all trouble in my thoughts.
Lord. I must translate that compliment, and owe
All that is cheerful in myself to these
All-quick'ning smiles. And rather than such bright
Eyes should repent their influence upon me,   30
I would release the aspects and quit the bounty
Of all the other stars. Did you not think me
A strange and melancholy gentleman
To use you so unkindly?
Celestina.   Me, my lord?
Lord. I hope you made no loud complaint. I would not   35
Be tried by a jury of ladies.
Celestina.   For what, my lord?
Lord. I did not meet that noble entertainment
You were late pleased to show me.
Celestina.   I observed
No such defect in your lordship, but a brave
And noble fortitude.

---

19. *phlegm*] the humour which causes dull and lethargic behaviour; see
IV.i.52n.

29. *All-quick'ning*] See IV.iii.146n.

30. *influence*] literally, 'an etherial fluid' thought to be exuded by the stars
and planets; 'hence, exercise of personal power regarded as something akin to
astral influence' (Onions).

31. *aspects*] 'the relative positions of the heavenly bodies as they appear to
an observer on the earth's surface at a given time, and the influence attributed
thereto' (Onions, 2).

36. *Be . . . ladies*] the fate of the notorious misogynist, Joseph Swetnam, as
dramatised in *Swetnam the Woman-Hater* (1620), ed. Crandall (1969),
V.ii.218-344.

Lord.   A noble folly!   40
    I bring repentance for't. I know you have,
    Madam, a gentle faith, and wo' not ruin
    What you have built to honour you.
Celestina.   What's that?
Lord. If you can love, I'll tell your ladyship.
Celestina. I have a stubborn soul else.
Lord.   You are all   45
    Composed of harmony.
Celestina.   What love d'ee mean?
Lord. That which doth perfect both. Madam, you have heard
    I can be constant, and if you consent
    To grace it so, there is a spacious dwelling
    Prepared within my heart for such a mistress.   50
Celestina. Your mistress, my good lord?
Lord.   Why, my good lady,
    Your sex doth hold it no dishonour
    To become mistress to a noble servant
    In the now court Platonic way. Consider
    Who 'tis that pleads to you: my birth and present   55

54. now] *Q;* new *Schelling.*

---

50. *mistress*] Here the word is undoubtedly used 'in the wanton sense' (see l. 158), even though Lord Unready is quick to interpret it, when pressed, in the 'Platonic way' (l. 54).

54. *now*] here used as an adj., meaning 'present; of the present time' (*O.E.D.*, 16). Since this usage was 'very common' in the seventeenth century, Schelling's emendation, though tempting to the modern ear, should be resisted. Cf. Shakespeare, *All's W.*, II.iii.177–8: 'this contract, whose ceremony / Shall seem expedient on the now-born brief . . .'.

Platonic way] James Howell provides a useful description of the fashion in a letter to Mr Philip Warrick, dated at Westminster, 3 June 1634; see *Familiar Letters*, ed. Jacobs (1890), pp. 317–18: 'The Court affords little News at present, but that there is a Love called Platonick Love, which much sways there of late; it is a Love abstracted from all corporeal gross Impressions and sensual Appetite, but consists in Contemplations and Ideas of the Mind, not in any carnal Fruition. This Love sets the Wits of the Town on work; they say there will be a Mask shortly of it, whereof Her Majesty and her Maids of Honour will be part.' By alluding to the new fashion, Lord Unready assumes that he can give the word 'mistress' an entirely innocent coloration: a 'mistress' in this context is a woman who commands the devotion of and exercises spiritual influence over 'a noble servant' (l. 53). Cf. G. F. Sensabaugh, 'Platonic Love in Shirley's *The Lady of Pleasure*', *A Tribute to George Coffin Taylor*, ed. A. Williams (1952), pp. 168–77.

Value can be no stain to your embrace;
But these are shadows when my love appears,
Which shall in his first miracle return
Me in my bloom of youth and thee a virgin,
When I within some new Elysium   60
(Of purpose made and meant for us) shall be
In everything Adonis, but in his
Contempt of love, and court thee from a Daphne
(Hid in the cold rind of a bashful tree)
With such warm language and delight till thou   65
Leap from that bays into the queen of love
And pay my conquest with composing garlands
Of thy own myrtle for me.
Celestina.   What's all this?
Lord. Consent to be my mistress, Celestina,
And we will have it springtime all the year,   70
Upon whose invitations, when we walk,
The winds shall play soft descant to our feet
And breathe rich odours to repure the air,
Green bowers on every side shall tempt our stay,
And violets stoop to have us tread upon 'em.   75
The red rose shall grow pale (being near thy cheek)
And the white blush (o'ercome with such a forehead).
Here laid, and measuring with ourselves some bank,

66. bays] *Q subst.;* bay *Neilson.*

---

58. *miracle*] Cf. III.i.115–16n.

62. *Adonis*] the beautiful youth whose reticence in love was all but overcome by the blandishments of Venus; cf. IV.i.78–9n.

63. *Daphne*] the nymph who escaped the amorous pursuit of Apollo by turning into a laurel tree. The story is told in Ovid's *Metamorphoses*, tr. Golding, i.545–700 (*Shakespeare's Ovid*, ed. Rouse, 1904, pp. 31–4), where Apollo caresses the tree with surprising results: 'And as he softly layde his hand upon the tender plant, / Within the barke newe overgrowne he felt hir heart yet pant' (i.679–80).

66. *bays*] 'leaves or sprigs' of the laurel tree, 'especially as woven into a wreath or garland to reward a conqueror or poet' (*O.E.D.*, sb.1, 3).

queen of love] i.e., Venus.

68. *thy . . . myrtle*] 'the myrtle was sacred to Venus, as the bay laurel was to Apollo' (Spencer).

73. *repure*] an obsolete and rare word meaning 'to purify again' (*O.E.D.*, citing this example).

78. *bank*] hillside (*O.E.D.*, sb.1, 2b).

A thousand birds shall from the woods repair
And place themselves so cunningly behind   80
The leaves of every tree, that while they pay
Us tribute of their songs, thou shalt imagine
The very trees bear music and sweet voices
Do grow in every arbour. Here can we
Embrace and kiss, tell tales, and kiss again,   85
And none but heaven our rival.
Celestina.   When we are
Weary of these, what if we shift our paradise,
And through a grove of tall and even pine
Descend into a valley that shall shame
All the delights of Tempe, upon whose   90
Green plush the graces shall be called to dance
To please us, and maintain their fairy revels
To the harmonious murmurs of a stream
That gently falls upon a rock of pearl.
Here doth the nymph, forsaken Echo, dwell,   95
To whom we'll tell the story of our love
Till, at our surfeit and her want of joy,
We break her heart with envy. Not far off
A grove shall call us to a wanton river
To see a dying swan give up the ghost,   100
The fishes shooting up their tears in bubbles
That they must lose the genius of their waves –

---

82. Us] *Gifford;* As *Q.*

---

90. *Tempe*] a valley in Thessaly widely celebrated as a pastoral retreat (Papousek).

91. *the graces*] See III.i.222–3n.

95. *forsaken Echo*] in Ovid's *Metamorphoses,* tr. Golding, iii.442–500 (*Shakespeare's Ovid,* ed. Rouse, 1904, pp. 71–2), Echo is the nymph who falls in love with Narcissus, but is unable to court him except with fragments of his own speech. After being rejected, Echo retreats to the woods, 'And ever sence she lyves alone in dennes and hollow Caves' (iii.491). Cf. Shirley's retelling of the story in *Narcissus, or the Self-Lover* (*Wks,* VI, 463–89).

99. *wanton*] luxuriant (Onions, adj., 3).

100.] and, presumably, to hear the exquisite song which (in legend) the swan sings as she dies. Cf. II.ii.211–12.

102. *genius*] 'the tutelary and controlling spirit . . . connected with a place, an institution, etc.' (*O.E.D.,* 1); as Harrier points out, the *genius* referred to here is the swan (l. 100), in her role as 'generative spirit of the water'.

And such love, linsey-woolsey, to no purpose.
Lord. You chide me handsomely. Pray, tell me how
     You like this language. [*Offering to embrace her*]
Celestina   [Resisting him] Good my lord, forbear.   105
Lord. You need not fly out of this circle, madam.
     [*Aside*] These widows are so full of circumstance.
     [*To Celestina*] I'll undertake, in this time I ha' courted
     Your ladyship for the toy, to ha' broken ten,
     Nay twenty colts (virgins, I mean) and taught 'em   110
     The amble or what pace I most affected.
Celestina. Y'are not my lord again – the lord I thought you –
     And I must tell you now, you do forget
     Yourself and me.
Lord.   You'll not be angry, madam.
Celestina. Nor rude (though gay men have a privilege)   115
     It shall appear. There is a man, my lord,
     Within my acquaintance, rich in worldly fortunes –
     But cannot boast any descent of blood –
     Would buy a coat of arms.
Lord.   He may, and legs
     Booted and spurred to ride into the country.   120
Celestina. But these will want antiquity, my lord,
     The seal of honour. What's a coat cut out
     But yesterday to make a man a gentleman?

---

107. are so] *Con. MS, Gifford;* so are *Q.*   112. not my lord again – the]
Baskervill; not my Lord agen, the *Q;* not, my lord, again, the *Gifford;* not, my
lord, again the *Knowland.*

---

   103. *linsey-woolsey*] 'a strange medley in talk or action; confusion, non-
sense' (*O.E.D.*, 2–3).
   107. *circumstance*] 'the "ado" made about anything; formality, ceremony,
about any important event or action' (*O.E.D.*, sb., 7).
   109. *toy*] The sexual meaning is inescapable; cf. Giovanni's reference to
'this pretty toy called maidenhead' in Ford's *'Tis Pity*, ed. Roper (1975),
II.i.10.
   110. *colts*] adequately glossed by Lord Unready.
   111. *affected*] fancied, desired.
   115. *gay*] 'addicted to social pleasures and dissipations' and implying (euphemistically) 'loose or immoral' behaviour (*O.E.D.*, adj., 2, citing this
example).
   119. *Would*] who (understood) would like to (Abbott, § 244, 329).
   buy . . . arms] For an account of this practice and its attendant corruptions,
see L. Stone, *The Crisis of the Aristocracy, 1558–1641* (1965), pp. 66–71.

Your family, as old as the first virtue
That merited an escutcheon, doth owe   125
A glorious coat of arms; if you will sell now
All that your name doth challenge in that ensign,
I'll help you to a chapman that shall pay
And pour down wealth enough for't.

Lord.   Sell my arms?
I cannot, madam.

Celestina.   Give but your consent.   130
You know not how the state may be inclined
To dispensation; we may prevail
Upon the heralds' office afterward.

Lord. I'll sooner give these arms to th'hangman's axe –
My head, my heart, to twenty executions –   135
Than sell one atom from my name.

Celestina.   Change that,
And answer him would buy my honour from me:
Honour that is not worn upon a flag
Or pennon (that without the owner's danger
An enemy may ravish and bear from me),   140
But that which grows and withers with my soul;
Beside the body's stain, think, think my lord,
To what you would unworthily betray me.

---

134. arms] *Gifford;* armess *Q.*   139. danger] *This ed.;* dangers *Q.*

---

125. *escutcheon*] heraldic shield. See A. Favyn, *The Theater of Honour and Knight-hood* (1623), sig. A6v: 'the Scutcheon or Shield, (to speak uprightly) is the essential note of a Nobleman, as also of an Esquire and Knight'; its shape is 'broad above and in the midst, but finished in a point'.

    owe] 'i.e., own' (Gifford).

127.] your entire claim to bear these heraldic arms.

128. *chapman*] 'purchaser, customer' (Onions, 2).

133. *heralds' office*] i.e., the College of Arms, especially those officers 'whose duty it was to smother new wealth beneath a coat of arms and a respectable pedigree. Since the heralds made their living by the issue of these certificates of gentility, and since the number of aspirants was increasing at a tremendous pace, it is hardly surprising if a large element of venality soon crept in' (L. Stone, *The Crisis of the Aristocracy, 1558–1641*, 1965, p. 66).

134. *these arms*] i.e., his literal, physical arms.

139. *pennon*] A particular kind of heraldic flag, 'the pennon was the personal ensign of the knight who bore it. It was small, pointed or swallow-tailed at the fly, and was borne immediately below the lance-head' (C. Scott-Giles and J. Brooke-Little, *Boutell's Heraldry*, revised ed., 1966, pp. 246–7).

If you would not for price of gold, or pleasure
(If that be more your idol), lose the glory   145
And painted honour of your house – I ha' done.
Lord. Enough to rectify a satyr's blood.
  Obscure my blushes here.

                    Enter SENTLOVE *and* HAIRCUT.

Haircut.   Or this or fight with me.
  It shall be no exception that I wait
  Upon my lord. I am a gentleman;   150
  You may be less and be a knight. The office
  I do my lord is honest, sir; how many
  Such you have been guilty of, heaven knows.
Sentlove. 'Tis no fear of your sword, but that I would not
  Break the good laws established against duels.   155
Haircut. Off with your periwig, and stand bare. [*Assaults
    Sentlove.*]
Lord. [*To Celestina*]   From this
  Minute I'll be a servant to thy goodness.
  A mistress in the wanton sense is common;
  I'll honour you with chaste thoughts, and call you so.
Celestina. I'll study to be worth your fair opinion.   160
Lord. Sentlove, your head was used to a covering
  Beside a hat; when went the hair away?

---

147. *satyr's blood*] i.e., the lust of a satyr. 'Being made up of a human trunk
on the body of a goat, a satyr was extremely lecherous' (Harrier).

148. *Obscure*] conceal, keep secret (*O.E.D.*, vb., 4).

Or . . . or] either . . . or.

149. *exception*] 'objection (to a person's status or fitness)' (Onions, 1).

150–1. *I . . . knight*] an allusion to the proliferation of knighthoods during
the reign of James I, a policy which had meanwhile been checked by Charles.
According to L. Stone (*The Crisis of the Aristocracy, 1558–1641*, 1965, pp.
75–6), 'a current joke told how "two walking espyed one a farr off; the one
demanded what he scholde be, the other answered he seemed to be a gentleman. No, I warrant you, says the other, I think he is but a knight".'

155.] 'James I . . . regarded duelling as a "vaine that bleeds both incess-
antly and inwardly", and resolutely discountenanced the practice; his *Proclamation against private Challenges and Combats* appeared in 1613 (in conformity with which Lord Sanquhar was executed for the "murder" of his
fencing master), and in 1615, when Bacon was attorney-general, the Star
Chamber "with one consent did utterly reject and condemne the opinion that
the private duel in any person whatsoever had any ground of honor"'
(*Shakespeare's England*, II, 405–6).

Sentlove. I laid a wager, my lord, with Haircut
    (Who thinks I shall catch cold) that I'll stand bare
    This half hour.
Haircut. [*To Celestina*] Pardon my ambition, madam.   165
    I told you truth: I am a gentleman,
    And cannot fear that name is drowned in my
    Relation to my lord.
Celestina.   I dare not think so.
Haircut. From henceforth call my service duty, madam;
    That pig's head that betrayed me to your mirth   170
    Is doing penance for't.
Sentlove.   Why may not I,
    My lord, begin a fashion of no hair?
Celestina. Do you sweat, Sir William?
Sentlove.   Not with store of nightcaps.

            Enter ARETINA, BORNWELL.

Aretina. Heaven has dissolved the clouds that hung upon
    My eyes, and if you can with mercy meet   175
    A penitent, I throw my own will off
    And now in all things obey yours: my nephew
    Send back again to th' college, and myself
    To what place you'll confine me.
Bornwell.   Dearer now
    Than ever to my bosom, thou shalt please   180
    Me best to live at thy own choice. I did
    But fright thee with a noise of my expenses:
    The sums are safe, and we have wealth enough
    If yet we use it nobly. My lord – madam,
    Pray honour us tonight.
Aretina.   I beg your presence   185
    And pardon.
Bornwell.   I know not how my Aretina
    May be disposed tomorrow for the country.

165–6. ambition, madam. / I] *lineation of this ed.;* ambition / Madam, I
Q.   185. us] *conj. Gifford; not in* Q.

---

   170. *pig's head*] 'closely shorn head' (Harrier), revealed by the removal of
his periwig at l. 156 above.
   173. *store*] over-abundance; cf. V.ii.70n.

Celestina. You must not go before you both have done
      Me honour to accept an entertainment
      Where I have power; on those terms, I'm your guest.   190
Bornwell. You grace us, madam.
Aretina.   [*Aside*] Already
      I feel a cure upon my soul, and promise
      My after life to virtue; pardon, heaven,
      My shame yet hid from the world's eye.

Enter DECOY.

Decoy.   Sweet madam.
Aretina. [*Aside to Decoy*] Not for the world be seen here: we are
      lost!   195
      I'll visit you at home. [*Aside*] But not to practise
                                        [*Exit* DECOY.]
      What she expects. My counsel may recover her.

Enter ALEXANDER.

Alexander. [*To Aretina*] Where's madam? Pray, lend me a little
      money;
      My spirit has deceived me; Proserpine
      Has broke her word.
Aretina.   Do you expect to find   200
      The devil true to you?
Alexander.   Not too loud.
Aretina.   I'll voice it
      Louder, to all the world your horrid sin,
      Unless you promise me religiously
      To purge your foul blood by repentance, sir.

---

191. *grace*] confer honour upon (Onions).
    199. *spirit*] i.e., the 'she-devil' (V.ii.157) who, Alexander claims, appeared
to him in the form of an old hag. For comparable uses of the term, all of them
including the general sense of 'evil spirit', see Burton, 'A Digression of the
nature of Spirits, bad Angels, or Devils' (*Anatomy*, I.ii.1.2, pp. 157–76).
    Proserpine] Referred to by Spenser in *The Faerie Queene*, I.i.37.4 and
I.iv.11.2 (*Works*, ed. Greenlaw *et al.*, 1932–57, I, 14, 45), as 'blacke *Plutoes*
griesly Dame' and as 'sad *Proserpina* the Queene of hell', Proserpine can claim
a sufficiently infernal reputation in Renaissance folklore to make her name an
appropriate one for Alexander's 'she-devil'. The story of Proserpine's abduc-
tion by the gods and her marriage to Pluto is told in Claudian's *The Rape of
Proserpine*, tr. Digges (1617).

Alexander. Then I'm undone.

Aretina.   Not while I have power   205
      To encourage you to virtue; I'll endeavour
      To find you out some nobler way at court
      To thrive in.

Alexander.   Do't, and I'll forsake the devil
      And bring my flesh to obedience; you shall steer me.
      My lord – your servant.

Lord.   You are brave again.   210

Alexander. [*To Celestina*] Madam, your pardon.

Bornwell.   Your offence requires
      Humility.

Alexander. [*Kneels*.] Low as my heart. Sir Thomas,
      I'll sup with you: a part of satisfaction.

Bornwell. Our pleasures cool. Music! [*Music sounds*.] And
      when our ladies
      Are tired with active motion, to give   215
      Them rest, in some new rapture to advance
      Full mirth, our souls shall leap into a dance.   *Exeunt*.

FINIS.

---

210. *brave*] splendidly dressed; see IV.ii.143n.

APPENDIX A

The Cockpit in Drury Lane

The playhouse in which *The Lady of Pleasure* was first performed came into being when Christopher Beeston, a prominent member of Queen Anne's company at the Red Bull, planned and sponsored the construction of the Cockpit in Drury Lane in 1616 and 1617. On 9 August 1616 he leased for thirty-one years 'All that edifices or building called the Cockpittes and the Cockhouses and the shedds thereunto adjoining . . . Togeather alsoe with one tenemant or house and a little Garden thereunto belonging next adjoyning to the said Cockpittes . . . and one part or parcell of ground behinde the said Cockpittes'.[1] Within seven months the buildings had been renovated and the new playhouse was in operation. But not for long. On Shrove Tuesday, 4 March 1616/17, an unusually vigorous apprentice riot interrupted Beeston's enterprise; one part of the mob, 'making for Drury Lane, where lately a newe playhouse is erected, . . . besett the house round, broke in, wounded divers of the players, broke open their trunkes, & what apparell, bookes, or other things they found, they burnt & cutt in peeces; & not content herewith, gott on the top of the house, & untiled it, & had not the Justices of the Peace & Sherife levied an aide, & hindred their purpose, they would have laid that house likewise even with the ground'.[2]

Undaunted by this disastrous beginning, Beeston set about having the damage repaired, and within three months (by 3 June 1617) the playhouse was ready to open again.[3] Perhaps the alternate name for the theatre, the Phoenix, was Beeston's attempt to make good publicity out of the near destruction and quick revival of his edifice. In any case, the public continued to prefer the traditional name, the Cockpit, as the habitual usage of such playgoers as John Greene and Sir Humphrey Mildmay will attest.[4] On this question of usage I have chosen to follow Caroline taste, so that 'the Cockpit' (unqualified) may be understood as referring to Beeston's theatre, and should not be confused with the Cockpit-in-Court, of which more later.

No direct documentary evidence about the design of the Cockpit has been discovered. The earliest verbal description occurs in James Wright's *Historia Histrionica* (1699), cast in the form of a dialogue between Truman, an 'Honest Old Cavalier' who remembers a great deal about the good old days, before the closing of the theatres, and Lovewit, a persistent interrogator who today might be either the host of a talk-show on daytime TV or a Professor of Oral History. 'What kind of Playhouses had they before the Wars?' asks the genial interviewer. Truman replies:

> The *Black-friers, Cockpit,* and *Salisbury-court,* were called Private Houses, and were very small to what we see now. The *Cockpit* was standing since the Restauration, and *Rhode's* Company Acted there for some time.

'I have seen that', Lovewit interposes, and the old gentleman continues:

> Then you have seen the other two, in effect; for they were all three Built almost exactly alike, for Form and Bigness. Here they had Pits for the Gentry, and Acted by Candle-light. The *Globe, Fortune* and *Bull,* were large Houses, and lay partly open to the Weather, and there they alwaies Acted by Daylight.[5]

Since a great many of Truman's assertions have been confirmed by modern scholarship, we ought to treat his claim about the resemblance between the Cockpit and the other 'Private Houses' with some respect. If it is true that the 'Bigness' of the Cockpit was roughly the same as that of Blackfriars, then we might suppose it to have occupied a space 46 feet by 66 feet with a seating capacity not much in excess of 500 spectators.[6] If it is true that the 'Form' of the Cockpit resembled that of the other two, then we can suppose it contained a platform stage somewhat smaller than that specified in the Fortune contract (43 feet by 27 feet 6 inches);[7] that the stage was flanked on either side by high-priced gentleman's boxes; that opposite the stage was a pit, furnished with benches 'for the Gentry' instead of a yard for the groundlings in the outdoor manner; and that the pit was surrounded on three sides by a U-shaped configuration of galleries, in either two or three tiers.[8] Some of these inferences by analogy can be confirmed by indirect evidence drawn from plays performed at the Cockpit. In the Prologue to *The Example*, Shirley refers to the man of wit who 'rules the Box' from which he observes the play, and contrasts him with a less officious spectator who 'has a place / Here, on the Bench'. The Prologue continues with a reference to a stage-keeper who 'bears / Three-footed stooles in stead of Juory chaires'.[9] This allusion to the practice, peculiar to the private houses, of allowing some spectators to sit on the edges of the stage, is consistent with other available evidence, like the imaginary portrait by Hemminges and Condell of a gallant who 'sit[s] on the Stage at *Black-Friers*, or the *Cock-pit*, to arraigne Playes dailie'.[10] Finally, in asserting indirectly that the private houses were alike in being indoor theatres, and directly that their stages were lit by candles, Wright is making quite uncontroversial claims which are nonetheless pertinent to the design of the Cockpit.

But there is one highly controversial inference to be drawn from Wright, and I shall mention it without presuming to solve the problem it creates. If the Cockpit was anything like Blackfriars or Salisbury Court in 'Form', then it should be visualised as a rectangular structure. No matter how diligently the Burbages renovated the Upper Frater of the Blackfriars monastery, the result must have been a rectangular auditorium. And since the builders of Salisbury Court began with a barn on a plot of ground measuring 42 feet by 140 feet, it is difficult to imagine them achieving anything but a rectangular playhouse.[11] Yet it has been a favourite belief among students of the Cockpit that they are dealing with a round or octagonal structure.[12] This belief is based on three separate kinds of evidence: (1) the conventionally circular or polygonal shape of buildings used for cockfighting in the seventeenth century, and hence the plausible assumption that the cockpit leased by Beeston was also 'round';[13] (2) the hazardous assumption that Inigo Jones's drawing of the octagonal interior he designed for the Cockpit-in-Court bears a rough resemblance to the design of Beeston's Cockpit; and (3) the hasty supposition that references to 'this sphere of love' in Cockpit plays can be understood as describing the shape of the galleries.[14] The second and third lines of argument are, without documentary support, little more than fanciful guesswork. The first hypothesis, based on what is known about the design of cockhouses, does bear on a crucial question: namely, what was Beeston up to when, in 1616 and 1617, he converted a plain ordinary cockpit into *the* Cockpit in Drury Lane?

A tempting solution to this problem has recently become possible, thanks largely to D. F. Rowan's discovery of the Jones/Webb theatre project which, in one of the few ironies of theatre scholarship, can no longer be described as 'neglected'.[15] After a thorough review of the evidence connected with the Jones/Webb drawings themselves and some speculation about their significance, Rowan concludes that 'there can be no doubt that they represent a real or proposed private "professional" theatre'.[16] This conclusion, though temperate enough to invite eager assent, is also decisive enough to affect in significant ways our interpretations of staging practices in the private houses. The elevation showing the stage, as reproduced on this page, becomes the single most reliable guide to recapturing the experience of being a spectator in an indoor playhouse of the time.

But at present my concern is with the ground-plan in the Jones/Webb project. This drawing shows a semicircular shape (housing the pit and galleries) combined with a square shape (enclosing the stage, boxes, and tiring-house). John Orrell has argued, on

Architectural plan for the interior of a Jacobean or Caroline indoor playhouse; from item 7C in a series of drawings by Inigo Jones and John Webb in the Library of Worcester College, Oxford. By permission of the Provost and Fellows of Worcester College, Oxford.

what is admittedly 'circumstantial evidence', that this ground-plan and the drawings which accompany it are in fact the designs for the Cockpit in Drury Lane.[17] If Orrell is right, then we have encountered a highly unusual compromise between the rectangle and the circle. The ground-plan is in one sense a rectangle, with two of its corners rounded: enough of a rectangle, that is, to allow James Wright to compare its 'Form' without qualification to Blackfriars and Salisbury Court. But the ground-plan includes a semicircle as well; enough of a circle, that is, to betray the cockhouse origins of the edifice and to allow its galleries to be referred to as a 'sphere'. Still, to make the association between the Jones/Webb drawings and the Cockpit, though highly enticing, remains a temptation rather than a virtue, at least until there are further documentary witnesses.

In view of the tenuous status of the 'facts' as they stand, modern readers who wish to imagine the Cockpit stage as it might have looked during a production have no choice but to enlist the supplementary assistance of indirect visual and verbal evidence. In addition to the elevation showing the stage in the series of Jones/Webb drawings, there are three notable and familiar specimens of visual evidence: the frontispiece for *The Wits* (1662), and the vignettes from the title pages of *Roxana* (1632) and *Messalina* (1640).[18] It is possible that none of these visual specimens is based on the stage of the Cockpit in 1635, but even if that is the case, as indubitable representations of indoor stage conditions, they become significant in so far as they illuminate or corroborate the evidence drawn from the stage directions of Cockpit plays.

My understanding of the verbal evidence (stage directions and the like) is heavily indebted to three works of scholarship, all of which are acknowledged in full in the table of abbreviations (pp. x–xii) and repeatedly in the notes to this edition. The three works in question are William B. Markward's unpublished Ph.D. thesis on the Cockpit, T. J. King's incisive article on staging practices at the Cockpit, and the seven-volume gathering of indispensable resources by Gerald Eades Bentley. The scholars just named would, in varying degrees, be at odds about how the available evidence should be treated. Markward's thesis, for example, is based on all of the conceivably relevant information: on texts of plays written specifically for the Cockpit, on texts of plays revived at the Cockpit and on texts of plays possibly staged at the Cockpit though not published until the interregnum. King's enquiry is based on a selection: that is, on plays incontrovertibly written for and staged at the Cockpit, whose texts or manuscript copies bear marks of association with performance in the theatre. By calling Markward's a promiscuous and King's a chaste interpretation of the evidence, I am admitting something about my own predilections.

The process of reconstructing the essential features of the Cockpit stage can safely begin with a platform, thrust forward from the tiring-house wall, and surrounded on three sides by spectators. The façade of the wall in all four of the relevant visual specimens is divided into two levels: a level contiguous with the stage and an 'above'. The design of the above varies significantly from drawing to drawing, but on the evidence of the Cockpit plays we can infer that it was often used as an observation post from which one or more actors could look down on and comment upon the action on the platform below.[19] Communication between the platform and the 'above' was remarkably rapid and easy, to judge by such evidence as the final act of Davenport's *A New Trick to Cheat the Devil* (1639), where Master Changeable, after announcing that the Devil will soon appear, says to his Wife: 'will you ascend and guide my Lord to a / Convenient place, where you may view this object?' The stage direction which follows is uncompromising: '*They ascend*'.[20] Eight lines of dialogue cover the ascent, after which the Wife and three other characters '*Enter above*'. At the climax of this scene the Wife offers to leap down to the platform below, but is warned that she may break her neck and advised that 'The Stair-case will doe better'.[21] This is presumably a permanent, backstage staircase which allowed the ascent to be made in the first place, and which allows the Wife to descend while twelve further lines of dialogue cover her actions.

To judge by the evidence of all three specimens of visual evidence other than the Jones/Webb drawing, the lower façade of the Cockpit stage would have been entirely or partly covered with hangings. The presence of these is nowhere better confirmed than in Celestina's insistence that her Steward provide her with finer and more fashionable 'hangings' than the 'arras' she finds in place (I.ii.11–12). In addition, though of the drawings only the Jones/Webb project provides for them, the tiring-house façade required doors for entrances and exits. If Jones was in fact designing the Cockpit, he certainly wanted three doors: two of normal size at either edge of the façade, and a larger arched doorway at upstage centre. Three doors are stipulated by Markward, whose argument exploits the possibly contaminated evidence offered by Nabbes's *Covent Garden* and Heywood's *The English Traveller*.[22] King's analysis of the thirty pure Cockpit plays yields only two necessary doors. This debate could be prolonged by citation of and interpretation of stage directions. I propose to suspend it, for the present, by leaving the left-hand and right-hand doors exactly where they are in the Jones/Webb project, and by drawing the hangings from either side of the stage façade neatly together until they meet, thus enclosing the arched aperture at upstage centre. Now, at least, we have accommodated the stage direction from *The English Traveller* (1633): '*Enter at one doore an* Usurer and his Man, *at the other,* Old Lionell *with his servant: In the midst* Reginald'.[23] The compromise offered here has the advantage of giving Heywood credit for knowing the difference between a door and an aperture which is not a door. And an entrance '*In the midst*' need be nothing more serious than what is going on between the two panels of hangings in the frontispiece to *The Wits.*

The features of the Cockpit stage thus visualised are perfectly adequate for a company of actors engaged in producing *The Lady of Pleasure.* Many further problems would of course need to be solved, since the play calls for splendid and extravagant costumes, hand-held properties ranging from Littleworth's ubiquitous box of 'sugar-plums' (I.i.195) to the 'light' required by Madam Decoy in the bewitching scene (IV.i.18), and a few large properties – notably a '*table, and looking-glass*' (III.i.0.2) – which would need to be placed in advance. But such matters can be left to the ingenuity of any competent theatrical troupe, especially one as experienced in social spectacle as Queen Henrietta Maria's men. And for Shirley himself, craftsman that he was, these problems of stage management and their solutions had no doubt become routine by 1635, as the years of practice in stagecraft were absorbed into a professional second nature.

NOTES TO APPENDIX A

1 Bentley, VI, 48.
2 The account is contained in a letter by Edward Sherburne (8 Mar. 1616/17), and is printed in Bentley, VI, 54.
3 Bentley, VI, 56.
4 See, for example, the references to the Cockpit from the diaries of John Greene and Sir Humphrey Mildmay as quoted in the Introduction, pp. 23–4.
5 The relevant extracts are printed in Bentley, II, 694. Readers with a taste for genealogical small-talk will wish to be informed that in James Wright they are encountering the son of Abraham Wright, the author of the commonplace book referred to in the Introduction, p. 5.

6 The dimensions are those given by Richard Hosley in his essay on 'The Playhouses' (*Revels History*, III, 206). Irwin Smith estimates the capacity of Blackfriars at 516 in *Shakespeare's Blackfriars Playhouse* (New York, 1964), p. 297. The highest known receipt for a single Blackfriars performance is £19 15s. (see Bentley, VI, 22). At the putative average price of a shilling per admission, this would mean 395 spectators. But of course, on the occasion in question, the house may not have been full or even very near to full. The estimate of 516 would seem to be a safe maximum, if there is any truth in Wright's claim that the Caroline private houses were 'very small' compared to Restoration playhouses; Wren's Drury Lane held about 600 to 800 spectators, or so Richard Southern claims (*Revels History*, V, 110).

7 For a review of the evidence concerning stage sizes, see Leonie Star, 'The Middle of the Yard, Part II: The Calculation of Stage Sizes for English Renaissance Playhouses', *Theatre Notebook*, XXX (1976), 65–9. Star estimates the dimensions of the Blackfriars stage as 30 feet in width by something less than 30 feet in depth; this compares favourably with Hosley's calculations of 29 feet by 18 feet 6 inches (*Revels History*, III, 210) and with William A. Armstrong's observations about the relative smallness of the stage at Blackfriars in *The Elizabethan Private Theatres: Facts and Problems* (London, 1958), p. 5.

8 This is not the place to demonstrate that these features were common to both of the other private houses mentioned by Wright, but a good case could be made by comparing Hosley's carefully documented reconstruction of Blackfriars (*Revels History*, III, 205–17) with the evidence assembled by Bentley (VI, 86–115) pertaining to the Salisbury Court theatre.

9 *The Example* (London, 1637), sig. *2. I quote from the quarto in this instance to avoid repeating Gifford's unhappy rendering of the final phrase as 'ivory chairs' (Shirley, *Wks*, III, 282).

10 From the address 'To the Great Variety of Readers' prefixed to *Mr William Shakespeares Comedies, Histories, & Tragedies* (London, 1623), sig. A3.

11 See Bentley, VI, 88–92.

12 See Markward, pp. 182–3, 363–4; and Bentley, VI, 50.

13 For a review of the evidence, see John Orrell, 'Inigo Jones at the Cockpit', *Shakespeare Survey*, XXX (1977), 163–5.

14 See the Prologue to *The Coronation* (Shirley, *Wks*, III, 459).

15 See 'A Neglected Jones/Webb Theatre Project, Part II: A Theatrical Missing Link', *The Elizabethan Theatre*, II (1969), 60–73. See also 'A Neglected Jones/Webb Theatre Project: Barber-Surgeons Hall Writ Large', *New Theatre Magazine*, IX (1968–9), 6–15, and an abridgement of the same article in *Shakespeare Survey*, XXIII (1970), 125–9.

16 'Missing Link', pp. 72–3.

17 'Inigo Jones at the Cockpit', pp. 157–68.

18 All three illustrations are often reprinted, most conveniently in *The Riverside Shakespeare*, ed. G. Blakemore Evans *et al.* (Boston, 1974), pls. 8 and 10 following p. 494.

19 See King, pp. 159–60.

20 Sig. K1.

21 Sig. K2.
22 Markward, pp. 329–32.
23 Sig. FIv.

APPENDIX B

Press Variants

The copies of Q collated for the present edition, together with the abbreviations used in referring to them, are listed below.

BL 1	British Library, c.12.f.16/2.
BL 2	British Library, 644.c.51. (Lacks B3–C1 and G4).
Bl 3	British Library, Ashley 1707.
D	Victoria and Albert Museum, Dyce Collection.
Bod 1	Bodleian Library, Malone 255(5).
Bod 2	Bodleian Library, Douce S 192.
Bod 3	Bodleian Library, Art 4° T.38.
W	Worcester College, Oxford.
E 1	Eton College Library, Plays A 4.2(6).
E 2	Eton College Library, Plays A 3.8(2).
C	Cambridge University Library.
B	Boston Public Library.
Ch	Chapin Library, Williams College, Williamstown, Massachusetts.
Con	Library of Congress, Washington, D.C.
F	Folger Shakespeare Library, Washington, D.C.
H	Houghton Library, Harvard University.
Hunt	Henry E. Huntington Library, San Marino, California.
M	Pierpont Morgan Library, New York.
N 1	Newberry Library, Chicago, Y 135.S.62875a.
N 2	Newberry Library, Chicago, Y 135.S.62875.
NY	New York Public Library.
Penn	Van Pelt Library, University of Pennsylvania.
Pf	Carl H. Pforzheimer Library, New York.
T	Humanities Research Center, University of Texas, Austin.
Y	Beinecke Library, Yale University.

The list which follows tabulates in detail, and forme by forme, the discrepancies between uncorrected (Qa) and uncorrected (Qb) states of Q. The reading before the bracket is that of the corrected state. Variants obviously caused by uneven inking are not recorded. Also omitted from the tabulation is a series of variants in the outer forme of sheet E which appears to have been caused by an improperly trimmed or badly aligned frisket. In two copies of Q (B and N 1), a few words at the righthand margin of E2v have been partly obscured by the frisket. The same is true of 'fortitude' (III.i.208) in the right-hand margin of E4v; the frisket has reduced this to 'fortit' in the following copies: BL 2, BL 3, Bod 1, Bod 3, W, E 2, C, B, Ch, Con, F, H, Hunt, M, N 1, Penn, Pf, T, Y. Thus, in the list below, only those variants which constitute genuine press corrections are recorded.

SHEET A (inner forme)
Corrected: BL 1, BL 2, BL 3, D, Bod 2, Bod 3, W, E 1, E 2, C, B, Ch, Con, F, H, M, N 2, NY, Penn, Pf, T, Y.
Uncorrected: Bod 1, Hunt, N 1.
Sig. A2.
  Epistle, l. 4 *present*] *presant*

SHEET A (outer forme)
Corrected: BL 3, Hunt.
Uncorrected: BL 1, BL 2, D, Bod 1, Bod 2, Bod 3, W, E 1, E 2, C, B, Ch, Con, F, H, M, N 1, N 2, NY, Penn, Pf, T, Y.
Sig. A2v.
  Epistle, ll. 11-12 *Lordship will onely crowne*] *Lordshipps will onely crownes*

SHEET C (outer forme)
Corrected: BL 1, D, Bod 1, Bod 2, Bod 3, W, C, M ,N 1, N 2, NY, T.
Uncorrected: F, Hunt, Penn, Pf, Y.
Partly corrected (at I.ii.77 but not at I.ii.119): BL 2, BL 3, E 1, E 2, B, Ch, Con, H.
Sig. C2v.
  I.ii.77. Here] Her
Sig. C3.
  I.ii.119. these] thee

SHEET D (inner forme)
Corrected: BL 1, BL 2, BL 3, D, Bod 1, Bod 2, Bod 3, W, E1, E 2, C, B, Ch, Con, F, H, Hunt, M, N 2, NY, Penn, Pf, T, Y.
Uncorrected: N 1.
Sig. D2.
  II.i.163. how (broken *w*)] how
Sig. D4.
  II.ii.131. A] a

SHEET D (outer forme)
Corrected: Bl 1, BL 2, BL 3, Bod 2, Bod 3, W, E 1, E 2, C, B, Ch, Con, H, NY, Penn, Pf, Y.
Uncorrected: D, Bod 1, F, Hunt, M, N 1, N 2, T.
Sig. D2v.
  II.ii.34. lharge titles,] charge titles
Sig. D3.
  II.ii.61. justice] justifie

SHEET E (inner forme)
Corrected: BL 1, BL 2, BL 3, D, Bod 1, Bod 2, Bod 3, W, E 1, E 2, C, Ch, Con, F, H, Hunt, M, N 2, NY, Penn, Pf, T, Y.

Uncorrected: B, N 1.
Sig. E2.
    II.ii.277. not, your person you] not your person, yon
Sig. E3v.
    III.i.101.1. *Ex.*] not in Qa.
    III.i.133. Though all the yeare were] Where all the yeare is
Sig. E4.
    III.i.143. bawd] bawds
    III.i.164. know't?] know't,
    III.i.169. her] your

SHEET F (inner forme)
Corrected: BL 3, Bod 2, E 2, B, Ch, Con, Hunt, N 1, Penn, Pf.
Uncorrected: BL 1, BL 2, D, Bod 1, Bod 3, W, E 1, C, F, H, M, N 2, NY, T, Y.
Sig. F1v.
    III.ii.19. is convenient] is so convenient
    III.ii.21. And] Such
    III.ii.25. must] may
    III.ii.33. evening?] evening
    III.ii.40. with ore pride . . . favor?] with meere pride . . . favor.
Sig. F2.
    III.ii.57. her?] her.
    III.ii.58. not, if] not if
    III.ii.65. made the times] made times
Sig. F3v.
    III.ii.171. be as ignorant] be ignorant
    III.ii.182. boast] least

SHEET F (outer forme)
Corrected: BL 2, BL 3, D, Bod 2, E 2, B, Ch, Con, F, Hunt, M, N 1, N 2, NY, Penn, Pf, Y.
Uncorrected: BL 1, Bod 1, Bod 3, W, E 1, C, H, T.
Sig. F1.
    III.ii.12. love] lovə
Sig. F2v
    III.ii.97. *C'est*] *Cest*
    III.ii.104–5. *supplie . . . permettoz*] *supplis . . . permiettoz*
Sig. F3.
    III.ii.144. power,] power
    III.ii.164. instruct] iustruct

SHEET K (inner forme)
Corrected: BL 1, BL 2, BL 3, D, Bod 2, Bod 3, W, E 1, E 2, C, B, Ch, Con, F, H, M, N 2, NY, Penn, Pf, Y.
Uncorrected: Bod 1, Hunt, N 1, T.
Sig. K1v.
    V.iii.135. head,] head
    V.iii.142. Lord] Lord.
Sig. K2.
    V.iii.158. common,] common

Glossarial Index to the Commentary

Words and phrases are listed in the form in which they occur in the text. Most entries are followed by a single reference pointing to the note in which the word or phrase in question is most fully explained. More than one reference is provided when a word is used in more than one sense or in widely divergent contexts. An asterisk before a word indicates that the note contains information supplementing that given in the *O.E.D.*

a, I.i.243
adamant, IV.ii.192
Adonis, IV.i.78–9, V.iii.62
affect, III.ii.33, IV.ii.103
affected, II.i.134, V.iii.111
affront (someone's) lip,
   IV.ii.111–12
agree, II.ii.95
air, free as, III.ii.31
ambition, II.ii.276
and, IV.i.95
angle, V.ii.72
antic, I.i.78, II.i.72
any, IV.ii.85
apocryphal, in proof, III.i.185
appliable, III.i.49
applies, V.ii.42–3
argent, III.ii.183–4
arrant Epicure, II.ii.155
arras, I.ii.12
as, I.i.276
aspects, V.iii.31
at a fault, II.ii.149–50
at gaze, V.i.98
ay, I.i.283

back, mortal, III.i.193
backrag, V.i.75
bag-pudding, I.i.40
bailiffs, IV.i.11
baldness, III.i.79–80
ball, the, I.i.114
ballads, IV.ii.54–5

bank, V.iii.78
banquet, IV.iii.165
Banstead downs, I.i.228
Barbary, III.i.112
barley-water, III.ii.316
bawd, III.i.53–5
bays, V.iii.66
beadle, III.ii.318
bear, III.ii.220
Bear at the Bridge-foot,
   IV.ii.146
beard (*vb*), III.ii.193–4
beaver, II.i.152
beldam, V.ii.161
Belgic gentleman, II.i.25
bellies, great, V.ii.101
belt, sword and, III.ii.146
bias, II.ii.185–6
black, on, I.i.197
bled … in a master vein,
   II.ii.248
*blistermaker, II.ii.153
block, II.i.153
blood, IV.ii.222
blood, satyr's, V.iii.147
blossom, IV.iii.130
*blown up, IV.ii.178
bodkin, cloth o', III.ii.172
bona roba, V.ii.26
bones, V.i.14
bone-setter, V.i.16
bow (*sb.*), III.ii.240
box (*sb.*), I.i.105

brave, IV.ii.143
bravery, I.i.275
brawl (sb.), III.ii.302
break ... jests, IV.ii.84
breath, out of, II.ii.265
breath, stinking, II.ii.197
bribed, III.i.193
bring off, III.i.224
brisk, IV.ii.148
brusheth all the table, V.i.20
Bucephalus, IV.ii.138
burden of ... innocence,
 III.ii.217–21
busk, I.i.188
but, I.i.155
but with, III.i.224
buy a coat of arms, V.iii.119
by the tapers, I.i.94

camel (adj.), I.ii.28
camphire ball, II.ii.167
Candlemas, III.ii.304
canvas tragedies, III.ii.233
capons, I.i.307–11
career, V.ii.46
carriage, III.i.94
carted, III.i.59
carve, III.i.141
case is altered, the, II.i.121
caster, V.i.6
cat, IV.i.88
catched, II.ii.212
cent, III.ii.346
cette langage, III.ii.92
Chamber of London, V.ii.115
chapman, V.iii.128
character, III.ii.287
character, save my, II.ii.168
chargeable, II.ii.28
Charing Cross, I.ii.91
circumstance, V.iii.107
city bonfire, II.ii.34–6
clean, V.ii.99
clean from the bow,
 III.ii.160–1

clean Mercury, I.i.255
clean tobacco, III.ii.317
cleave the pin, III.ii.161
client, II.ii.82
cloth o' bodkin, III.ii.172
cloth of gold, V.i.60–1
cloth of silver, I.i.91
coat, III.ii.182–3
coat of arms, buy a, V.iii.119
cocking, I.i.222
coiner, IV.i.26
cold, IV.i.51
colts, V.iii.110
comfits, II.i.81
common market, IV.i.68
compare thus, IV.ii.195
complexion, III.ii.313
compliment, I.i.196
composition, vulgar, IV.iii.124
compound (v.b.), IV.iii.102
conclude me, V.iii.13
condition (vb), II.ii.93
confer, III.ii.270
conformity, in ... due,
 V.ii.98–9
constitution, II.ii.223
consuls, III.ii.61–2
consumption, III.i.180
converse (sb.), IV.ii.221
copy (sb.), II.ii.79
copies, III.i.174
coranto, III.ii.261
cork brain, V.ii.15
corruption of the blood, II.ii.37
court shuttlecock, II.ii.179
courtoisie, III.ii.101
courtship, II.ii.116
coyness, I.ii.127–9
credibly, V.ii.17
Crow, III.ii.193–4
cuerpo, in, IV.ii.28–9
current (adj.), IV.i.27
customer, IV.i.37
custom of the country, the,
 II.i.67

dancing on the rope, III.ii.264
Daphne, V.iii.63
darks, I.i.122
d'ee, II.ii.236
deal (sb.), V.i.75
dearer, . . . nearer, III.i.58–9
desert (sb.), III.i.19
decks, false, III.i.194
defies, II.i.125
dependances, V.ii.98
determine, III.i.201
*device, V.ii.26
discharge the first maturity,
    II.ii.143
diseases that offend you,
    III.ii.280
dogdays, III.i.133
do the trick, IV.i.38
doves, I.i.225
doublet, II.i.44, IV.ii.18
drags (sb.), V.ii.13
drawer, IV.ii.147
drawn a stake, V.i.22
drink . . . tobacco, III.ii.317
duels, V.iii.155
dying swan, V.iii.100

echo, foresaken, V.iii.95
Elephant, III.ii.193–4
embroidered, V.i.60–1
ends (sb.), V.ii.90
engagement, III.i.17–18
engine, III.ii.4
engines, I.i.77, III.ii.297,
    V.ii.13
English, IV.ii.131
Epicure, arrant, II.ii.155
equal to my thought, III.ii.74
ermine's, IV.i.77
escutcheon, V.iii.125
Ethiopia, III.i.131
exalted, I.i.311
exalt it with, I.ii.86
exalt your blood, II.i.159–60
exception, V.iii.149

expect, II.ii.65
expensive, II.ii.66
eyes, III.i.30–1
eyes and judgement,
    III.i.152–3

fall away, III.ii.335
false decks, III.ii.194
false glass, V.ii.178
familiar (sb.), IV.i.39
family of love, I.i.118
fancy (sb.), II.ii.78
*fantastic, IV.iii.178
fashions, II.i.68–72
fault, at a, II.ii.149–50
fetch a priest out of the fire,
    II.ii.244–5
fetched, IV.ii.196
fever, III.i.109
fire, give, I.ii.173–4
firks, V.ii.27
first hair, o'th', II.ii.230
Flandrian trotters, II.ii.32
fools are a family, IV.ii.102
foot-cloths, III.i.80
forsaken Echo, V.iii.95
fort of sturgeon, IV.ii.151
foul, IV.ii.20
free as air, III.ii.31
freedom of a sense, III.i.195
French Cardinal, II.i.23
French tailor, IV.ii.2
fret, II.ii.172–3
fright, III.ii.211–12
*fripperies, IV.ii.60
frolic (adj.), V.i.112
full of powder, II.ii.107

gamboling, II.i.6
Ganymede, IV.ii.147
garb, IV.ii.8
garters, V.ii.98
garters, your own, III.ii.319
gay, V.iii.115
gaze, at, V.i.98

genius, II.i.41, V.iii.102
gentleman, V.iii.150–1
*geometrical, IV.ii.11
gilt, single, I.ii.36
girdle, Venus', V.ii.44
give day to, IV.iii.104
give fire, I.ii.173–4
give ... the wall, III.ii.301
glorious, I.i.273, II.i.34, V.ii.89
gloriously, III.ii.173, IV.iii.127
godwits, IV.ii.150
gold, cloth of, V.i.60–1
Goth, II.i.105
go to, II.ii.227
grace (vb), II.ii.280
graces, the, III.i.222–3
grannam, IV.i.58
great bellies, V.ii.101
Greek wine, I.i.298
green disease, III.ii.307
gross, I.i.193
gum, II.ii.172–3

hair, o'th' first, II.ii.230
halberdiers, III.i.64
hangings, I.ii.11
have a heart, V.ii.157
heard, II.i.36
Hecate, IV.i.95
hell-cat, V.ii.169
herald, IV.iii.67
herald's office, V.iii.133
heraldry, school of, IV.ii.88
her idea, III.i.169
Hesperian fruit, IV.iii.131
hiccup, III.ii.211–12
hobbyhorse, I.i.14
honest, III.i.68
honesty, in, III.ii.228
honour, IV.iii.69–70
hooded, V.ii.162
horse-leeches, III.ii.284
hot i'th' mouth, III.ii.317
hot-reined, IV.ii.17
humour, II.i.1

humour, try his, II.ii.265
Hyde Park, I.i.182

idea, her, III.i.169
*in-and-in, V.i.19
in court, II.ii.60
incubus, IV.i.51
in cuerpo, IV.ii.28–9
in ... due conformity, V.ii.98–9
infected, II.ii.173
infidel, III.i.181
influence (sb.), V.iii.30
ingenious, III.ii.219
ingrateful, II.ii.192
in honesty, III.ii.288
innocence, burden of...,
    II.ii.217–21
in proof apocryphal, III.i.185
in stock, II.ii.72
in view, II.ii.149–50
Irish, wild, I.ii.16
Islington, I.ii.44

jest, but love not, II.ii.17
Jewish stories, I.ii.15
John, poor, V.ii.71
judgement, eyes and,
    III.i.152–3
julep, V.ii.13
jury of ladies, V.iii.36
justify, II.i.57

keep a table, II.i.122–4
kennel, I.i.301
kidneys, III.ii.335
knight, V.iii.150–1
knight bachelor, II.ii.231

Lachrimae, tuning, V.iii.8
lady of pleasure, III.i.42
laid out, IV.ii.42
lamp, smell o' the, III.ii.182
langage, cette, III.ii.92
laundry ladies, II.i.154
*lay (sb.), V.ii.25

lay (*vb*), V.ii.138
learned, IV.iii.69–70
leather tenements, V.i.81
leiger, IV.ii.104
legs, rotten, III.i.79–80
library at Westminster,
    II.i.165–6
linsey-woolsey, V.iii.103
lip, affront (someone's),
    IV.ii.111–12
little honesties, II.ii.217–21
Long-lane Lombard, IV.ii.30
love, queen of, III.i.222–3
low, III.i.194

Macedonian, IV.ii.144
magazine of sauce, V.i.74
maidenhead, II.ii.217–21
Maid Marian, I.i.15
March beer, I.i.300
Mars his, I.i.223
master, V.i.17
master of the college, III.ii.221
maturity, discharge the first,
    II.ii.143
melancholy, II.i.36
*men-mules, I.ii.52
Mercury, I.i.255
mercy, III.i.127–8
Mile-end, I.ii.42
mille basia, III.ii.126
miracle, III.i.115–16
mistress, II.ii.132, III.ii.37,
    V.iii.50
more, III.ii.40
morris, I.i.12
mortal back, III.i.193
motley, I.i.81–4
motion, IV.ii.8
mount of ... Saturn, V.ii.45
mount of Sol, V.ii.45
murderers, III.ii.194
mushrooms, III.ii.325
myrmidon, V.ii.8
myrtle, V.iii.68

my wonder, IV.iii.122

name's up, thy, III.i.138
nap, III.ii.295
napkins, I.i.14
narrow, III.i.173
nearer ... dearer, III.i.58–9
nectar, IV.ii.148
nods (*sb.*), III.ii.66
noses, quarter, III.i.79–80
not devour, III.i.186
notes, III.ii.270
not for the table, V.ii.104
now, V.iii.54
nurse-child, I.ii.33

obscure (*vb.*), V.iii.148
observe still, III.i.182
officer, III.i.41
officers, IV.ii.50
on black, I.i.197
or (*sb.*), III.ii.183
or blush, II.i.64
ordinaries, III.ii.63
oringado, I.i.194
or ... or, IV.ii.70
o'th' first hair, II.ii.230
outlandish, II.i.20
out of breath, II.ii.265
owe, V.iii.125
own (*vb*), II.ii.134

painted cloth, III.ii.252
palate, V.ii.50
palmistry, V.ii.42
Pandarus' works, IV.ii.58
pantables, V.i.61
particular (*sb.*), III.i.17–18
parts, II.ii.185
pennon, V.iii.139
perspective, III.ii.352
Peru, III.i.132
petticoat, I.i.296
pewter candlesticks, throw for,
    I.i.11

Phaeton, V.i.114
philosopher's stone, IV.ii.97
phlegm, IV.i.52
physic, II.ii.222
piece, III.i.151
pieces, I.i.223
pie-wench, IV.ii.52–3
pig's head, V.iii.170
pike, trail a, V.i.100
pilchards, III.ii.292
pile (sb.), III.i.186
pin, cleave the, III.ii.161
pink (sb.), III.ii.192
plant (sb.), IV.ii.133
Platonic way, V.iii.54
player's boy, IV.ii.117
pleasure, lady of, III.i.42
plot (sb.), III.ii.223
plough (sb.), IV.ii.142
plume, I.ii.92
plushes, I.i.91
poor John, V.ii.71
poor Knight of Windsor,
    V.i.107
posset, V.ii.77
posy, I.i.269
powder, full of, II.ii.107
practised, III.ii.27
practised upon, III.i.25
prefer, III.i.42
present (vb), I.ii.172–4
priest out of the fire, fetch a,
    II.ii.244–5
prisoner, III.i.225–6
proclamations, II.ii.28
prodigal, story of the, I.ii.59
promotion, II.ii.94
proneness, III.i.69
proof apocryphal, in, III.i.185
Proserpine, V.iii.199
protect, III.ii.68–9
providence, IV.ii.64
publish, III.ii.68–9
pulse, III.i.47
puppet, III.ii.230

quarter noses, III.i.79–80
quarters, IV.i.49
queen of love, III.i.222–3
quick'ning, IV.iii.146
quicksilver, I.ii.98
quotidian, I.ii.152

rapture, III.ii.69
ravish, II.ii.213–14
read, IV.ii.145
reed, IV.ii.32
regalias, V.i.65
repure, V.iii.73
reversion, II.ii.91
rivelled, IV.i.76
rooks, V.i.20
rope, dancing on the, III.ii.264
roses, V.ii.98
rotten legs, III.i.79–80
royal luminaries, IV.iii.180–1

sable, II.i.53
sack, I.i.290
satin, II.i.44, III.ii.172
Saturn, mount of, V.ii.45
satyr's blood, V.iii.147
save my character, II.ii.168
'scape ambassador, II.ii.146
scarfs, I.i.14
scarlet, III.ii.172
school of heraldry, IV.ii.88
scruple, II.ii.152
scurrility, III.ii.68–9
seal (sb.), III.ii.67
Sellinger's round, I.i.10
sense (sb.), IV.i.72
sense, freedom of a, III.i.195
sentinel, stand court, II.ii.90
servant, II.ii.105
several, II.ii.187
shape, II.i.61, III.i.91
shaver, IV.iii.14
shirt, IV.ii.20
shoe (a) horse with gold, I.ii.48
show their teeth, III.ii.124–5

shuttlecock, II.ii.179
sibyl, III.ii.251
silk stockings, V.ii.98
single gilt, I.ii.36
skink, IV.ii.148
smell o' the lamp, III.ii.182
smelts, V.i.21
so, III.ii.249
Sol, mount of, V.ii.45
Spain, III.i.130
Spanish gravity, IV.ii.23–5
spectacles, II.ii.15
spirit, V.iii.199
spirits, V.ii.151
spoon meat, I.i.16
stake, drawn a, V.i.22
stand court sentinel, II.ii.90
state (sb.), II.i.100, IV.iii.19
Stillyard, V.i.74
stinking breath, II.ii.197
stone, philosopher's, IV.ii.97
store (sb.), V.ii.70, V.iii.173
*story, IV.ii.94
story of the prodigal, I.ii.59
Strand, I.ii.79
Strand bridge, IV.ii.164
strange, III.i.30
strike, III.ii.192
strong waters, II.i.80
sturgeon, fort of, IV.ii.151
succubi, IV.i.183
*sugar-plums, I.i.195
sumer ... service, I.ii.156
Superintendent Bailie, I.i.34
surgeon, II.ii.236
Susanna, III.ii.232
swan, dying, V.iii.100
sword and belt, III.ii.146

table, not for the, V.ii.104
taffeta, III.ii.171
take place, IV.ii.86
take the wall, III.i.80
take water, IV.ii.163
tall, III.ii.181

tapers, by the, I.i.94
tasters, II.ii.92
teeth, show their, III.ii.124–5
Tempe, V.iii.90
Temple Bar, I.ii.95
tender (sb.), II.i.142
tenements, leather, V.i.81
that, V.i.16
think me, IV.ii.124
throughly, II.ii.30
throw for pewter candlesticks,
    I.i.11
thy name's up, III.i.138
Tiger, III.ii.193–4
tilter, I.ii.92
Time, IV.i.42–3
tires (sb.), I.i.78
tissue, III.ii.172
tobacco, III.ii.317
told tales out of school,
    V.ii.174–5
top and top-gallant, III.ii.196
torch, IV.iii.146
toy, V.ii.127, V.iii.109
tract, I.i.142
trade (sb.), V.i.111
traduce, II.ii.9
traffic, II.ii.96
trail a pike, V.i.100
trained band, IV.ii.150
trick, do the, IV.i.38
Trojan, IV.ii.58
try his humour, II.ii.265
*tumblers, I.ii.43, V.ii.25
tun, V.ii.60
tuning Lachrimae, V.iii.8
twelvescore, III.ii.162
Tyburn, III.ii.290

unbuttoned, IV.ii.19
undone courtier, II.ii.38–9
unprovided, I.i.200
unready, III.i.0.1
use not, II.ii.278

vagaries, V.ii.27
Vandal, II.i.105
Venus' girdle, V.ii.44
Venus' wild-fowl, II.ii.89
very (*adj.*), III.i.48
view, in, II.ii.149–50
vulgar composition, IV.iii.124

wall, give ... the, III.ii.301
wall, take the, III.i.80
wanton, V.iii.99
wanton boy, IV.iii.146
ware (*vb*), II.i.55
water, take, IV.ii.163
watermen, V.ii.12
water-spaniel, V.ii.75
w'ee, II.ii.181
Westminster, library at,
   II.i.165–6
Westphalias, V.i.77
what, III.i.41

whelp, III.ii.193–4
where, IV.ii.94
whipped, III.i.50
whiskin, IV.ii.51
whitepots, IV.ii.52–3
Whitsun ales, I.i.13
wild-fowl, Venus', II.ii.89
wild Irish, I.ii.16
Windsor, poor Knight of,
   V.i.107
winter service, I.ii.156
wit, IV.iii.72
witches, V.ii.151
with safety, I.i.95
wonder, my, IV.iii.122
wonders, III.i.115–16
wo' not, II.i.135
would, V.iii.119

your own garters, III.ii.319